CW01546198

Ian Andrew Isherwood is Visiting Assistant Professor at Gettysburg College, PA. An expert in modern history with a focus on war and memory studies, his articles have appeared in *First World War Studies*, *War, Literature and the Arts*, the *Journal of Military History*, and *War in History*. He gained his PhD at the University of Glasgow and is the editor of the online resource 'Great War Writing' and the digital history project Jackpeirs.org.

'*Remembering the Great War* re-writes the First World War story with an original and realistic twist: analysing war books from the point of view of the commercial publishing houses and their editors. Ian Isherwood's account goes beyond broad cultural speculation to make proper historical sense of the war books boom.'

Simon Ball, Chair of International History and Politics at the University of Leeds

REMEMBERING THE GREAT WAR

Writing and Publishing the Experiences of World War I

Ian Andrew Isherwood

Published in 2017 by
I.B.Tauris & Co. Ltd
London • New York
www.ibtauris.com

Copyright © 2017 Ian Andrew Isherwood

The right of Ian Andrew Isherwood to be identified as the author of this work has been asserted by the author in accordance with the Copyright, Designs and Patents Act 1988.

All rights reserved. Except for brief quotations in a review, this book, or any part thereof, may not be reproduced, stored in or introduced into a retrieval system, or transmitted, in any form or by any means, electronic, mechanical, photocopying, recording or otherwise, without the prior written permission of the publisher.

Every attempt has been made to gain permission for the use of the images in this book. Any omissions will be rectified in future editions.

References to websites were correct at the time of writing.

International Library of Twentieth Century History 91

ISBN: 978 1 78453 567 4
eISBN: 978 1 78672 103 7
ePDF: 978 1 78673 103 6

A full CIP record for this book is available from the British Library
A full CIP record is available from the Library of Congress

Library of Congress Catalog Card Number: available

Typeset in Garamond Three by OKS Prepress Services, Chennai, India
Printed and bound by CPI Group (UK) Ltd, Croydon, CR0 4YY

CONTENTS

Acknowledgements	vii
Introduction	1
1. Writing the War	12
2. Publishing the War	36
3. War Memories: The West	62
4. War Memories: The East	86
5. War Experiences: Suffering	110
6. War Experiences: Heroism	138
Conclusion	158
Notes	165
Bibliography	190
Index	206

CONTENT

ACKNOWLEDGEMENTS

It seems appropriate that the first people I should thank are those who survived the Great War and left behind their memoirs for the public as well as the publishers who released their accounts. Without war books, the public, both then and now, would know far less about the many experiences of the Great War.

I owe a professional debt to the many archives and staffs who assisted me in researching this book. They are: the Trustees and Staff of The Imperial War Museum, Department of Printed Books and Department of Documents; University of Reading Special Collections; the Random House Archive; Somerville College Library Special Collections, University of Oxford; The University of Glasgow Library; The John Murray Archive and William Blackwood Collections, National Library of Scotland; the Somerset Heritage Centre and the South West Heritage Trust; Churchill Archives Centre, Churchill College, University of Cambridge; the Brotherton Library, University of Leeds Special Collections; The Guildhall Library, London Metropolitan Archives; The Liddell Hart Archive, King's College, London; The US Army Heritage and Educational Center for selecting me as a Ridgway Fellow in 2011; and finally the entire staff of my home institution, the Musselman Library, Gettysburg College.

I would like to thank the editors and reviewers of *War in History*, *First World War Studies* and *War, Literature and the Arts*, where my work on Great War memoirs has appeared. A portion of Chapter 6 appeared in *First World War Studies* and I thank Taylor & Francis Group for permission to publish that material here. I am also indebted to the following copyright holders and archives for permission to quote from manuscript collections: A.P. Watt and The Trustees of the Robert Graves Copyright Trust; Special Collections, Leeds University Library; The National Library of Scotland, John Murray Archive and William Blackwood Collections; the Random House Group Ltd for permission to consult and quote from the Jonathan Cape and Allen Lane archives; and Mark Bostridge and T.J. Brittain-Catlin, literary executors for the Estate of Vera Brittain.

This project began as a PhD thesis and would not have been completed but for the excellent support I received from my supervisor, Simon Ball, who taught me how to write a PhD. Without his sage advice and continued mentorship this project would never have been realised. I received excellent secondary supervision from Kate McLoughlin who helped frame the direction of this project in its early stages. At Glasgow, the Department of History and Faculty of Arts provided research funds and made me feel welcome over the course of my study. Both Richard Vinen and Sönke Neitzel provided helpful advice during my viva examination for the eventual book. Finally, I am thankful to editors Lester Crook and Tomasz Hoskins at I.B.Tauris, Ken Moxham for his excellent copyediting, and to the external reviewers who offered detailed advice on its completion.

I am especially grateful to my employer, Gettysburg College. Over the last six years, my students have informed the way that I see history (and write it) and I am thankful for each and every day I have spent in the classroom. The support of the senior administration has been invaluable: thank you Janet Riggs, Chris Zappe and Jack Ryan. I would like to thank my colleagues of the last four years at the Civil War Institute and Civil War Era Studies Program – Peter Carmichael, Allen Guelzo, Jill Titus, and Diane Brennan – for their encouragement and support. My colleagues and friends at the college – Michael Birkner, Tim Shannon, William Bowman, and Christopher Fee – have each been models of the balanced scholarly life and I am grateful for their friendships. I was fortunate to have summer research assistance from Sarah Marianne Johnson, who went through every part of the manuscript, offering advice from commas to content, and who helped get me through writing days that felt attritional. That being written, any and all mistakes in this book are mine alone.

Personally, I am grateful to many family member and friends on both sides of the Atlantic. Jack and Judy Isherwood, John and Kathy

Isherwood, James and Izumi Isherwood, Daniel and Sue Bogdan Jewett, Peter and Sandy Gregg, Jason and Katie Gregg, Bud and Betty Murphy, Mildred Saurs, Thomas Powers, Amy Murphy, Amy Roch, Alan MacLeod, Rob Shearcroft, Amy McKnight, Alex Leithead, Allison Herrmann, Natalie Sherif and Johnny Nelson, all of whom have offered support. Most importantly, my wife Sam has lived with the ups and downs of the academic life for over a decade and never wavered in her faith in me and in our future together. It is to Sam, Penny and our young gentleman, Henry, that I dedicate this book with all my love.

INTRODUCTION

C.S. Lewis reflected upon his experiences in the British Army in World War I with a degree of paradoxical puzzlement. 'I am surprised I did not dislike the Army more,' he wrote in his autobiography *Surprised by Joy*. 'It was, of course, detestable. But the words "of course" drew the sting.'[1] Despite suffering the miseries of trench life and a severe wound that left shrapnel in his body, as a middle-aged man in the 1950s Lewis appeared un-disillusioned by his early life's encounter with war. Reflecting the sense of camaraderie that he remembered from the trenches, he wrote of the men with whom he served not as victims but as 'fellow-sufferers' participating in a destructive war that was unfortunate, but as he described it an 'odious necessity, a ghastly interruption of rational life'.[2] However destructive and dislocating the war was, to Lewis it was an experience that he remembered for its 'guns and good company', the horrors of the western front reconstructed in generalities in his memoir that seem banal, that existed 'rarely and faintly in memory' afterwards.[3] To C.S. Lewis the war was one of many bad experiences that could befall a person, violence a condition that mere individuals did their best to overcome with some semblance of human spirit intact.[4]

Twenty-first-century minds have a distinct image of what World War I was like. The names are familiar enough – Verdun, the Somme, Ypres – and these places elicit associations of visceral carnage, of human waste in an industrially corrupted landscape. The images we have inherited – trench desolation and destruction, broken bodies and minds, perpetual mourning by families and the tortured memories of survivors – are the Great War's legacy passed down to us. The dark muddy stalemate of the western front is well known to any with an appreciation for history: the Great War's horrors have reverberated through generations that have questioned its meaning, debated its impact and tried to understand what it was like for those who lived through it.[5]

Much of what we know of the war has been passed down to us through its books. More than through any other form of expression, the war is remembered through its writers, many of whose names are well known: the embittered and tragic Wilfred Owen; the brave but disenchanted Siegfried Sassoon; the clever and esoteric Edmund Blunden; the wry and mischievous Robert Graves; the mournfully poetic Vera Brittain – these writers' works represent something of a canon of British war literature that has come down as iconic portraiture of the experience of war. Beyond anything else, their works remind us that the war was a great cultural event, a muse for writers who managed to reconstruct their dreadful memories for readers hungry to know what such an event was like for those who lived through it.

Today the war is remembered largely from accounts by survivors who wrestled with its legacy. In its aftermath it was clear that two worlds had been defined. The pre-war period was idealised because of the age of many who fought and later wrote about it; their youth in the Edwardian age reinforced the public school middle-class mythology of an antebellum England.[6] For many like Lewis, who went to war after a very brief stint at Oxford, the war itself proved to be a violent catalyst to adulthood. The postwar period was marked by dislocation: men and women sketching out new lives, building careers, and restoring civilian relationships with friends and families. In ways that are not altogether unfamiliar to twenty-first-century readers, the men and women who survived World War I found their third and fourth decades on earth challenging, uncertain and difficult because their maturation had been upended by violence. At no point in the interwar period was the war forgotten; at no point, the idea of a future world war thought to be impossible. It is altogether understandable that Gertrude Stein believed the war generation to be 'lost', perpetually resigned to a dislocated existence because of the war.[7] To those who survived and lived through the tumultuous 1920s and the fearful 1930s, the war's legacy was being formed as a product of their own insecure maturity.

INTRODUCTION 3

It was in the decades after the war that the first draft of its history was written by memoirists who returned from the front with stories to tell of both great tragedy and great adventure. Rather than writing history, exactly, returned servicemen and women wrote accounts of what they witnessed, memoirs and thinly veiled novels describing war experiences that many admitted to be indescribable. The glut of war literature created in the interwar period came from expositional necessity: the war was the most significant event of the age and it was the most important event to write about; certainly the most meaningful for those who survived to mourn their lost comrades. It was through this glut of expansive prose that the war gained its imagery – its feeling and voice – the war's human face articulated through life-writing, its ramifications and legacy understood in terms of individual memories and personal transformations.

This book is about war memoirs and the way some writers remembered their war experiences. Though sources of great value for historians, war memoirs are not the same thing as history. Expressive prose intersects with historical events and tells us stories about the past, but those stories are all filtered through the imaginations of their authors, who have different ways of looking at similar events. As such, memoirs present a fundamental methodological problem for historians: they are individualistic, often flawed and sometimes fallacious. They are difficult to work with because of the many distortions of individual memory, whether they are intentional or accidental. Compounding the methodological difficulties, war memoirs are also records of trauma: men and women in war face all manner of hardships and dangers. Fear takes its toll on those who are resurrecting memories. Kipling wrote of some of these difficulties in his *The Irish Guards in the Great War:*

> When to this are added the personal prejudices and misunderstandings of men under heavy strain, carrying clouded memories of orders half given or half heard, amid scenes that pass like nightmares, the only wonder to the compiler of these records has been that any sure fact whatever should be retrieved out of the whirlpool of war.[8]

Though they pose methodological difficulties, memoirs are gems of interpretative meaning; they contain descriptions that show us something about the way people felt about historical events. They are a way that we can see Kipling's messy 'whirlpool of war'.

Though vastly different from one another, memoirs all tell stories of individuals struggling to make sense of the terrible events they witnessed. Rather than writing to forget, many men and women of the war generation wrote to remember their war experiences. Repatriated soldiers were all living with war memories; some desired to get them down on paper so that others could understand what they went through. One such veteran, Charles Douie, wrote of the need to tell the story of other soldiers for the next generation, writing, 'the spirit of the soldier is ever present in our midst, that his courage and devotion, have become the heritage of generations yet unborn.'[9] Through understanding their memories, we learn something about the way that all wars are remembered.

This book is a history of the way the Great War was written in the 1920s and 1930s. Before the concept of a 'modern memory' was posited, there were hundreds of individual memoirists writing with an earnest goal: to make sense of what they experienced. Their books, collectively called 'war books' at the time, were printed and released in a commercial marketplace friendly to war memories. Rather than affirming any particular zeitgeist, war books instead reflected a broad spectrum of interpretations of the Great War, most somewhere in the middle of the wide gulf between abject disillusionment and propagandist patriotism. The war literature created in the interwar period is simply too vast to easily generalise, but this study is an attempt to offer some additional context and clarity to the way the war was remembered by its generation through their writings.

The genre of the war memoir has been chosen because there is a distinct difference between writing a book presented as a truthful story for the public and one that is presented as fiction, however thinly veiled. Though there was a glut of war novels in the interwar period, everything from patriotic children's books to 'death of a hero'-style disillusioned tomes written for adults, the memoir remained a distinctive type of war book. This certainly does not mean that all memoirists wrote completely truthful accounts – personal memories failed or changed as years went on, sources were lost and some writers no doubt exaggerated or even fabricated parts of their work – but the idea of truthfulness was important to the veterans who did the writing.

Accuracy was not the same thing as historical exactitude; the genre of the memoir was one of the 'impression of eyewitnesses', recollected events filtered through an author's own beliefs, ideals and feelings.[10] Over time, changes in memories altered the contexts in which authors viewed their war experiences.[11] Yet even with these issues, memoirs are important sources for historians because of the veracity claimed by their authors. By defining the work as a true-to-life account, the author was telling the reader that the events not only happened, but that the author's opinions on the war mattered; that their recollections were valuable enough to be remembered as historical sources later. By placing emphasis on the war memoir as a distinctive genre, this study hopes to present a panorama of war memories that add clarity and nuance to the way that the war was remembered by those who lived the events that they wrote about. It does so in three ways.

First, this study examines the phenomenon of the British war book in the interwar period and the publishing industry. War books were released in their hundreds in a commercial marketplace full of readers interested in accounts from the recent war. Yet, the publishing industry's relationship with war writers has received scant attention from scholars.[12] Through examining the literary marketplace we can ascertain the place of war books within the industry, the practicalities of writing and publishing for veterans, and the way that certain books became privileged over others. Over time Britons were forming opinions on the memory of the war largely through the British publishing industry's efforts; editors were contracting and releasing books to make a profit off war memories, and the public was reading these accounts. In the process of selling books, publishers gave veterans a forum for their opinions on the importance and legacy of the war.

Secondly, this book examines the types of memoirs published about two distinct geographic theatres of war: the western front and the war's eastern 'side shows'. Stories from particular theatres and their distinctive landscapes helped to cement images of the war in the minds of the public but also stereotyped soldier experiences of those theatres. Readers became accustomed to understanding concepts like futility, stagnation and attrition on the western front because writers emphasised these ideas in the materiality of their depictions. In the East the story was different. Despite the grave hardships suffered by combatants in Palestine and Mesopotamia, accounts from the 'side shows' emphasised adventure and exoticism. Eastern accounts were often romances and fit within a longer tradition of imperial war literature. By comparing the myths created by particular landscapes of war, we learn something about the way the fronts were being remembered.

Thirdly, this book examines two prominent tropes in war literature: suffering and heroism. The war's scale and duration unleashed levels of suffering upon Britons unthinkable in 1914. With casualties reaching into the millions, Britons were affected on a very personal level by the war's conduct, families living with its legacy for decades. Veterans were very interested in the war's literary legacy because it was not only an event in which they had participated, but also one in which they had sacrificed and suffered. Participants had distinct opinions about the way the war was being remembered, and two ways that veterans frequently described their experiences were through the tropes of suffering and heroism. These chapters consider how the war was depicted by participants with shared experiences — the infantry officer, the medical aid worker, the prisoner of war and the pilot — whose memoirs tell of different faces of battle. Through understanding the memorial importance of both suffering and heroism we can see how the war generation hoped their experiences would be remembered.

This study has been both framed and bolstered by the work of generations of literary scholars and historians who have wrestled with the cultural memory of the war. Rather than attempting to fit war books into particular ideological camps of interpretation, which is artificially deterministic, this study attempts to build a portrait of the era using a broad base of printed memoirs and by paying close attention to what writers said they were doing by writing a war memoir. It is altogether easy to get caught up in the gruesome depictions found in the literature of this particularly horrific war, but to do so is to get stuck a bit in the quagmire of war imagery, and miss the message that many memoirists hoped to get across: that the war was a great generational trial, but one endured for a purpose. It is that sense of purposefulness that this study hopes to emphasise; that men and women endured odious hardship and wrote their stories to leave behind a legacy, a human voice of the war, for our understanding.

No scholarship exists in a vacuum and all scholars build their houses on the foundations of others. The historiography of experiential war literature is dense, that of World War I especially so. Both historians and literary scholars have contributed greatly to the study of the war and the variations on its memory. Each discipline has its own methodologies and focus. As such, there are conflicting ideas on the role of literature in the interpretation of the war.[13] The myth of the British war poet has long dominated what many think of as the experience of World War I, though the myth itself has been debunked time and time again.[14] Regardless, elite war poet-memoirists have influenced the public memory of the war in Britain and remain the most influential conduits on the experience of the war. What that memory is, exactly, is a debatable concept, but literature continues to be one of the most important ways in which contemporary Britons interpret the conflict's importance.

Central to this study has been work by historians on the experience of war. Forty years ago, John Keegan's *The Face of Battle* helped shift the methodological focus of military history from tactical developments and grand strategy to a more intimate history of combatants.[15] Keegan's work identified the deficiencies of military history in order to approach the idea of battle from the perspective of the common soldier enduring hardship and trauma, but who also felt the tight bonds of comradeship and *esprit de corps* in service.[16] Keegan wrote of the military historian's challenge to approach the idea of war experience 'in light of what all, and not merely some, of the participants felt about their predicament', a concept that meant, in practice, examining sources from all facets of battle to understand something of the broader picture of war 'as it actually was'.[17] His work has influenced scholars since who have sought to move their critical gaze forward from the headquarters chateau to the front of the firing lines to understand how wars were fought and remembered by those who suffered their hardships. Keegan helped turn the history of warfare and open the door for social and cultural historians to examine the way wars were fought and remembered.

Since Keegan wrote in the 1970s, the historiography of World War I has changed to include wider discussions of social and cultural history, studies of gender and race, and the importance of memory in understanding the public history of conflicts. At the dawn of the new millennium, historians Stéphane Audoin-Rouzeau, Annette Becker and Gary Sheffield wrote important books on the war generation and our perceptions of the war's conduct and memory.[18] Their works have had a significant influence on this and many other studies that seek to engage with the idea of the war's experience to the generation who did the fighting. Equally important has been Jay Winter's work, in particular his *Sites of Memory, Sites of Mourning* and *Remembering War*, books that are essential to understanding the ways in which Europeans have conceptualised the Great War's changing legacies.[19] Winter's emphasis on generations of memory and the physical act of remembrance as having tangible meaning are concepts all too apparent when considering war writing.[20] All of this excellent scholarship forms part of the methodological basis of this study.

From literary scholars, there has been no shortage of writing on the legacy of World War I. Paul Fussell's landmark *The Great War and Modern Memory* helped define literature's importance to our understanding of the war, its generation and the idea of the cultural impact of the war's writers. Fussell's work focused on the notion of cultural change: to him World War I ushered in a new way of understanding not only war, but culture and society's response to the war more broadly. Fussell's analysis of elite writers remains convincing, but his overall framework for understanding the war itself fits within a deeply disillusioned school of literary historiography. Though other scholars have debated and debunked some of his ideas in the last 30 years, his work still remains influential.[21] Even with such criticism, Fussell's work demonstrates the importance of literary culture in creating myths about historical events, ones that have proved lasting to our understanding of the war's literary impact.

Similarly, literary scholar Samuel Hynes's important work has been influential in helping to conceptualise the notion of literary myths and their importance to history. In both *A War Imagined* and *The Soldiers' Tale*, Hynes discusses how elite writers framed the popular history of World War I, what he calls 'The Myth of the War', which is not 'the war entire' but the most influential part of its legacy – a cultural response to the war that emphasised powerful myths like innocence lost, conventions of heroism destroyed, and idealism shattered.[22] Hynes's work helped guide a central question to this research: if the 'myth of the war' was only one facet of the war's memory, then what other myths are out there? This book complements Hynes's work by showing that a single literary 'myth of the war' was not something universally subscribed to by veterans, at least in the 1920s and 1930s, but was a product of later generations of Britons accepting a particular imprint of the history of the war.

One of the most significant of the war's great literary myths – the trope of generational disillusionment – has been discussed and debated by critics and scholars since the war itself. Defined here broadly, disillusionment meant a rejection of the war's purposefulness by those who fought or witnessed the war's suffering. Feeding into this powerful feeling was disenchantment with cause, country, or conduct of the war, all of which were demonstrated in different ways by different people; but the concept of cultural malaise, of weary dissatisfaction with war service and feelings of futility and purposelessness, was one that developed as a reaction to the experience and legacy of the war. Disillusionment was prominent in some of the war's literature despite the fact that these feelings were not truly indicative of the morale of soldiers in the British Expeditionary Force (BEF) while the war was ongoing.[23] The popularity of the trope increased in the interwar period as writers adapted their war memories in light of the social and political changes of the 1920s and 1930s.[24]

There have been notable works by military and cultural historians written in the last 20 years that have challenged the notion of the disillusioned British war writer. Historian Brian Bond has written on war literature extensively and published an important study of war memoirs, *Survivors of a Kind*, a book that examines the complexities in the way that men remembered their war experiences in light of their duties performed and personal lives after the war.[25] Bond is one of the few authors to have examined the memoir as a genre distinct from its more imaginative cousin, the war novel. Hugh Cecil's *The Flower of Battle* is a study of popular novelists who returned from the war to write, mostly, patriotic accounts of their service.[26] His work, like Bond's, is biographical in its focus, and demonstrates that the literary marketplace was not uniformly full of disillusioned accounts in the 1920s, but that patriotic books continued to be popular after the war. Rosa Maria Bracco's work on middlebrow print culture demonstrates the importance of war novelists to the literary marketplace in the 1920s and places particular emphasis on writers who were vaguely patriotic about the war and found their service meaningful despite its hardships.[27] Like the novelists she describes in her *Merchants of Hope*, many memoirists, too, were middlebrow writers; they shared the same publishers and garnered the same readership. The middlebrow was a space where traditional notions of middle-class suffering, interpreted as a virtuous and even heroic attribute, were still culturally prominent even in an age of 'modern memory' created by World War I.

Social and cultural historians have demonstrated that war books reflected the culture in which they were written as much as they did the war that they represented and that British culture was hardly uniform in its recollections. Michael Roper writes that war stories involve 're-remembering' events in light of both past and present and war books react to the war's memory as it changes culturally.[28] As such, books tell us much about the way that Britons were actively remembering the war in the 1920s and 1930s, how the war was being, to some degree, reimagined by writers who believed that they were writing truthful stories. Work in memory studies, particularly on the changing culture of memorialisation in the interwar period, has been helpful to understanding the period more generally by showing the different ways that Britons dealt with the war's legacy.[29] Recent work on masculinity and emotional history, particularly the work of Joanna Bourke and of Jessica Meyer, in addition to Roper, has emphasised the importance of gender in men's lives and in their descriptions of the ordeal of battle.[30] War books were written in a culture in which the virtue of manhood was important, but also, importantly, challenged by the experiences of war that had altered the image of the soldier-hero. Along these lines, the work of Alexander Watson on combat endurance and Edward Madigan on courage has demonstrated the many coping mechanisms soldiers used to deal with combat, and that the heroic ideal did not die in the trenches, but was importantly altered by the conditions of mechanised warfare.[31] These themes are all reflected in postwar literature, and this recent scholarship has helped to bolster what was essentially a study in book history with current research on morale and survival in the trenches. As such this book is about not only war writing, but also the way writers remembered their experiences of World War I.

In a broader context, war literature's lasting impact is a subject that has garnered significant attention from scholars interested in charting the war's legacy. Daniel Todman's work has shown that the memory of the war has changed with the generations since the Armistice, the war creating many differing myths that were altered to speak to new generations of Britons wrestling with notions of the war's meaning within their perception of national identity.[32] Similarly, David Reynolds has argued that the war's legacy itself changed drastically as a result of

World War II, and that British memories of the Great War are largely refracted back through that prism, so that the first war seems even more futile, even more unfinished, as it failed to achieve a lasting peace.[33] Certainly, for memoirists, the idea of the war being an endeavour to preserve peace was an important factor in their understanding of its purpose. The disappointment felt by the war generation in 1939 cannot be overstated and it is largely for the reasons Reynolds indicates that this study is confined to the interwar years. The issues of interpreting the war generation's feelings after 1945 are too much for one book; they exist in a different world entirely, a post-imperial world, where the idealistically liberal reasons for war in 1914, as well as the realities of heroic sacrifice venerated during the war, have not worn well in postwar Britain.

During the interwar period, things were less certain. The war's memory was far more malleable than how it has been interpreted since. The stakes for writers were great because they believed themselves to be agents of memorialisation and with that came the burden of interpreting their memories for readers. 'And I am left alone with Memory,' Ralph Mottram reflected on Armistice Day in *Through the Menin Gate*. 'Yet not alone, for all around me are survivors like myself who have their memories too, absorbing, almost sacred. No, we shall never be able to forget.'[34] Like attending a memorial dedication or observing the two minutes' silence on Armistice Day, writing a war book was also a means of memorialisation, a way to resurrect old and powerful memories, to offer both clarity and a sense of sacredness to the idea of the war. At its heart, writing a war book was about remembering.

CHAPTER 1

WRITING THE WAR

In November 1918, Captain Angus Buchanan, MC, was in a Red Cross hospital for officers in Brighton. He was being treated there after his return from the war in East Africa. In the previous three years, his body had been through the hardships of life on campaign in a difficult theatre of war, one which deteriorated both men's spirits and their bodies. He had suffered deprivation and disease; he had also dutifully served his nation and empire in a remote corner of the world war. He was a competent young officer, earning promotion and being decorated for bravery. Now with the war seemingly behind him, he took up his pen and while recovering in hospital he wrote a memoir of his war experiences for publication. A week before the armistice that marked the ending of a war in which he had sacrificed his health and risked his life, his manuscript, entitled *Three Years of War in East Africa*, was accepted by publisher John Murray.[1] Buchanan's book was one of the few published depicting the war in Africa, an important work demonstrating the war's global reach, a chronicle of men who served not only their country, but also their empire beyond the western front.

As Buchanan was convalescing in Brighton, Captain Charles Carrington, MC, was in England. He had grown despondent from the boredom of being at home. Carrington had served on the western front since 1915 and had seen much action in the 1/5 Battalion of the Warwickshire Regiment. After fighting and suffering in the abysmal mud of Passchendaele in 1917, Carrington's nerves were strained, and he was granted an extended leave where he was assigned to a reserve training battalion in England. Though lucky to be on leave, he disliked the experience so much that he longed to go back to the front.[2] After three years of war, Carrington was used to being busy, performing the hundreds of tasks required of a junior officer in a good battalion in the line. Now idle in his hut, he began to write essays about his experiences and 'bad romantic verses about death and the trenches', while he pined for a return to his men and the troglodyte home he knew in France.[3] Carrington found life in wartime England unappealing; the sense of alienation was powerfully acute between a combat soldier and civilians at home who knew little of what life was like in the trenches. Being away from the front, though, had got him writing; indeed the first draft of his *A Subaltern's War*, which he would wait ten years to publish, was inspired by the bored mulling of a combat officer home on leave who was waiting to go back to his men. Carrington eventually got his wish and was given orders to the front. At the time of the Armistice, he was on a train en route to the Italian front.

In Italy, Captain Charles Douie, MC, was standing on the side of a road watching on as a weary British infantry brigade marched past. Like Carrington, for three years Douie had fought on the western front and had witnessed the destructive war as it developed around him. Like so many other subalterns, Douie was young, commissioned as a teenager just out of Rugby. Despite his youth and inexperience, he had grown into command. Unbeknownst to him, on 11 November 1918, the war was over. Reflecting back on that moment – so significant later but one whose meaning he was unconscious of at the time – he wrote of the dust-covered men walking past. 'These men have lived long in the Valley of the Shadow; they had learned there to distinguish between the false and the true.'[4] Over the next decade, Douie would ponder the meaning of the 'true' war, the one that he survived. Eventually, mustering the courage necessary for all authors, he published his war memoir *The Weary Road* in 1929, a book that was as much a manifesto on the war's generational impact – the legacy of the war to those who lived through it – as it was a record of his own experiences.

Three men, all officers in the British Army, subalterns who had been decorated for bravery and who had grown into their adult lives as soldiers of their empire's war against Germany. They were also authors who wrote and published accounts of their service. Their books – *Three Years of War in East Africa*, *A Subaltern's War* and *The Weary Road* – were attempts by young amateur authors to convey something very difficult to write for the public: the experience of war. Each of their stories tells us something about the way that war experiences are remembered. Buchanan wrote his account soon after he returned from Africa. His book is documentary; he told a story of a theatre that was not particularly well known and he published the work quickly within a literary marketplace full of stories of the war. His would be one of many memoirs released in the first two years of peace depicting the war's other fronts, its trials and adventures for imperial soldiers. Douie and Carrington's experience was different. They would each mull over their war recollections for a decade before publishing them in 1929. They had the advantage of hindsight to offer context to their experiences, an advantage used to editorialise on the meaning of the war and its changing memory in the 1920s. What was common to all three authors was a similar challenge: to make sense of events that seemed chaotic, traumatic, and often difficult to recall with any degree of clarity. With remembering and narrating came an intellectual process of creating linear stories from disjointed memories, attempts to make sense of a world war that destroyed as much a person's ability to think clearly as it did anything else.

***

The Great War was a catastrophic world event that affected millions of people in direct and indirect ways. For returning soldiers, volunteers or conscripted civilians in uniform, the experience of war was intensely and traumatically carried forward into their peacetime lives. John Keegan's sentiment that the war was a 'monstrous cultural aberration' was clearly demonstrated by the way the war was remembered throughout the twentieth century in Britain.[5] The Great War was believed by many to have been an event of widespread social and cultural transformation, often referred to as a type of Armageddon, a pronouncement that dramatically described the feelings of many that British society was forever changed, altered by a sense of social trauma that ran deep in its mournfulness. Modris Eksteins writes that at the end of the war, 'Europe slumped into a monumental melancholy.'[6] The dramatic importance of the war itself – as well as the feeling of drastic rupture garnered by it – was certainly felt as it was ongoing, its grandness and scale widely commented upon. But similar to the way memoirists recall the events of their earlier lives, the wider significance of the war was not truly understood until it was juxtaposed with the altered world that emerged from its destruction.

One way to understand the war's impact is through the way it was written by men like Buchanan, Douie and Carrington. War memoirs – defined here as retrospective personal narratives – document the experiences of individuals and their opinions on the events that they witnessed.[7] In the decades following World War I, British publishers released hundreds of non-fiction accounts of the recent war by veterans who were interested in making their war experiences known to the public. These books were incredibly varied in their depictions, but all writers contemplated the meaning of the war against the backdrop of their postwar lives. In hundreds of ways the war was written and remembered by men and women who witnessed it: their stories a mosaic of war experiences, a panorama of war memories released at a time when the dramatic story of the war was more akin to memory than history. The new war literature chronicled the way the war affected individuals, their personal stories a guide to the way that Britons were actively remembering the war in the 1920s and 1930s.

Writing a war memoir was an exercise in retrospection. To do so pitted the author's past with their present knowledge of the world.[8] Yet, war writers were not divorced from the culture in which they lived, but instead functioned within it. To Jay Winter and Emmanuel Sivan the war generation created a culture of remembering: through their similar experiences, writers were 'participant in a social group constructed for the purpose of commemoration', and this impulse to remember was one that was shared by nearly all that penned the war's story.[9] Because they were written, in part, to commemorate, war books carry the baggage of the postwar years as much as they depict the actual war; they are documents that intercede between the reader and the war's experiences through a commemorative filter. The story of the war gleaned from memoirs is one that was retold – and as such reimagined – through the peace that followed.

This chapter considers the writing of British war memoirs in the 1920s and 1930s. The war's history – the very first draft of it – was composed in the 20 years following its conclusion by those who survived its many different fronts and came home with a story to tell and a story to sell. Though varied in their motivations, the war's authors all sought to do two things by writing a war book: to tell a true story about events they believed to be historically important; and to interpret those experiences for the public.[10] As such, memoirists had both documentary and editorial motivations for writing. Writers hoped their books would be of historical value; that their stories would serve as an adjunct to the history of the war. Writers also hoped to leave their impressions on the war's conduct, to engage with the complicated notion of the war's memory at a time when it was only just being formed, and leave an impression of the war's lasting meaningfulness in the most personal way possible, by discussing its human impact.

Memoirs and history

Historical posterity is an important impulse for memoirists. According to Samuel Hynes, the feeling of being a part of history is particularly acute for veterans. He writes: 'For most men who fight, war is their one contact with the world of great doings.'[11] While serving as a second lieutenant in an infantry platoon might be an insignificant experience outside of a particular section of the line, when this experience is published, it becomes something more permanent, perhaps something more meaningful as it is bound, printed, and sold to the public. In terms of the British experience in World War I, the returned soldier's story, through publication, was connected to a long tradition of other war stories; an important part of a legacy of martial publishing into which the memoirs of the Great War fit.[12] Many authors were certainly aware of the importance of their memoirs to history and they wrote so that their stories would become a contributing part of it. Whether authors were writing polemically to prevent future wars, memorially to pay tribute to lost comrades, or adventurously telling the story of a far-flung theatre or experience, the historical motivation – to leave an impact on the emerging history of the war – remained of paramount importance.

Memoirists wrote their accounts at a time when the publishing industry released all manner of war books to readers.[13] 'War books' in their many forms formed a niche within the interwar literary marketplace. Readers were interested in accounts of the war; the British public was trying to make sense of the events through which they had just lived and both histories and memoirs were published to meet the demand, ones that detailed not only the military campaigns of the war, but also what it was like to fight in those campaigns. *The Bookseller* records no shortage of war books announced as new releases and had a special category, 'Naval and Military', for books about war.

Much of the war's literature was actually written as history. The massive undertaking of the Official Military Histories under the direction of General Sir James Edmonds is probably the best-known historical effort, for it saw the publication of 29 volumes of military history between 1922 and 1948.[14] These Official Histories were meant to be read by both the public and Armed Forces.[15] Edmunds personally wrote 11 of these volumes and directly supervised the others.[16] Other histories, both general and specific, were published, some written by veterans, politicians or by well-known literary figures such as Arthur Conan Doyle and John Buchan.[17] Regimental and battalion histories were also published, usually in small runs, but important for veterans of distinguished units. Britain was a nation awash with printed war books in the 1920s.

Memoirs were complementary to the vast efforts of historians to document the war. While the historian could describe the great events of a campaign, war memoirists recorded the emotional history of eyewitnesses, explaining how historical events impacted on and changed people.[18] The distinction between the writing of history and the writing of a memoir was one widely commented upon and few war memoirists would have seen their autobiographical attempts as history, though many saw the historical value in writing their stories.[19] Yet the potential usefulness of the war memoir to future historians was a compelling motivation to write and publish a war story because it offered the veteran an opportunity to show how their lived experience influenced history. Charles Carrington's *A Subaltern's War* was one of many memoirs that the author hoped would be important for the eventual story of the war. He wrote in his preface, 'I have decided to offer them [his memoirs] to the public, because no war book written now, ten or fifteen years after the event, can secure the authenticity attached to these stories.'[20] Carrington's principal motivation to publish his war book was to preserve what he believed were authenticated memories for the historical record and to release a book of value in an age of sensationalist war literature. Carrington wrote from sources and approached writing his memoir in a similar way to that of an historian.[21]

For memoirist E.J. Thompson, historical posterity was also an important motivation for writing. Thompson was the chaplain of the

2nd Leicestershires and served with his battalion in Mesopotamia. He wrote a type of personal history of his regiment entitled *The Leicestershires Beyond Baghdad* (1919). Thompson's methodology was that of a military historian in the first person: he constructed the book from his own memories, from his notebooks, the battalion war diary, and from conversations with his men.[22] He believed his memoir to be a valuable future historical source, writing: 'From a multitude of such narratives the historian will build upon his work hereafter.'[23] Historical record was a primary motivation but so was memorialising his unit. Though concerned with the legacy of his unit's conduct in the war, Thompson was clear to distinguish his book as a personal history, one that he believed was of value for its accuracy.[24]

The connection between lived memory and history was not an exact one and not all memoirists went to the same lengths to validate their memories as Carrington and Thompson. There were many constraints to writing about the war afterwards: lack of documentation, imperfect memories, and social conventions among them. Though some publishers exercised scepticism towards sensational accounts, there was no standard for validating individual memories outside of the author's reputation, which was certainly at stake in an age when veterans clearly read one another's books. Some authors wrote from memory alone, believing their impressions of the war were more important than the exact recalling of the facts of their service. One former subaltern wrote that because he composed his recollections in hospital, 'I was forced to rely mainly on my memory for dates, names of places, incidents, etc.'[25] He then added, 'If they have failed to be exact in some cases it is largely due to hypothesis, which is sure to creep in. Also, impressions vary with time and temperament and it is in this light that I hope to pacify my critics.'[26]

Surgeon Arthur Osburn believed his memoir could offer 'feeling and outlook', traits much more important to him than strict factual accuracy.[27] For Osburn, the war memoir's purpose was primarily interpretative. Describing *Unwilling Passenger* as a 'test of memory' he wrote, 'it is not intended to pit accuracy against the more complete and carefully documented diaries of those who wrote down their experiences at the time, and have since published them.'[28] Though not a war diary, Osburn's 'test of memory' included clear depictions of the retreat from Mons in 1914 and vivid scenes of battlefield surgery recalled 18 years afterwards. He was clearly interested in telling a story about his intersection with history, but was careful to disclaim his memoir as strictly that.

Osburn's recollections were not about specific troop movements, dates of significant events, or divisional personalities or politics; instead, his book was a deeply personal account of a career army doctor witnessing the effects of splinter shells and cordite burns on wounded men. Similar to many other veterans, he sought to convey a sense of authority gleaned from his experiences that went far beyond that of historians or even eyewitnesses.[29] He wrote critically of the Official Histories: 'Several other incidents are, if I may say so with all due respect, described in the Official History rather as the English would have had them happen than as they actually occurred.'[30] He was clear to contrast his memories from August 1914, events punctuated by confusion, chaos and high casualties, with more sanitised depictions of the war as it appeared in the official histories. His impressions of war were exactly that: chaotic and desperate. In this way Osburn used his memoir as a complement to official military history, but also, as a corrective to sanitised depictions that left out a significant part of the war's history, how it impacted individuals and their emotions. He was conscious that his 'imperfect record' was one of interpretative historical value even if it was not strictly history.

Memorialising the experience of war

Memoirs not only leave behind a record of service, they also memorialise the experience of war itself for future generations. Writing of his service in the Scots Guards, Stephen Graham described his motivations for writing as, 'I have thought I could perform no better service than describe the social life and the spirit in these historic regiments of the British army.'[31] To him, both the history of the events he lived, but also the morale or *esprit de corps* of the men with whom he served, were worthy of remembrance. Graham was not alone: tributes to comrades and the war dead were extremely common, particularly in book dedications. The desire to remember what soldiers went through, what they suffered and endured, was a natural response to the experience of the war. The brutal nature of a war of attrition took its toll on minds, bodies and memories, and soldiers had to adapt to carnage, fear and the lingering prospect of death in order to cope with losses and trauma. After the war, when men and women began to write their war books, they invariably had to confront difficult memories within a society that still felt acutely the war's losses, a society that did not always understand what veterans went through.

It is impossible to divorce the war memoirist of the interwar period from the culture of war memory in Britain that was created by the war's wake. Jay Winter writes that war books 'are indispensable guides to how some contemporaries tried to come to terms with the slaughter'.[32] Coming to terms was an exercise in remembering, often memorialising, a shared experience of comradeship. All veterans who decided to pen a memoir had to confront memories of traumatic events, and many wrote to further public understanding of the war so that their sacrifice would not be overlooked.

The phrase 'traumatic events' is perhaps too abstract. Veterans were reliving memories that were impossible to fit into tidy narratives, yet they often tried to do so. Past and present often blended together in battlefield descriptions as writers attempted to make sense of the war's suffering afterwards. In *Up to Mametz,* Llewelyn Wyn Griffith wrote that whenever he smelled freshly cut wood, he remembered a severed human limb hanging in the boughs of a tree broken by bombardment.[33] Griffith recalled the war's imagery through his sensory memory, which was still powerful a decade after the war's conclusion. A peaceful and pastoral experience, the cutting of green wood, reminded him forever afterwards of the horrors he witnessed. Remembering battle meant trying to explain the inexplicable: to make coherent narrative memories from the fragments of the past reimagined in the present.

Because of the vast suffering of the war, the impulse for memorialisation was strong, and tributes to comrades in war memoirs were common. 'For indeed men have suffered things in this war which no individual "on his own" could possibly endure. But our men have endured them because others were suffering with them,' wrote Stephen Graham.[34] Feelings of suffering manifested themselves in writing, which was a memorial reaction to trauma by veterans, who longed to show that the war had purpose and was both personally and generationally transformational. To some degree, war books are written so that veterans can 'create meaningful narratives of their wars', and the search for such meaningfulness came in many different forms in the

1920s.[35] Many memoirs emphasised endurance at the front, more often than not a trial of human endurance over appalling conditions and high casualties. Friendship – often referred to as comradeship – was another way to find meaning in the war's trial.[36] John More, who served in Palestine, wrote his account as a 'reminder of the strenuous times when all were working together for the common cause'.[37] He wrote of service and suffering by men who together believed that these experiences had value. By demonstrating the close bonds formed by men who fought and survived through terrible experiences, the implicit virtues of loyalty, charity and friendship were emphasised as important aspects of the martial fraternity. Memorialising comrades ensured their place in the history of the war; men and women whose suffering would otherwise be insignificant in the broader scheme of the war's millions of individual acts of cruelty were remembered in print by individuals who knew what they went through, so that they could show that these experiences mattered.[38]

An example is R.T. Rees's 1935 infantry officer memoir, *A Schoolmaster at War*. In it, Rees described how the process of writing brought back conflicted memories of service that were beginning to fade in 1935. He wrote, 'the mere handling of my pen recalls at once the close smell of the dug-out, the scampering of rats, the rat-tat-tat of machine guns, the ear-splitting bark of guns, the horror of the gas cloud, and the chilly stillness of No Man's Land just before dawn.'[39] These images of the western front were familiar to all his readers in the 1930s; they were the ordinary realities of all junior officers in that theatre and were ubiquitous depictions in the war's literature. Rees continued, 'Happily, it also recalls good fellowship in trench and billet, feasts and concerts behind the lines, and above all, the sense of loyalty and comradeship which illuminated even the squalid gloom of war.'[40] In his account, Rees was interested in showing the war's hardships but also the 'good fellowship' of his comrades-in-arms. Comradeship was an important corrective to the unpleasant realities of service; in memory, it became a central part of the war's reinvented martial virtue afterwards.

Akin to comradeship, pride, affection and loyalty towards regiments was common. Even as wry a writer as Robert Graves adored his unit and memorialised the traditions and elitism of the Royal Welch Fusiliers in *Good-bye to All That*.[41] More important, perhaps, was the notion of the morale of a good battalion, referred to as 'spirit' by Graves; he wrote that despite appalling attritional losses in the Royal Welch, 'Regimental spirit persistently survived all catastrophes.'[42] Unit identity, particularly within elite regiments or service branches, accentuated feelings of comradeship. This sense of pride was remembered fondly in many war books, some of which had the unit within the title itself; 19 published memoirs used the preposition 'with' to convey the centrality of unit identity to individual experience. Some authors even wrote specifically to tell the story of a unit. Colonel Neil Fraser-Tytler, author of a collection of edited letters entitled *Field Guns in France* (1922), prefaced his book by writing that it was of primary interest to artillerymen, and 'anyone else who buys the book does so at his own peril.'[43] Similarly, Ardern Beaman found *esprit de corps* a motivation to publish his cavalry memoir *The Squadroon* (1920). In his foreword, Beaman attributed the writing of his book to his uncle coaxing him: 'Now you've been with a Cavalry Brigade through the most stirring time of the war, why don't you write an account of their life out there.'[44] With modesty he assured his uncle that he would try to tell a faithful story of the gallant doings of his unit. Beaman wrote: '[the] purpose of this narrative, however, is not unduly to extol the occasional performances of the Cavalry, nor to excuse their many failures and their long periods of seeming inutility. It aims only to paint in plain and faithful colours the life and sentiments of [...] a squadron of Cavalry in the field.'[45] Beaman wrote to both convey his own experiences, but also those of his unit, an attempt at faithfully reconstructing their conduct in the war filtered through his own lens as a witness.

Just as some were comfortable writing on behalf of their comrades, others found this task difficult. Journalist and former sergeant in the Black Watch William Linton Andrews, author of *Haunting Years: The Commentaries of a War Territorial* (1930), found the balance between memoir and battalion history difficult.[46] Initially, Andrews wanted to write history but found the task daunting so he turned to writing a memoir. He wrote: 'For I want very much to tell you about my comrades – great-hearted comrades – many of whom did not come home [...] This will be my own story. I shall tell it because it is also the story of thousands upon thousands of others, not in particulars, but in broad essentials.'[47] The desire for personal recollection, remembrance and collective history was important to Andrews – important, yet still very difficult to write well due to the social restraints and burden of writing on behalf of others, an imposing task for all who write of small units in war. Former prisoner of war H.C.W. Bishop recalled the limits of telling the story of men that he knew and served with at Kut. He wrote firmly that his was an individual account: 'It is not intended to generalize in any way, since an individual, unless of exalted rank, sees as a rule only his own small environment and cannot pretend to speak for the majority of his comrades.'[48] Yet Bishop hoped his book would be of informational interest to the 'relatives and friends' of his fellow prisoners of war.[49] The essential point is that many writers saw the process of writing a war memoir as inherently memorial: an opportunity to earnestly reflect upon their comrades with hope of telling a faithful story of their own war experiences despite knowing the limitations of being one voice of many.

Writing the truth of the war

In their desire to record for posterity their experiences, memoirists invariably framed their books in ways that interpreted the conflict for readers. Though often earnest in their desire to tell truthful stories, literary imagination and the fallibility of individual memories has led many historians to view postwar literature with a healthy dose of scepticism. There is nothing new to this criticism, but it does raise the issue of the importance of truthfulness in war stories. There are different types of truths in war books, and many memoirists were conscious of this fact. The experience of war is one shared by many, but remembered individually; it is a subjective experience that can be interpreted in starkly different ways.

Remembering combat was often a confusing and emotionally jarring experience. When his own veracity was questioned, Robert Graves famously wrote to his critics that 'High-explosive barrages will make a temporary liar or visionary out of anyone.'[50] Graves's distinction was that men who fought and wrote their war experiences deserved a degree of critical leniency when it came to the details. For men recalling what was likely the most traumatic experience of their lives, truth would be something certainly valued, but also contested by others who had lived through the same events. Graves saw no small amount of futility in the process of validating memories. In as gifted hands as his, the very notion of a 'truthful' or 'authentic' war memoir was an opportunity to question the notion of truth itself, or to ascertain which truths, if any, were important. To Graves, truth was not necessarily found in strict factual accuracy of events lived and witnessed, but instead deep within the overall transformation of men in battle in the context of their later lives, a form of emotional truthfulness that was far more impactful on readers than accounts of troop movements or strategy.

It is worth noting that Graves was largely an exception. There was something self-defeating in contesting the idea of truth while writing an autobiographical account that would be marketed and sold to the public as such. Graves was accounting for what he called 'the old trench mind', or the confusion found in the psychological disruption of battle.[51] Both factual details and author's impressions are integral to autobiography, and author's prefaces from this period are replete with discussions of methods and disclaimers. Former medical officer David Rorie wrote his memoir from his diary and excused the fact that many of the technical details in his memoir, *A Medico's Luck in the War,* were 'monotonous' because he felt obliged to include them, writing that 'historical accuracy demands it.'[52] It was not uncommon to write from sources, and many other writers felt a keen desire to be accurate in their depictions. M.C.C. Harrison and H.A. Cartwright's 1930 account of their prisoner-of-war escapes, *Within Four Walls,* was an exceptional story, but one that the authors felt a need to validate in their preface. 'Even though the narrative was not put together until this year the authors have not had to fall back, therefore, upon memory, but have each had the facts before them as they were written down at the first possible moment.'[53] That they felt the need to explain their authenticity to the reader demonstrates something about the different types of war memoirs released and the widespread critical questioning of the veracity of war books.

Somewhere between the liar and the visionary was the earnest British war memoirist, diligently reconstructing their war experiences from limited sources and relying, as their first and most important source, on their emotional impressions resurrected from memories that had been fractured by war. However problematic the notion of truth was for writers, it was a virtue important to many if not most who wrote. Max Plowman wrote that his book's appeal came from his 'candid and truthful' depictions, without which 'authorship on such a subject as the European War will, in any case, be valueless.'[54] His connection between candidness and value is important: memoirs had a truthfulness that went far beyond historical events. They were interpretative and transformational texts, recounting what Alfred Pollard called 'thoughts and sensations when going into battle'.[55] Novels could offer a perspective on truth; poetry and plays could as well. But there was something inherently different about authors writing autobiographically, especially in a literary marketplace where veterans both read and reviewed war literature. Writer and historian Guy Chapman saw the idea of sincerity as the principal virtue of English war books, one which he lauded as he compiled his collection of international war writing, *Vain Glory*, in 1937. 'Whether he tells it with greater or less skill, the English narrator is painstakingly trying to put down the thing as he saw it. He is interested in fact, not for the sake of truth but because he wants to get the fact clear in his own head.'[56] Chapman had served in the war, wrote a war memoir, and understood well the difficulties in trying to put fragmented memories into clean narrative.

As shown above, some authors wrote self-consciously of their attempts at reconstructing their memories, often humbly offering their recollections to readers through disclaimers in their prefaces or forewords. Philip Gosse, son of the critic Edmund Gosse and friend of Siegfried Sassoon, described his war memoir as being a collection of 'experiences and impressions of a very unmilitant individualist who, like thousands of others, suddenly found himself taking part in the great catastrophe'.[57] His war experiences were mildly described as a series of personal 'impressions' to be taken exactly as such. Former prisoner of war John Still wrote that his book consisted of 'both facts and opinions', a healthy qualification against the work being understood as an objective history.[58] Cambridge don H.G. Durnford wrote that his memoir was justified by the banality of its story. He wrote, 'The plainness of the story must be its justification. It is subjective and carries no moral.'[59] Former 51st Highland Division Medical Officer David Rorie concluded his memoir, 'So there you have the tale, such as it is.' He hoped his book would recall pleasant memories of those with whom he served, adding an apology: 'if I have told the tale badly – well, *mea culpa*; but, let me add, *sit meritum vuloisse*. For in the years to come a rough and ready record may be better than none.'[60] Many were conscious that their works were grounded firmly in the subjectivity of their own recollections, while at the same time they attempted to give truthful impressions of witnessed events, however rough their recollections of those impressions might have been.

The authority of the war memoirist was predicated on the idea that their opinions were formed through their trials and that they could be believed because they had lived through the events described.[61] Chapman wrote in the introduction to *Vain Glory* that there was little reliable truth to be found in the histories of the war, but instead, 'The nearest contacts with truth are the accounts of eye-witnesses of incidents from which a general picture can be built up.'[62] Like many other veterans, Chapman's preference was for works by authors who had witnessed combat, who had survived and reflected upon their experiences. Though Chapman understood well the difference between history and autobiographical writing – he became a professional historian later in life – he believed the value of literary contributions lay in their ability to supplement the historical record with impressions of participants with the emphasis on feeling and the truth that came through reflection. He reinforced the narrative agency of individuals who had seen the war, in all its aspects, as being cultural interpreters in the interwar period of the experience of war for subsequent generations. This is not altogether different than how some historians see the cultural value of these texts for students interested in warfare.[63] For a memoirist, publisher and historian like Guy Chapman, the eyewitness account was of utmost importance to understanding the war, if it could be understood, and offered something far different, but equally of value, to history.

Writer Rowlands Coldicott prefaced his *London Men in Palestine* (1919) in a similar vein. 'You will not find in this book the full-fig military narrative,' he wrote. *London Men*, though not military history, was still an important contribution, he argued:

> comments upon strategy, divisions rehandled in words, talk of the characteristics of a general. The net of prose is set in sight of smaller birds; chiefly a mass of private sorrows and rejoicings are entangled here. Out of a number of personal narratives of this kind some ultimate history of the war may be compiled.[64]

His memoir was meant to be exactly that – one work of many in which the eventual story of the war would be written – personal memories as something that could be compiled as the true chronicle of the Great War. 'We require all the personal narratives we can get; and, in my opinion, the more personal and intimate the better,' recalled Thomas Hope Floyd in his 1920 memoir *At Ypres with Best-Dunkley*.[65] He continued, 'Only thus can we see the recent war in all its aspects.'[66] Each war memoir was one part in understanding what men and women went through in the war. Samuel Hynes writes in *The Soldiers' Tale* of 'the truth of war experiences as being the sum of witnesses, the collective tale that soldiers tell'.[67] Hynes's description of the universal soldier's tale, a type of Braudelian sum of all possible war stories, fits closely with the contribution men like Coldicott and Floyd believed they were making to the war's legacy – one part of many from which an eventually true story could be understood, however visionary it was in its storytelling.

Interpreting truth

There was a strong desire by many writers not only to report on the war's conduct, but to also interpret the war's meaning to the next generation. This is not an uncommon response by those who witness any manner of traumatic events. 'Bearing witness is an aggressing act,' writes Kalí Tal.[68] 'The battle over the meaning of a traumatic experience is fought in the arena of political discourse, popular culture, and scholarly debate.'[69] Then as now, veterans were motivated to 'speak out' or truth-tell about their experiences, engaging with the concept of the living memory of events that they had witnessed. With emphasis on the inherent authority of the combat witness to interpret war, often a volunteer civilian or conscript in uniform, the war book was an influential cultural symbol of the 'real' or authentic war experience for those who have not experienced combat. The confessional aspects of war literature are particularly prevalent in World War I books; the idea of an outpouring of truthful emotions after the war is a prominent trope. In part this was because censorship during the conflict fostered distrust afterwards and feelings that the true suffering of soldiers was not accurately reported. As the era progressed, some feelings of bitterness became heightened and expressed in war literature. War bitterness, something found in nearly all war literatures, was not unique or uniform in British war books. Instead, war memoirs broadly reflect the same ambiguity consistent with the general population's varying beliefs on the war's greater meaning.[70]

The motivation to 'speak out' was one shared by some memoirists in this period. Many Great War books were disillusioned and/or darkly graphic in their portrayals of combat and the psychological effects of war. If the memoir was not history, exactly, then it was meant to reflect authentic experiences and feelings; yet emotional authenticity was something impossible to reconstruct through hindsight. Vera Brittain was one of many who felt a sense of generational burden in writing her war memoir *Testament of Youth* (1933). Describing her own youth as being smashed up by the war, Brittain's emphasis was on truth-telling about the war's horrors and its lasting trauma upon her generation, a polemical motivation for penning a memoir.[71] Writing from her letters and diaries, Brittain reconstructed her war experiences and put them within a wider context of her feelings about the war afterwards, using sources to reconstruct memories that she put within the context of her life and beliefs in the early 1930s. Truth was exceptionally important to her story, but her truths were not universal ones. Brittain's authority as a writer was limited to the events that she witnessed, her insight important but filtered through her postwar feelings about the war's legacy.

As Brittain reconstructed her memories she looked through old papers to piece together her narrative.[72] She was not alone: many others drew from documents or physical ephemera to write their accounts. Rooting through old letters, diaries and trench kit was a way to connect memories to composition, handling artefacts a means of authenticating memories. Material culture played a significant role in the process of reconstruction – of remembering – and, especially as the years went on, it became a vital way to show the reader that the author had not only lived the events described, but went through a physical process of remembering. Mottram recalled handling his old revolver and webbing as he sat down to write his 'personal record' of service. 'Like everyone else, I write without final authority. Only the Dead know the ultimate fact about War.'[73] Handling personal mementoes was a way to spark those memories, yet also an emotional process of reinvention for the writer as they confronted their memories. Objects were powerful props aiding the memoirist, but also conveying a sense of legitimacy to the reader.

One way to lend credibility to one's memoirs was to have an authoritative person or celebrity write an introduction. Writers turned to general officers and well-known literary figures to authenticate, endorse and contextualise their books. General Sir Hubert Gough, former commander of the Fifth Army on the western front, wrote the preface to Geoffrey Dugdale's slim memoir *Langemarck and Cambrai* (1932).[74] Similarly, Major General Rt Hon. J.E.B. Seely authored the foreword to Alfred Pollard's *Fire-Eater: Memoirs of a V.C.* (1932). Seely wrote a firm statement of martial spirit in keeping with Pollard's message: 'Every boy must long to receive the Victoria Cross. In this book he will learn how to deserve it.'[75] No less a figure than Field Marshal Allenby wrote the preface to Bernard Blaser's *Kilts Across the Jordan* (1926). Blaser served in Palestine and his book is a somewhat rare account by a common soldier in that theatre. Allenby commended the accuracy of the work and added his firm endorsement, 'I recommend to everyone this book.'[76] This was warm praise from the highest ranks of the British Army towards the common soldier. Though there was certainly criticism towards generals and politicians by soldiers during and after the war, the fact that many veterans had generals write on their behalf demonstrates that the surviving men of the war generation were not uniformly disillusioned with their commanders, but instead, many of them relied upon these commanders to preface their books.

A general could offer unique interpretative insights into the book that followed. Major General Sir Ernest Swinton, who after the war became the Chichele Professor of the History of War at Oxford, wrote the introduction to Charles Douie's *The Weary Road* (1929). He wrote:

> His book, written from the heart, with deep conviction, is cheering. It is essentially an act of justice and a tribute to our million dead. It tells us something of what they cannot tell us, of what the vast inarticulate majority of those who still live cannot tell us.[77]

Swinton's endorsement came with the message that Douie's work was meant to tell the story of those who could not tell it themselves, an indication of the historical importance of the work to follow. This type of preface lent vast credibility and distinction to an individual's war story.

Like former commanders, literary luminaries sometimes contributed prefaces. Arthur Conan Doyle, who lost his son in the Great War, wrote the introduction to Captain J.L. Hardy's prisoner-of-war memoir *I Escape!* (1927). Doyle complemented Hardy's prose and labelled him a courageous 'man of action'.[78] Hardy was one of the great serial escapers of German captivity, his story sensational and adventurous, and Doyle's endorsement lent the work authority. The American cowboy novelist Owen Wister, a popular fiction writer of the early twentieth century, was so taken with a dinner talk given by Major Vivian Gilbert on the Palestine campaign that he wrote the preface to his *The Romance of the Last Crusade* (1923). He wrote:

> none have I heard who could hold an audience in public with a war tale as Major Gilbert did. Such tales should be told and should be set down. They set to remind us of the greatness in man at a time when his littleness seems chiefly to the fore.[79]

As the title would suggest, Gilbert wrote a heroic account of his experiences in Palestine, which Wister put into the perspective of early 1920s war weariness.

Praise could also come from established relatives. Journalist Philip Gibbs wrote the introduction to his brother Hamilton's book *The Grey Wave* (1920). Philip Gibbs had been a war correspondent and was generally critical of the war's conduct by its general officers. His brother witnessed the war from the front lines as a junior officer. Philip wrote of his brother's experience:

> He had not the same broad vision of the business of war – appalling in its vastness of sacrifice and suffering, wonderful in its mass-heroism – but was one little ant in a particular muck-heap for a long period of time, until the stench of it, the filth of it, the boredom of it, the futility of it entered into his very being, and was part of him as he was part of it. His was the greater knowledge.[80]

Gibbs verified the truthfulness of his brother's book and spoke of the ability of the witness to add something more valuable about the human condition of war than the journalist or the historian. The 'greater knowledge' was the moral truth of the survivor to speak on the war's legacy.

A good preface could also offer a bit of panache that would distinguish a book or create a framework for understanding the text that followed. Osbert Sitwell wrote the introduction to Carrol Carstairs's *A Generation Missing* (1930). Carstairs's book was a memoir of service in the Guards Division and rather similar to many other junior officers' accounts that had been published. Sitwell gave the book a glowing introduction speaking to the authenticity of the work that followed. He used his preface to editorialise his own bitter memories of the war, hoping that more disillusioned books could lead to world peace: 'one would like to see, even in war books [...] a little more contempt and scorn, as well as hatred, for the war.'[81] Though Sitwell characterised *A Generation Missing* as a thoroughly disenchanted text – certainly the book shows no great affinity for war – Sitwell's preface framed the book darkly for readers.

As the 1920s wore on and more war books glutted the literary marketplace, prefaces began to discuss and debate the phenomenon of the war book itself. With so much ink spilled by war writers, the preface was a way to discuss the work that followed in light of other books in the same genre and to separate one account from the many others. The bestselling novelist Ian Hay wrote in the foreword to R.T. Rees's *A Schoolmaster at War*, 'For the last yen years we have been submerged by a flood of so-called war books, which depict the men who fought as brutes and beasts – as living like pigs and dying like dogs – disillusioned, drunken, and godless.'[82] The purpose of these books, to Hay, was to present the war in such a bad light that it could not happen again.[83] Hay viewed war as a test of 'human virtue', one which his generation had passed. Like many authors, he lamented much of the popular literature of the Great War because he saw it as being harmful to the memory of the soldiers who served.

As participants in the same conflict, many of whom shared similar experiences in combat, authors were bound to have different opinions about their service. These feelings became even more acute in the decades following the war when the legacy of military service was considered against lives in peacetime. Feelings of disillusionment and war-weariness were discussed and debated. When Carrington eventually published *A Subaltern's War* in 1929, he did so with a polemical epilogue where he addressed his concerns over the war's representations in popular culture. Disillusionment to Carrington was a misinterpretation by the public of soldiers being 'fed up' at the end of the war – tired and cynical but not disillusioned with cause or country. He saw disillusionment as a cultural trope, in his words a 'legend' that had developed as a means of explaining something that was much more complicated, the feeling of soldiers as they adjusted from war to peace.[84] Like Douglas Jerrold's pamphlet *The Lie About the War* (1930), Carrington's epilogue demonstrates the importance of the public debate over the memory of the war as it was played out from within war books themselves. Carrington was not fundamentally a militarist, but like Hay, he found the turn in public sentiment from celebration of victory in 1918 to regret in the interwar period decidedly problematic for members of his generation who had paid dearly for their victory.[85]

One way that authors reacted to 'sensationalist' war literature was by tempering their depictions of carnage. Though it was popular for writers in the late twenties to use grotesque scenes of 'battlefield gothic' in their works, many authors found graphic images of the war's gruesomeness tasteless, and they adopted milder imagery out of decency.[86] Geoffrey Dugdale deliberately sought to avoid grotesque depictions in his book. He wrote, 'I have avoided as much as possible the gruesome and disgusting side of the war; these episodes are dim in my memory and thankfully forgotten.'[87] Dugdale contrasted his memories, or as he called them, his 'plain statement of facts', with those of other writers: 'I never saw an officer drunk in action, nor did I have any of the unpleasant experiences which many authors of war books seem to have had, although I was in France for eighteen months.'[88] Some portrayed the war positively as an adventure. Thomas Hope Floyd's memoir *At Ypres with Best-Dunkley* was full of positive recollections of service, with occasional bouts of terror. 'For any boy who, like this boy, craved for excitement, and, while hating war theoretically and disliking it temperamentally, was not blind to the romance and drama of it all, there was ample satisfaction in the Great War,' he recalled.[89] H.G. Durnford, who was imprisoned by the Germans at Holzminden camp, wrote on the reissue of his book *The Tunnellers of Holzminden* (1930) that his book seemed quaint in hindsight, especially when he compared it to more sensationalist texts released at the time. 'It barely touches the battlefields, recounts no actual horrors and does not emphasise the spirit of good-bye to "all that".'[90]

Another way that authors engaged with the memory of the war was to discuss aspects of service that they believed had been neglected by the public. Captain Alfred Pollard, author of the obviously heroic *Fire-Eater: Memoirs of a V.C.*, indicated that he wrote his memoir to reclaim the virtues of military service despite the war's many tragedies. Pollard seemed to enjoy fighting, but acknowledged that his men thought him a bit mad for his bloodlust.[91] He, like Carrington and Dugdale, was frustrated with the way postwar literature was depicting soldiers, but to him there was another side to the coin that was not being depicted in war literature. 'The War is said to have brought out the beastliest instincts in man,' he wrote. 'It certainly brought out the noblest – self-sacrifice, unselfishness, comradeship.'[92] Though Pollard thrived in the military and exhibited great courage under fire, he knew he was an anomaly and believed that war, in general, was to be avoided for the best of humanity.[93] Pollard disliked war in an abstract sense, but found combat to be an adventure, a word also used by Carrington to convey the high spirits and positive morale of soldiers as they endured terrible combat on the western front.

The desire to write of the war's purpose runs against the stereotype that the war generation saw only futility in their experiences. Historian Daniel Todman has written in *The Great War: Myth and Memory* that many veterans saw purpose in their war experiences and that ideas of the war's futility were not universally felt.[94] The literary record demonstrates this variety of opinions. For memoirists, the impulse to show purposefulness and meaningfulness was strong, and functioned in tandem with their intentions to memorialise comrades. The desire to pass on their insights to the next generation is consistent with Jay Winter and Emmanuel Sivan's observation that the veteran, or witness to war, is an agent of these memories to the greater society.[95] For authors in the interwar period, a case can be made that their transmission of war experience to the wider public, whatever its objectives or intentions on the part of the author, created a collective body of works of remembrance that defined the experience of war for the public at large as a war that was hard fought, but ultimately meaningful to its generation.

For some memoirists, writing had a more pragmatic purpose than the complexities of the war's legacy. A war book could convey lessons for the next generation. Former ranker John Gibbons wrote his *Roll On, Next War!* (1935) to tell his son what he needed to know about army life: 'the Next War will come in his time, and I wish to give him a fair chance of deciding for himself whether or not to join the army.'[96] Gibbons found army life difficult. He wrote to teach his son of the hardships of combat and to give him the benefit of the practical tips he learned in the army. From scrounging to shirking, his book is written as an old soldier's advice to a new recruit. Similarly, Hugh Bayly's memoir *Triple Challenge* (1935) decried the decline in British manhood since the war, the author asking British women to expect more martial spirit from boys.[97] Another author concluded his memoir with a call for rearmament in 1923 as a means to promote the 'gospel' of peace by preparing for war. He wrote, 'A weakly armed nation of un-drilled and decadent males cannot with any hope of success preach this gospel.'[98] As the 1920s turned into the 1930s, these messages become more substantial. In Douie's memoir *The Weary Road*, he hoped, rather modestly, that his book would influence his comrades and future generations alike. He wrote:

> My hope is that its publication may induce other soldiers of wider experience and greater literary merit to put on record their memories of the war. The record of our tragic experiences may help our children: we could not save ourselves; we may yet save them.[99]

This tone of sacrificial reminiscence was unmistakably mournful, but it was also hopeful that a future war could be prevented.

***

Since the war itself, British memoirists have engaged with the public memory of the war, attempting to shape the ways in which the war was being remembered. In the interwar period, memoirists helped to write a new story for readers, that of the war's impact on individuals. They wrote conscious of historical legacy and to contribute their own voices to the war's legacy as it was first being considered. Essential to the memoirist's sense of identity was the personal 'voice' of the author, noted by Paul Edwards to be the true lifeblood of these texts, a voice that has now faded completely from direct memory.[100]

The motivations for writing a war memoir were varied and individual, but the desire to record events witnessed and to interpret their meaning for the wider public remained essential. The notion of truth was an important virtue: the authenticity of autobiography something that separated the genre from fiction. By giving the war a human voice, memoirists created a supplemental archive of war recollections for the emerging history of the war in the 1920s and 1930s as that history was written.

Though selective reconstructions, war memoirs were written to convey and preserve a life-changing experience, one written about in a commemorative literary marketplace that allowed veterans' many different voices to be heard. Veterans engaged with the concept of the memory of the war in their books, placing their work within the context of others. Though varied and individual in their interpretations, all memoirists were conscious of the importance of the events they were describing for history. As such, war memoirs remain for historians what they were at the time that they were published: a contested and debatable collection of varying opinions on the most significant event for the war generation.

CHAPTER 2

PUBLISHING THE WAR

By 1933 the British war book had become a cliché. The familiar figure of the infantry subaltern fighting in abominable conditions on the western front had sunk into the British reading psyche as deeply as any popular image of war previously. France and Belgium, with their muddy fields of shell-holes and corpses, were sensationalised in fiction and non-fiction war books that brought human suffering and deprivation to the fore. Depictions ranged from the sentimental and patriotic to the deeply disillusioned, with everything in between. The war book had become a cultural symbol, a guide to the personal trials of men and women who had returned from the war with tales to tell of destruction, despair and, for some, disillusionment.

Poking fun at the glut of war books available to readers in his *England, Their England,* A.G. Macdonnell wrote that in his book:

> there will be no terrific descriptions of the effect of a chlorine-gas cloud upon a party of nuns in a bombarded nunnery, or pages and pages about the torturing remorse of the sensitive young subaltern who has broken his word to his father, the grey-haired vicar, by spending the night with a mademoiselle from Armentieres.[1]

The important aspect of Macdonnell's satire was not necessarily that the British war book had become something familiar, but that his joke was good enough to be understood by its audience. Many war books were hackneyed, the experience of war stereotyped in the hundreds of similar scenes of the war, that, when taken together, told an unrelentingly violent story of a generational tragedy shown through the dashed heroic hopes of subalterns and the broken landscapes of France and Flanders.

When Macdonnell wrote in the early 1930s, the British public had grown fatigued with war books, and not for the first time. For nearly two decades – since the very first months of the war – war books had been released by British publishers, and by the 1930s they had simply lost something of their former edge. Commenting upon the social utility of the most graphic of this war literature, Ian Hay wrote: 'Their object of course is obvious and understandable – to paint war in such horrible colours that nobody will ever fight again.'[2] War depictions were still poignant and culturally relevant: lost innocence, battlefield carnage, and the psychological trauma of veterans who had returned from the Great War would always provoke reviews and discussion. Yet, graphic images of the war had grown somewhat tiresome, collectively grotesque, and disillusioned war experiences had become so ordinary by the 1930s that the impact of the war's sensationalism on British culture had gradually dissipated. Individual memories, which by their nature are complex and convoluted, were lost to the idea of the war's legacy of human destruction, its 'battlefield gothic' reigning supreme, cementing together the idea of the war's memory with its literary depictions, reimagined, by war writers.

In part, the reason for this gradual martial malaise was that war's tale was told hundreds of times over. When veterans returned from service after the war, some with manuscripts in their hands but many more with book ideas rattling around in their heads, they began the process of interpreting war experiences in the context of lives that were now forever changed. Publishers were eager to profit off the popularity of the genre and released hundreds of varied accounts: from the patriotic to anti-war, traditional to modernist, conventional to avant-garde, the war's tale was told in so many different ways.[3] The war's relevance to readers was what drove the publishing sensation of the war book, and, for 20 years following the Armistice, British booksellers' shelves were never empty of dust jackets depicting the many images of the war: aerial dogfights, sympathetic nurses, escaped POWs and the ubiquitous trench scenery of mechanised siege warfare.[4]

The war, with its millions of tragedies, generated hundreds of British war books about its experiences – well over 350 non-fiction war books alone – each telling a different story. As commercial commodities, war books did not exist in a vacuum, but instead were published within a literary marketplace that valued autobiographical writing. This chapter considers the way that the publishing industry responded to the war, or perhaps more appropriately, how the industry published the war's memory in the years when that memory was first being formed, the interwar period. In order to understand the commercial side of the war's memory, this chapter is divided into three sections to clarify certain aspects of the non-fiction war book market in Britain: first, the types of autobiographical war books released and trends in martial book publishing in the 1920s and 1930s; secondly, the popularity of martial literature with publishers and the public; and thirdly, attempts by British veterans at canonising war books, or separating quality from quantity.

Publishing war books

War books have a long publishing history. For centuries European soldiers and statesmen have written accounts of the great events of their age, and war was a part of commercial publishing long before the twentieth century.[5] Accounts from imperial wars were common in the nineteenth century and there was no shortage of soldier stories in circulation before the war's outbreak in August 1914. There were differences between previous wars and World War I's literary output. Though professional soldiers did write about their war experiences, the majority of Great War books were written by men and women who were civilians before the war and returned to civilian life afterwards. These new authors largely sought to describe the impact of the war upon their lives – juxtaposing their experiences of war with those of peace – and were not necessarily interested in writing the histories of their campaigns or the battles that they witnessed.[6] The new war memoirs went hand in hand with an increased penchant in the growing book business for autobiographical novels and memoirs, which had become popular with readers.

The war came at a time when British publishing was a stable industry and readership was growing.[7] Increased literacy led to a boom in commercial publishing in the nineteenth century that catered to many different demographics of readership. When war was declared in August 1914, the British Empire mobilised and a highly literate population volunteered for the armed services. Mass mobilisation introduced a new pool of potential writers – citizen-soldiers – who both during and after the war wrote accounts from the war's many fronts. As an event that changed the lives of so many Britons, the war became an important subject for the publishing industry to exploit.

The British publishing industry recognised the war as a commercial opportunity and was quick to respond to it despite the many trials that the war brought to the industry.[8] After an initial slump, the war helped boost sales in a period when there was uncertainty in the literary market over whether the public would still buy books in a time of insecurity.[9] Though the war led to challenges in the industry, it also proved the muse for thousands of poems in penny papers, essays and stories in periodicals, and books for major publishers on the fighting. The war opened up many opportunities for new writers, both men and women.[10] It also led to an expansion of the juvenile marketplace, particularly as martial stories were marketed to boys, a genre that had never been a stranger to adventurous tales of imperial adventure, a trend that continued afterwards.[11] The interwar British literary marketplace was inundated with stories of the war across all genres, and the subject published widely to meet the public demand.

Though many publishers certainly made a profit off the war, this is not to suggest that the industry did not face hardship due to the instability caused by the conflict.[12] The book industry traditionally had narrow profit margins and the war destabilised publishers, particularly, in terms of their available manpower and materials for production. Publishing houses were dependent on the availability of supplies at their printers and bookbinders to manufacture new books. Material shortages caused by the war and the associated rising costs were serious concerns. By 1918, publisher John Murray estimated that wartime paper prices had gone up 300 per cent.[13] Material shortages also affected other necessary items, such as binding materials of heavy paper, cardboard, and leather. Additionally, lack of manpower caused severe strains felt at publishing houses as men left their jobs for war: publisher Stanley Unwin lost three directors to war service.[14] The overall number of titles printed during the war fell.[15] Subsidiary industries, such as booksellers, binders and printers, also suffered. Faced with a drastic increase in prices and lack of supplies, some houses were barely able to survive. Publishing historian Jane Potter indicates that J.M. Dent nearly had to close his firm due to paper and leather shortages and lack of manpower.[16] Even with these obstacles, most London publishing houses survived the war. The firm Chapman and Hall not only survived, but also reported a record year in 1918 despite the limitations imposed on production.[17]

The demand for war literature continued after the Armistice, but war books faced a decline in popularity in the early 1920s. The years 1919 and 1920 saw a particularly high number of war novels and memoirs in print, books released by every major British publisher, reflecting a carry-over in martial publishing in the first two years of peace.[18] But fewer war books were released after 1920 and there was a feeling amongst publishers that the genre had passed its prime. In October 1920, George Blackwood, one of the most prolific publishers of martial literature, informed one of his more successful authors, Alan Bott, that 'War books seem to be deader than Queen Anne!'[19] Blackwood still published Bott's adventurous pilot POW memoir, *Eastern Nights – and Flights,* but the publisher had doubts about the genre's future sales. In *The Bookseller,* war books were reported to be in decline by Christmas of that year.[20] Predictably, in 1921 publishers accepted fewer war books and there was a major drop in those contracted and released.[21] Blackwood blamed the booksellers and the public for the turn, writing to an author: 'I am afraid that the booksellers are not giving us very much support, as they say the public will not take up War books.'[22]

The 'silent' 1920s

In 1929, the novelist Hugh Walpole wrote that he was stunned to see a revival in war literature after a decade of slump. 'Why, after almost complete silence for ten years, this sudden flood?' he asked readers of *The Saturday Review.*[23] Walpole believed that war books had disappeared in the early 1920s only to return after nearly a decade of silence. The logic was that, by 1929, veterans were finally able to speak their minds about the war after years of traumatised silence.[24]

The facts were very different. The war did not leave either the public mind or booksellers' shelves in the 1920s. Rather, war books were released in smaller numbers, but never completely disappeared from the market. Beginning in 1920, the downturn in martial literature can be attributed to both a fall in public demand and commercial factors. Book historian John Feather described publishers' conservatism as the 'dominant trend of the period' and publishers were cautious towards risk.[25] As soon as there was an indication that the demand for war books was decreasing, in 1920, publishers reacted by contracting significantly fewer of them. The decline was significant: 57 non-fiction war books were released in 1920 compared to 21 in 1921 and 14 in 1922. This was partly due to the pace of postwar recovery within the industry as the economy still proved sluggish. Wartime shortages carried over into the postwar period and books were more expensive to produce after the war than before.[26] Even by 1920 – two years after the war's ending – John Murray bitterly complained in *The Bookseller* that the cost of production was still three times more than it had been before the war.[27] There appears to have been no shortage of authors – Murray's firm was receiving three manuscripts a day in 1920 – but publishers simply could not afford to take risks on books that might not sell.[28] A saturated war book market and slow sales meant fewer book contracts for veterans with stories to sell.

Rather than the downturn in war books solely an ideological reflex – a type of mass turn in public mood against the war – it was also the result of the genre losing popularity because it had passed its prime. Since 1914, war books had been released in far greater numbers in Britain than ever before. 'So many people have written of their doings in the great war that it seems as if there were nothing more left to be said,' wrote Scottish nurse Henrietta Tayler in 1920.[29] The book industry had been publishing accounts of the war for six years – two years longer than the conflict itself – and in far greater numbers than these books had ever been contracted or sold to the public previously. The war not only dominated British life for its duration, it also saturated the book market with accounts of its conduct, and a downward trend was inevitable as public interest could not stay at the same levels as during the war. When publishers, such as Blackwood and John Murray, saw this interest beginning to decline, they decided that the public was 'off' war books and reduced the number of texts they were contracting.[30] The decline was in part market-driven and publishers were unwilling to contract books that involved greater risk at a time when they were still recovering from the war. Where just about any book about the war would have sold reasonably well in 1915, this could not be assumed to be the case in 1921.

As a result, fewer war books were released in 1922 than 1921. The decline in new titles does not signify that the public stopped buying war books, only that fewer were contracted and published. There were plenty of war books that sold well during the so-called 'years of silence' including some bestsellers. In January 1922, *The Blocking of Zeebrugge*, a historical account by Alfred Carpenter, and *The Escaping Club*, a war memoir by a former prisoner of war, A.J. Evans, were both listed as bestsellers.[31] In March 1922, four war books made it to the bestseller list of *The Bookseller*: two memoirs and two novels.[32] Ernest Raymond's patriotic war novel *Tell England* was very successful, selling out 11 imprints.[33] E.H. Jones's adventurous and sensational POW memoir *The Road to En-Dor*, which was originally published in 1919, not only sold multiple editions, but remained in print and selling a decade later.[34] Both patriotic and sensational war books were popular in 1922. It should be noted that this was the same year that C.E. Montague published his book *Disenchantment*, a popular collection of essays on the disappointments of the war generation.[35] Just at the time when all of these books were on the bestseller list, there was a trade rumour in 1922 that there was a 'ban' on war literature by British publishers.[36] One critic in May 1922 wrote: 'If you write well enough about the war, and truthfully enough; if you probe beneath its surface fallacies to the truths of its mental reactions, you will have readers enough to justify your publisher taking the risk.'[37] The war book was certainly not disappearing in the 1920s, but risk was clearly an issue for publishers.

In fact, the mid-twenties saw the publication of remarkable war books despite the downturn. Between 1924 and 1926, a total of 20 war memoirs were released. Though the wartime book boom was over, the war was not forgotten by book-buyers. In 1924, one critic wrote that there was still 'no end of new books about the Great War'.[38] Gerald Gould saw the difference between publication success and failure as hinging on quality. He wrote, 'Yet I do not think that the public (for whom too few good words are said) ever shrank from being reminded of the war, if the reminder came clothed in the vividness of a writer's genuine individuality.'[39] Celebrity authorship was certainly a factor. Macmillan published Kipling's regimental history *The Irish Guards in the Great War* in 1923. Winston Churchill's *The World Crisis*, a book for which he received an enormous £9,000 advance from Thornton Butterworth, made the bestseller list in 1924.[40] Works of quality fiction were released between 1922 and 1928 by R.H. Mottram, Ford Madox Ford and C.E. Montague. [41] All three authors wrote multi-volume works on World War I which gained significant public followings and made the bestseller lists. Ralph Hale Mottram was widely praised and thought by many to have written the great work of his generation in *The Spanish Farm Trilogy*.[42]

War books, in their many forms, had not disappeared in the 1920s. In 1926 one reviewer wrote, 'It is curious how these war-books continue to appear at intervals, although we have been assured, ever since about 1921, by publishers, theatrical producers and other experts that the public is sick of the war and never wants to hear it mentioned again.'[43] Despite their occasional pessimism towards the popularity of war books, publishers kept releasing accounts of the war.

The revival

The British war book began a mainstream publishing revival corresponding with the ten-year anniversary of the war's ending. The 1928–31 war book boom has been the subject of much attention because the period saw the publication of some of the best war memoirs and novels of the age by Siegfried Sassoon, Edmund Blunden, Robert Graves, Frederic Manning and Richard Aldington. Foreign authors, such as Erich Remarque and Ernest Hemingway, also released major works in this period, making it something of a golden age for World War I literature.

Though the revival of war books corresponded with an increase in book titles generally in the late 1920s,[44] the new war literature was seen by many as being darker and more cynical than what came before. As the 1920s waned, Britons, in particular those in elite political or intellectual circles, began to grow fearful of another European war. Richard Overy writes, 'future war was presented in remorselessly apocalyptic terms,' in particular, as a result of what the Great War generation had gone through.[45] The nature of warfare had been altered; the technological changes of battle had unmistakable human repercussions in the way in which Britons conceptualised the impact of war upon their society.[46] The ten-year anniversary of the Great War was a moment to redefine the war's meaning in light of an insecure future, rewrite, in part, its legacy in light of the fact that many Britons earnestly hoped to never go to war again. 'War-books suddenly came back into fashion in 1928–1929: but to "debunk" rather than glorify.'[47] The new war literature was seen by many to reflect a society frustrated and fearful of the future – a society yearning for peace.

The publishing industry released books that reflected complicated and changing memories of the war in the late 1920s. David Reynolds writes that 'the late 1920s was in general a moment ripe for reflection,' and the new war literature came out of the spirit of the anniversary that reflected a sense of 'seismic rift' felt by the war generation.[48] The book boom was a commercial opportunity for publishers to release accounts that catered to public demand. 'I am aware, there is a theory that as a nation we have grown graver since the war,' *The Bookseller*'s columnist wrote of war books in 1929. 'The question is simply one of demand and supply; and if the public were to show signs of having grown tired of such books, the publishers would speedily become aware of the fact. For the present, at any rate, the exact contrary seems to be the case.'[49] Rather than tiring of accounts that represented the 'filth, beastliness, and the demoralization of war', the public appeared ready for a revival of war literature to remember the war in light of a decade of rumination.[50] The 'new' war literature proved integral to the way the war has been remembered in Britain because of both the quality and tone of works released.

The revival of war literature began in the late 1920s and continued into the early 1930s. T.E. Lawrence's *Revolt in the Desert* was a bestseller in 1927 and Edmund Blunden's *Undertones of War* was very well received in 1928, beginning the new trend. It would be the success of Erich Remarque's *All Quiet on the Western Front* that created a boom out of a British revival of war books. Certainly, Remarque's book was exceptional compared to the British books in circulation: he represented an enemy soldier writing about the disillusionment and dehumanisation felt in the German Army on the western front. He was not a public school British subaltern, like Blunden, Graves or Sassoon, nor was he an eccentric hero like Lawrence. His work drove the revival in 1929, garnering much attention within the industry, and his widespread success sparked a debate on the legacy and meaning of the war.

Initially, the book industry was slow to notice Remarque's success.[51] Yet by May 1929 it was apparent that *All Quiet* was a bestseller. *The Publisher and Bookseller* wrote that it was a 'great piece of writing', but the industry's pre-eminent periodical was baffled by the German author's ability to sell 25,000 copies in month, a feat described as 'staggering and incomprehensible'.[52] There was no small amount of envy of Remarque's success, especially as his book continued to sell, outpacing

British authors that summer. By August 1929, Remarque's publisher Putnam advertised *All Quiet* as the 'Best Selling Book in the World'. The publisher advertised that the book sold nearly 195,000 copies, British booksellers selling more than any other nation but the author's Germany.[53] It was unusual for any book to remain on the bestseller list longer than a few weeks; Remarque remained listed from April to October. This type of success was an astonishing achievement for any book, in any genre, in this period.

Though Remarque's success eluded most British war writers, it also benefited them. In his wake, publishers contracted more war books, hoping for the next big success. In 1929, a total of 16 new war memoirs were released in Britain. This was only a slight increase from 1928. However, after Remarque's success that summer, British publishers released 35 new war memoirs in 1930.[54] The rise in new war book titles is, in part, attributable to the success of *All Quiet* and the hopes of publishers to strike while the iron was hot.

In addition to leading to a revival of war books in print, the 1929–31 book boom fostered an important debate over the way the war was being remembered, and *All Quiet* was at the centre of this controversy. The book was seen as 'an angry declaration about the effects of the war on the young generation that lived through it'.[55] The book's disillusionment and tragedy caused some British authors to write in the same vein, or write as a reaction to his work, and seek publication for their own stories.[56] The creative turn initiated by Remarque favoured books that were darker in their interpretations of the western front.[57] The 'realistic' war novel became largely a reflection of this theatre of war. Yet, some felt that the new war literature did not represent the spirit of men at the front and that the new literature tarnished their legacy. Douglas Jerrold wrote, 'Every one of these books is written under the illusion that the war was futile, and under the illusion that it was recognized as futile by those who fought it.'[58] To Jerrold this was one of the many 'lies' about the war, which had wider political effects upon society. 'These books simplify and sentimentalize the problem of war and peace until the problem tends to disappear in a silly gesture of complacent moral superiority,' he wrote.[59] To Jerrold the great risk of portraying the war as futile folly, where 'everything was lost and nothing gained', was that the next generation would grow up believing that peace was something easily attained.[60]

Complaints about the content found in war books were hardly new in 1929. Other scholars, most notably Janet Watson, have demonstrated that the war books debate of 1929, in which Jerrold was a key participant, focused attention on the trope of disillusionment, a concept that was widely contested.[61] The 'war books debate' of 1929–30 was multifaceted and largely focused on veterans critiquing each other's works because the war elicited strong reactions from those who served and sacrificed. Writing on the criticism and controversy surrounding R.C. Sherriff's *Journey's End* and Remarque's *All Quiet*, R.V. Dawson commented: 'Each man in his own way has shown us the reality of modern warfare, and has exposed it as animal reality, brutish, bestial, degraded, and unsupported by any hint of spiritual realism.'[62] Not all veterans, though, interpreted their war experience in such a way, and war books continued to be controversial because the war's legacy created strong feelings among those who had fought in it. The critic A.C. Ward wrote with hyperbolic relish in 1930: 'The affair of the War-books was the culminating episode of that Bloodless War between the Contents and the Not-Contents which divided the post-War generation into two camps as definitely as the Gospel divided Christian from pagan in the first century.'[63]

War writers were far more ambiguous in their interpretation than Ward was giving them credit for in his facetious polarity of contentment. Publishers, as well, demonstrated considerable breadth in the variety of books that they published. The late 1920s were not a uniformly disenchanted age, though many of the most popular war books reflected this theme. Disillusioned books were often present on the same publishers' lists as patriotic ones. Jonathan Cape published Thomas Marson's patriotic memoir *Scarlet and Khaki* in 1930, the year after they published Graves's contentious memoir *Good-bye to All That*. Faber, publisher of the disillusioned novelists Siegfried Sassoon and Henry Williamson, also published Frank Richards's *Old Soldiers Never Die*.[64] In 1928, Heinemann published Harold Dearden's *Medicine and Duty*, an edited diary containing positive reflections on the author's war service; in 1930, the firm released Carroll Carstairs's disillusioned memoir, *A Generation Missing*. On the bestseller lists too, there was variety: Charles Carrington, whose *A Subaltern's War* had an epilogue specifically contesting the notion of widespread cultural disillusionment, was listed as a bestseller in July 1929 in the midst of the

All Quiet boom.[65] The British war-book boom saw a revival of all types of war literature and not just anti-war tomes.

The 1929 debate had much to do with how veterans were interpreting the truth of the war. Truth was accentuated by reflection, it was thought, and a ten-year period of rest and contemplation had been long enough to germinate more realistic accounts of what soldiers went through.[66] Samuel Hynes likens this to an 'exorcism' of the war's demons by authors.[67] But there was an unmistakable commercial side to the debate as well. War writers were beholden to a literary marketplace: their contracts with publishers depended upon the quality of the work and its commercial prospects. Publishers in 1929 responded to public demand by doing what they had always done: they contracted more titles about the war to an eager public that seemed interested in the genre. Though certain authors may have kept quiet about the war during the 1920s, many others did not. An astute 1930 article in *The Times Literary Supplement* summarised the issue as one of tone, that recent war writing

> differs from what had gone before only in that it is a flood in place of a trickle and that the water has grown decidedly muddier. Its characteristics are brutality, cynicism, contempt for motives and for leadership in the council chamber and the field, an obsession with the disreputable.[68]

The flood of war books wrought by Remarque made issues of public war memory more apparent for mainstream book buyers and fed into concerns about the war's legacy. Controversy certainly benefited both writers and publishers.

In 1930, war books continued to be released in high numbers. Many were contracted in 1929 while the boom was ongoing and then put into print the following year. Reviewers speculated about the war book's continued popularity. 'What makes people, ten years after the War, write these books? Who are the people who read them? And by what literary law has it come about that they seem to get better and better every day?'[69] However, some critics were finding that by summer 1930 the genre had peaked and was losing ground.

> Some future historian of literature will perhaps write a chapter on the decline and fall of the English war novel. If he attempts to

discover why it declined and fell, he may decide that the process was due, not so much to the shortcomings of the writers, as to the jaded appetites of the readers.[70]

By the end of 1930, war books began to decline for the second time in ten years.

Similar to the early 1920s, war books did not disappear from the market in the 1930s but were reduced in numbers on publishers' lists. In 1930, a total of 35 non-fiction war books were published; in 1931 only 14 were. John Brown, writing for *The Publisher and Bookseller*, saw the 1929 boom as an 'artificial' one, driven mostly by the press. Brown also believed that the recession of titles was not the death of the genre, but instead a return to normalcy. 'After a river flood there is a drop in the level of the water – back to normal. The war-book boom is over, the public interest has slumped – back to normal.'[71] War books did recede back into their place within the publishing industry; throughout the 1930s, the industry continued to publish them, only in more limited quantities.

There were some notable memoirs released in the 1930s including Guy Chapman's *A Passionate Prodigality* (1933), Frank Richards's *Old Soldiers Never Die* (1933), Vera Brittain's *Testament of Youth* (1933), Cecil Lewis's *Sagittarius Rising* (1936) and John Lucy's *There's a Devil in the Drum* (1938). As the 1930s wore on, writers focused a bit more on the very real possibility of another European war. All memoirs, these were quality war books representing diverse experiences of the war.[72] Though Brittain's book was a vociferous indictment against war, the rest were more ambiguous in their interpretations. With each passing year of the 1930s, quality books were released, but there was no revival in the 1930s similar to that of 1929, where for one year war books dominated the publishing market as the public reconsidered and debated the legacy of the Great War in print.

Popularity

There is considerable difficulty in measuring the impact of war books on the public and gauging notions of readership in the interwar period. Publishing records are often incomplete and the book industry's consolidation has not always been kind to archival records. There were attempts to chart popularity in the interwar period by periodicals: since the early 1920s, *The Bookseller* has kept a monthly list of bestsellers. The bestseller list in the 1920s and 1930s was based upon booksellers writing in their bestselling books in any particular month.[73] Books were listed according to their popularity in select bookshops and not according to raw sales data. Though bestseller records are subjective, they can be useful to demonstrate popularity over a set time, but they reveal little in terms of specific sales numbers. Moreover, bestselling books are only an indication of copies sold in bookstores and not of the influence or impact of a work among readers. In a 1924 article entitled 'Why a best-seller', the mysterious nature of popularity was considered:

> It is perhaps as well that there is no certain prescription for the making or manufacture of a best seller [...] We may therefore be thankful that every best seller must, by necessity, be a rule to itself, and must attain the coveted place, if not entirely by good luck and good fortune, at any rate by the unfettered and unrestrained excellence of its own characteristics.[74]

Though there was no formula for making a bestseller, the industry did have certain marketing tactics that it employed to help book sales. Publishers often timed releases to coincide with summer or Christmas holiday buying and the industry would market books widely in periodicals to achieve notice. But there was no real way to predict the success or failure of a work. The fact that the trade seemed to be surprised by Erich Remarque's success in early 1929 is largely indicative of this fact.[75]

In November 1930, F.M. Harvey Darton wrote an analysis of books bought in the first nine months of that year for *The Publisher and Bookseller*.[76] Darton indicated that the book business had no way to predict what books would become bestsellers.[77] He also wrote that bestselling books only stayed at top sales, at most, for two months and that books sold were not an accurate indicator of books actually read or borrowed by the British public. His analysis, when applied to war books, rang true: of the bestsellers in 1930, H.L. Tomlinson's *All Our Yesterdays* was an early leader in January 1930, but the book's popularity waned with time. Other war books did well that year, such as Frank Crozier's bestselling memoir *A Brass Hat in No Man's Land*, Henry Williamson's

Patriot's Progress and Frederic Manning's *Her Private's We*, but they did not achieve the same lasting success as Remarque. Darton wrote that 'these [war books] were all rockets and are falling or fallen.'[78]

Success or failure in the book industry was dependent upon a number of factors. Genre played a role: in general, popular fiction sold better than other genres.[79] Fiction was the mainstay of the publishing industry and almost always outsold non-fiction: this applied to war books as well. It should not be surprising then that Remarque's *All Quiet* outshone British war memoirs in this period. His success was comparable to wartime novelists, like Ian Hay, 'Sapper' and John Buchan, whose popular fiction was reprinted widely throughout the interwar period.[80] Hay's *Carrying On After the First Hundred Thousand* was in enough demand in 1936 for William Blackwood & Sons to issue a 102,000 run of an affordable 1s. edition, a huge printing.[81] Other British war novelists too fared well in this period. As Hugh Cecil and Rosa Maria Bracco have demonstrated, middlebrow novelists such as R.H. Mottram, Wilfred Ewart, Oliver Onions and H.L. Tomlinson sold well in the 1920s.[82]

Although fiction dominated the market overall, nearly half of Great War literature released was non-fiction. Non-fiction was usually produced in smaller print runs than fiction: it was not uncommon for memoirs to be released in imprints of fewer than 5,000 copies and frequently as small as 1,000 copies. Print runs were larger for fiction and novels generally as they sold at a lower price than non-fiction, 7s. 6d., compared to upwards of 9s. or more for many war memoirs.[83] For example, Edward Arnold released seven non-fiction war books in the early twenties all of which were nearly twice the price of popular novels and each book was printed in a comparably small run.[84] Publishers had to take into consideration the market for a work and its likely sales and were careful in their estimates of printings, measuring the work's likely success against its price and print size.

Though most war books were printed in small runs, some were bestsellers and were marketed widely. Siegfried Sassoon wrote three volumes of fictional autobiography on the war compiled as *The Complete Memoirs of George Sherston*. Sassoon was a famous war poet and literary figure, factors that helped with the success of his works. His second volume, published in 1930, *Memoirs of an Infantry Officer*, was listed as a bestseller by *The Bookseller* as soon as it was released in mid-September.[85]

The book sold 24,000 copies in its first three weeks.[86] Faber advertised the book's success upon its debut: 'Over 20,000 before publication and selling 1,000 every day since.' [87] The fact that the book sold so many copies before publication is not terribly unusual. Faber had been advertising the book widely and this number accounted for pre-orders from booksellers who based their estimates on the success of his previous book, *Memoirs of a Fox-Hunting Man*. It should be noted that Sassoon's biographer indicates that *Memoirs of an Infantry Officer* did not outsell *Memoirs of a Fox-Hunting Man* and by 1935 had sold 48,000 copies in five years.[88] *Memoirs of an Infantry Officer* was out of print by 1945.[89] The fact that it disappeared from *The Bookseller*'s bestseller list soon after publication indicates that the book's sharp drop in sales was consistent, roughly, with the sales data cited by Sassoon's biographers. Even so, Sassoon's work has had lasting success and was in its period one of the bestselling British war books.

Robert Graves and Vera Brittain also had excellent sales. Graves's *Good-bye to All That* garnered five impressions in its first month in November 1929.[90] This was, perhaps, the best time in the interwar period for an author to release a war book as it was right in the middle of the Remarque boom. After a strong debut, *Good-bye*, like Sassoon's *Memoirs of an Infantry Officer*, began to waver. It sold only half of its fifth impression and sales dropped sharply by early 1930. As his book was non-fiction, Graves had a higher selling point than Sassoon (10*s*. 6*d*. to 7*s*. 6*d*.) but the book still sold 40,000 copies by 1931.[91] In comparison, Brittain's *Testament of Youth* went through 12 impressions from its release in 1933 until 1939, though, it had a bit of a slower start than both Graves and Sassoon. *Testament* seems to have done extremely well throughout the decade, Brittain's biographer noting that the book sold 120,000 copies in the 1930s.[92]

War poets were certainly not the only writers to sell books. First-time (and one-time) war memoirists also made the bestseller lists. E.H. Jones and C.W. Hill's *The Road to En-Dor* (1919) sold so well in the 1920s that John Lane issued a cheap edition in 1930 of 10,000 copies.[93] The book was still in its more expensive 8*s*. 6*d*. format, but the publisher felt confident it could sell out a cheap edition as well. The book was so successful it was generating modest royalties for the authors ten years after its debut.[94] Lasting success was relatively rare. With smaller print runs, non-fiction could usually sell out a first edition, provided that the publisher did not overestimate the size of the run. If sales were sluggish, the publisher could turn to marketing the work a bit differently. When sales of Alan Bott's *Eastern Nights – and Flights* began to wane in 1920, the author recommended his publisher, George Blackwood, target the book's marketing eastwards.[95] Bott thought the book would sell in India, where there were more soldiers who saw service in the Middle East, the theatre of war depicted in the book. Similarly, Bott recommended to Blackwood that the publisher market his flight memoir, *An Airman's Outing*, to serving cadets in the RAF, the author knowing where a book about flying would be most appreciated.[96] Bott's two books were certainly successful – they sold over 22,000 copies between 1917 and 1920.[97]

Bott's more modest success compared to authors like Ian Hay, Sassoon or Vera Brittain was not atypical. Publishers were often pleased when works sold out their initial runs, regardless of the print size. Publishers printed small runs for exactly this purpose and would selectively issue reprints based on successful sales. An example is Maurice Johnston's war memoir *450 Miles to Freedom* (1919). The book sold 4,424 copies for Blackwood and Sons. The publisher printed a large first run and then four subsequent smaller editions as needed.[98] Edition size decreased from 2,100 in the first printing to 525 in the final imprint as interest in the book waned.[99] Occasionally, reprints could yield greater success than the initial print run. Cartwright and Harrison's *Within Four Walls* (1930), a book about captivity and escape from Germany, sold just over 1,000 copies immediately after its debut in October 1930. From 1930 to 1940, the book sold only an additional 2,379 copies.[100] After the title was bought by Penguin during World War II, the book gained new life as it was reprinted in a cheap edition.[101] No doubt, the new war made an account of captivity and escape from a German prison popular again.

Though popularity was difficult to predict, many war books sold reasonably well during the interwar period, with the highest sales corresponding to the 1918–21 and 1928–31 periods. Bestsellers were regarded as something of a mysterious anomaly, though, they were usually written by established literary figures. Outside of the boom years, there were hundreds of memoirs and novels published in small runs in first editions and reprints, indicating that war books were in circulation, though their popularity depended upon the particular niche in which the book would fit. Though many authors were not bestsellers, many sold out their print runs, and earned modest royalties and some feeling of success from writing their war books.

Quality from quantity

In the March 1924 'Current Topics' column of *The Bookseller and Stationery Trades' Journal*, the question was posed: 'Are there too many books?'[102] In the mid-twenties the book trade began growing and recovering from the postwar economic slump. The concern was that Britain was producing too many books, many of them of low quality. Popular books spanning the 'brows' were in demand because of a growing level of literacy among the public.[103] But the number of books released was still high; in 1929 there were nearly 10,000 new books published by British firms. Considering reprints, there were 13,000 titles published that year alone.[104] The book industry was growing, but that growth was subject to criticism over whether all of these books were necessary and whether they had any lasting value.

Within this broad context of literary expansion, war books were one genre that expanded along with the rest. By 1929, there had been hundreds of war books printed since the Armistice, with many more to come. The numbers of war novels ran parallel to those of memoirs. The war's depictions varied as much as the tone of these books – there were dozens of books written by soldiers serving in exotic theatres, ones by pilots and prisoners, by medical officers and nurses, by spies and agents abroad – so many titles and so many differing stories. Critics began turning their attention to sorting quality from quantity.

Good from bad

The years 1929–30 witnessed significant coverage of war books in periodicals. Much of the coverage was by veterans objecting to the sordidness of sensational war literature. There was a general fear that Remarque's book would inspire imitators to publish overly graphic depictions of the war purely for shock value to sell books. T.H. Thomas in reviewing war memoirs in the *Journal of Modern History* in 1930 wrote that there was a 'quarantine' around war books cordoning off the bad from the good. 'The worse books, roughly speaking, have emerged as best sellers; the general public has pretty consistently maintained its favour for the most sensational and improbable narratives and for the obviously partisan and distorted histories (such as Winston Churchill's).'[105] The issue was not whether war books were being printed, it was the impression that the wrong message about the war was sinking in with readers.

Though for some of Bloomsbury's smart set the war was seen as culturally regressive, barbaric and destructive, there is little indication that these beliefs were widespread amongst critics, publishers or authors. Veterans did not share the same sensibilities as literary elites and many objected to war books that became polemical symbols of political causes. The book industry itself was full of veterans – editors and owners of firms had lived through the war and many had served – so they were not entirely divorced from having opinions on the books that they were releasing.

The reality of the marketplace was that publishers were caught in a bind between authors who wanted to publish war books of varying types and qualities and a reading public that had strong, but varying, feelings about the war. *The Bookseller*'s editorialist commented that it was difficult for publishers to strike a balance between works on either side of this debate.

> For while one of these bodies prefers the story of the war, and the experiences of the men who took part in it, to be more or less idealised – sentimentalised, if you will – the other approves of the most horrifying, repellent, and sordid details of every kind being revealed and described with a ruthless realistic frankness which need not, in fact should not, stop short of positive literary brutality.[106]

Publishers were likely catering to both groups: disillusioned books for those who were looking for confirmation of the war's horrors; patriotic depictions for those who wanted to be reminded of the war's heroism.

The sensationalism of the 'war books' debate was essentially about reception and the idea that the war's cultural impact could be measured in its literature. In many ways, literature was seen as the most powerful way for the war's meaning to be conveyed or compromised. In periodical reviews, works were almost always put into the context of this debate; how the book stacked up to the current war literature was a common way for reviewers to discuss its merits and detractions. Janet Watson writes that notions of postwar disillusionment were 'strongly and vociferously resisted at the time', mostly by former veterans.[107] This is largely true; the periodical literature from that year offered conflicted opinions on the role of literature and the war.

Reviewers in 1929–30 noted fatigue with the war books glut. Mostly, this was with the war's fiction rather than its memoirs, which were usually more balanced in their depictions. When Douglas Jerrold in 1930 attacked war books that in his view distorted the true meaning of the war, he listed almost entirely novels. Jerrold specifically singled out Graves's memoir *Good-bye to All That* which he criticised for its inaccuracies.[108] By February 1930, some critics were tired of bad war books. They described 'filthy' things, said one reviewer; 'the worse in this respect became the best of the best-sellers.'[109] Reviewing Williamson's *Patriot's Progress,* in July 1930, one reviewer wrote that it was 'one of the few war books that ought to be read, even after a surfeit of that sort of literature'.[110] War books did not just come in surfeits, but also in spates[111] and in floods.[112] The boom had created a weary critical response. Graphic war imagery, which was initially shocking to readers, had become banal. By July 1930, Osbert Burdett reflected the mood of exasperation at the spate of disillusioned war literature when he reviewed 'A Happy War Book'. He wrote, 'Here is that paradoxical and unexpected thing: a happy book about the war.'[113] Burdett was enthusiastic about Maurice Baring's *Flying Corps Headquarters*, largely a matter-of-fact memoir describing mundane staff work for the RFC. His enthusiasm to be reviewing a happy book indicates that war books had become very dark indeed.[114]

Canonisation

In 1930, there were two significant attempts to sort, categorise and rate war books. Both were to provide the British public with a list of books that should stand the test of time. The lists were an attempt to sort quality books from sensationalist tattle. These early attempts at canonisation were distinctive and erudite and were spearheaded by two intellectually rigorous men of different talents who served in the war: the poet Edmund Blunden and the historian/journalist Cyril Falls.[115] Though the two men came from different backgrounds and had differing opinions on war literature, Falls and Blunden both generally agreed on many titles. Both of their bibliographies demonstrate that in the 1920s and 1930s there was serious thought put into the genre's characteristics and that leading critics were attempting to canonise quality war books.

The Blunden bibliography was not his work alone. It was co-authored by Falls, H.M. Tomlinson and R. Wright. Blunden wrote the introduction and defined the contextual framework of the bibliography that included fiction, non-fiction memoirs, and history. An historical approach was important to Blunden and he saw continuity between the literature of the war in which he fought and a long tradition of military writing.[116] 'In short,' he wrote, 'the literature of the War began long before the War.'[117] Blunden believed many of the books published during the war were propagandist, what he called 'hate', and were unrealistic in their depictions as a result.[118] By 1917, the tone of writers toward the war had changed. 'Slowly, spokesmen appeared; and now the danger is, perhaps, that the horror and crime of war are being transformed into a glib axiom, a generalisation which may not work at the hearts of the new generation.'[119] Blunden was afraid that sensationalist writing about the war was just as unrealistic as that of the wartime propagandists.

Blunden judged authors according to their 'sincerity' and not their 'sensationalism'. He believed the former to be the essential trait for authors. 'Only a stern sincerity on the part of writers, and an open and wakeful mind on the part of readers, can produce a vital sense of the war as it was, and as it might be again,' he wrote.[120] Such sentiments demonstrate how seriously Blunden took his role as a bibliographer. Blunden believed that the literature of the war was an important part of educating the British people on the human experience of combat. A war book's truthfulness was demonstrated by the sincerity of its author. Blunden believed that the essential task of a war writer was to represent fairly the violence and human conditions of war. This was so the public could understand the high stakes of fighting. He also saw great virtue in portrayals of suffering and heroism, especially, for the next generation of Britons.[121] Blunden's idealistic hope that war fiction could set a moral example for 'heroism and self-sacrifice' contrasts greatly with feelings that the literature of the war was meant to evoke purely anti-war sentiment. Instead of widespread disillusionment, it demonstrates a more balanced approach. Blunden famously deeply hated war for its suffering; but in his bibliography he still believed in honouring the war's sufferers.

The Blunden bibliography was structured according to subgenres. They included: History, Personal Impression and Recollections, Psychological Interpretations, Prisoners of War, Fiction, Poetry, Drama, and Divisional and Regimental Histories. Though most of these categories would seem obvious, the separate subgenres for POWs and Psychological Interpretations stand out. POW books were a large group and Blunden listed nine important works from this subgenre, though there were many more of these books in print. The category of 'Psychological Interpretations' included Barbusse's *Under Fire*, A.P. Herbert's *The Secret Battle*, Montague's *Disenchantment* and Tomlinson's *Waiting for Daylight*. Such books, Blunden believed, demonstrated the war's impact on individuals, or, in the case of Montague, generational psychology. Fiction contained the works of R. H. Mottram, Ian Hay, Wilfred Ewart, Richard Aldington, Gilbert Frankau, F.M. Ford, Hemingway, Remarque and Edward Thompson amongst others. Many of these authors had been bestsellers. Blunden's list is a cross-section of, mostly middlebrow, British authors, with the occasional foreign author included.

The list includes Blunden's own work, *Undertones of War*, with a diverse pool of other writers. Bruce Bairnfather's wartime books made the list, as did the *Wipers Times*. Stephen Graham, Charles Carrington and Sassoon were listed. Included also were works by pilots, doctors and generals. Few of the books Blunden included would be considered sensationalist. Blunden praised historical accounts, particularly the *Official History*, Buchan's *A History of the Great War* and Churchill's *The World Crisis*. He also included 26 regimental histories. Blunden's analysis and his careful, diverse, cataloguing demonstrated the many forms the war book took in the 1920s. Overall, the Blunden compilation was an attempt to canonise war books in a way that would impart the wisdom of veterans with literary inclinations for a public that might not know a good war book from a bad one. In the prelude to the bibliographical listings, Blunden and his co-editors stated: 'This list is in no sense a complete bibliography, but aims at being a representative selection of books for those who would know why the War was and what it was.'[122]

Cyril Falls's bibliographical efforts were far more comprehensive. In 1930, Falls published *War Books: A Critical Guide* for the publisher

Peter Davies.[123] The Falls bibliography was the most comprehensive attempt by a British critic to annotate, rate and categorise war books during the interwar period. Falls had a significant bias. He had little time for disillusioned accounts or for those that questioned the war's purpose. However, in his compilation, he addressed the issues over the war's interpretations of memory fairly. He attempted to contextualise his argument in terms of his own war experiences. He rated books according to their ability to impart what he believed to be the 'truths' of the war from the perspective of the participant rather than of the back-of-the-lines critic. *War Books* is an unusual and rich book for Falls's annotations alone.

Falls was at heart a military historian. He had served as a staff officer with distinction in the 36th (Ulster) Division on the western front. After the war he helped write parts of the *Official History* and the history of the 36th Division.[124] Later he turned to writing for periodicals and newspapers and he was a prolific book reviewer for *The Times Literary Supplement*. His career as an historian was solidified by his appointment as Chichele Professor of the History of War at Oxford, a post formerly held by Major General Ernest Swinton.[125] He wrote widely on World War I. Falls believed the war justified, its soldiers worthy of honour. To defame their memory or sensationalise the war's horrors was anathema to his beliefs. Disillusionment reflected postwar bitterness more than anything felt during the war. What mattered to Falls was the accuracy of both the military details and the sentiment of works released in the interwar period. His rating system reflected this.

Falls's enormous task was to catalogue, describe and rate as many war books as he could from the 1920s. He did so through the means of genre: General Histories, Unit Histories, Reminiscences, and Fiction. He examined foreign books, those in German and French, as he had a reading knowledge of these languages. He did not include poetry or drama.[126] In his introduction Falls was very critical of war fiction and of embellished personal reminiscences. He believed such books had become formulaic. He dismissed much of the war fiction of the 1920s, with the intention of correcting the historical record, and re-establishing a sense of balance to books he thought went too far and became solely propagandist and exaggerated. He also believed that their content created a 'lust for horror' or a graphic effect of violent images in the minds of readers. He felt that novelists' repeated criticism of the motives of the nation and the conduct of the army was 'nauseous'.[127] Falls did not take issue with those who disliked war – he believed the conditions on the western front had been appalling – but he did not want sensationalist images in popular novels poisoning the legacy of the war or the reputation of the soldiers who fought it.[128] He believed that opportunistic writers were using the genre of the war novel for profit. His bibliography was an attempt to tell people who knew little about war what they should and should not read.

Falls's rating system was simple: one star for a good book, two for a very good book and three for one 'of superlative merit'.[129] His commentary was direct and repeated the themes of his introduction. Of the Master of Belhaven's war diary, a two-star book, he wrote, 'This is a diary of a quality and originality so remarkable that it makes many of the popular War books of to-day appear not only flat but childish.'[130] One superb book for Falls was Blunden's *Undertones of War*, a rare three-star work. He wrote of the poet:

> Those who know Mr Blunden as poet must have realised that the War has haunted him and that, however much he hates it, it has always had for him an extraordinary fascination [...] It is probably the only single book of its kind we have had in English which really reaches the stature of its subject.[131]

He compared Blunden's more modest sales with Remarque's by writing, 'Perhaps it is natural that the crowd should prefer a Doré to a Rembrandt.'[132] Remarque received one star. Frederic Manning got three for the fact that the 'horrors' of war were present, but 'incidental', their exposure not the focus of the narrative.[133] Robert Graves received one star. 'His War scenes have been justly acclaimed to be excellent; they are, in fact, among the few in books of this nature which are of real historical value. His attitude, however, leaves a disagreeable impression.'[134] To Falls, the sardonic Graves exhibited bad form. Falls tended to be more generous towards historical accounts or reminiscences that offered a balanced view of the war and its meaning. He sharply criticised books which had nothing good to say of the war or those who fought in it. His bibliographic selection and ratings were consistent with his opinions on the war.

Both Falls and Blunden attempted to catalogue war books according to the works' quality. They paid close attention to how those works represented the war to both former combatants and non-combatants. Each of their guides reveals certain prejudices: both valued the experiences of participants over non-participants and had discriminating literary tastes that rewarded the temperate and reserved while disliking the mawkish or sensational. Falls's work, in this respect, was biased towards men who served in the front lines; accounts by women receive little critical praise.[135] Falls and Blunden's works were early attempts to separate the good from the bad: they were functioning as literary guardians of the war's memory. Books that they believed should be read by the public contrasted with those they felt were distortive of the war or unworthy of public attention. They wanted to tell those who had not experienced the war what they should read about it. Through their eyes the experience of World War I was neither reductive nor was it limited to the clichés that had become the popular imagery of the soldier's experience. Instead it was best represented through accounts that demonstrated variety and nuance. Personal accounts that were valued demonstrated the endurance of the average soldier and fighting spirit of the BEF while not glossing over the horrors of the war. They also reinforced the personal transformation of participants under fire. To them the best war books were those that had a greater meaning or moral than just outrage or simple disillusionment. Each list is a healthy reminder that the conflict over the war and its representation was one addressed by participants in the interwar period who were not easily charmed by public sensationalism over war books. Historian Hew Strachan wrote in 1991 that Falls 'makes judgments which stand up well today and which are remarkable for their wisdom so close to the events'.[136] For historians, the lists tell us how two erudite critics of the interwar period attempted to rate books based upon their own experiences at the front and what they considered to be the meaning of the war they knew.

***

War books were an essential part of the publishing market for decades after 1914. In Britain, there was a vibrant publishing industry that met the demand for war books as the war was ongoing. Afterwards, as publishers confronted the realities of the postwar economy, war books lost some of their popularity. The interwar period was one of changing war memories in Britain that reflected growing concerns over the future of the nation and the possibility of another war, anxieties that were played out in the way that the war was written and remembered. In 1929, largely because of the anniversary of the peace and the publication of the international bestseller *All Quiet on the Western Front*, there was a revival of war books in the British marketplace. Publishers again printed the war's fiction and non-fiction stories in great numbers. The revival created a significant debate over the way war books represented the war. This debate continued into the early 1930s.

Throughout the interwar period, the war was a popular subject within the books business, its accounts generating much interest among publishers as well as the wider public. Critics, in particular Cyril Falls and Edmund Blunden, attempted to rate war books according to their accuracy and their tone. Veterans both, their concern for the war's representations was part of the 'war books debate' of the late 1920s, when soldiers discussed the war's memory through its memoirs. The debate coincided with the glut of war books in the British marketplace in 1929–30 and returned public attention to the war as a literary and commercial trope. The British publishing industry catered to public demand throughout the period and never stopped printing the war, though editors were careful in their selection of contracts. It is in no small part because of British publishers that the war was remembered in so many different ways.

CHAPTER 3

WAR MEMORIES: THE WEST

The western front is the dominant theatre depicted in Great War literature. In the words of Andrew Rutherford, it was 'the principal matrix from which war literature emerged'.[1] It was also the principal matrix that defined the idea of the British experience of World War I, one that was constructed and given life by war writers who depicted a subterranean hard existence defined by the iconic images of trench life. This chapter considers the way that war writers excavated the idea of the trenches from their own memories. Through writing about trench life, memoirists created a distinctive mythological landscape that defined the way Britons saw the experience of World War I for a century afterwards.

The logical explanation for the predominance of western front literature is a simple one: more British soldiers served in France and Flanders than anywhere else. When these soldiers returned, their war memories were of a static front, defined by darkness and sensory images associated with the trenches. Living through and surviving the western front came to dominate British conceptions of the war's memory because war memoirists chose to construct a landscape for readers that focused on the visceral rawness of survival and the physical transformation of men within a narrow, muddy spaces. Darkness, wetness, discomfort and death is the western front's great imaginary legacy. These images are found in all war books from this theatre, ones written by exhausted subalterns and their men, the 'Poor Bloody Infantry', who survived life beneath the parapet and remembered their service viscerally in print for readers.

The body of literature published in the 1920s – the trench tale – was remarkably similar in its temporal details, but often very different in its interpretative meanings. Western front books were more than just narrative retellings of the war: the trench was a trope, a means of understanding the war's illogical inhumanity. In the hands of a skilled war writer, the trench became a symbol of hardships endured and individual transformation in battle. The physicality of living underground provided innumerable trials for protagonists; men, mostly, writing their own stories that focused on the many small but emotionally draining discomforts of life in the line. The larger themes – such as the transition from youth to adulthood – developed through a narrative space where hardships were overcome daily. The nature of the trench itself and its effects on men's minds and bodies became a part of the war's unique story through this landscape's backdrop of suffering. With so many battles on the western front that seemed indecisive, the emotional battle of carrying on in the line, under fire, became as much a part of the war's story as its military history, if not more so. Surviving the trenches was its own victory for memoirists who might not have witnessed any other victories in battle in their months or years of service abroad.

As the years went by, trench memories became even more important to the way that the war was remembered publicly. In the process of remembering, memoirists created a version of history that emphasised hardship in the trenches, first and foremost, and created a distinct mythology defined by environmental challenges and personal change. In this context, western front memoirs represent Samuel Hynes's concept of the Myth of the War, which he defines as 'not a falsification of reality, but an imaginative version of it, the story of the war that has evolved, and has come to be accepted as true'.[2] In a larger sense, the landscape of the trenches came to represent an 'image of total annihilation' that 'is our tragic myth of modern war'.[3] The total annihilation – the pockmarked broken farmland of the Somme and the bogginess of Passchendaele – was creatively reimagined by writers from events they remembered, their war experiences recalled through the most trusted sources they had, their sensory memories, which even years afterwards remained acutely focused on what they had lived through.

The mythologised landscape of the western front has been a powerful trope in the public memory of the conflict since the 1920s. In this context a historical mythology is not a falsehood, but instead, an imaginative reconstruction of a true experience.[4] As memoirists remembered the war, they excavated sensory memories that had to be reformed imaginatively into prose. The trenches were a powerful part of a soldier's experiences, but certainly, not all of it. Their importance to the war's memory, however, is essential to understanding how landscapes form historical myths, which function not only creatively, but also have a lasting influence on the historiography of conflicts in popular perception. Daniel Todman writes that myths have a 'social function', one that helps explain historical events reductively, so that they can be easily digested by the public.[5] In this context mythologies are not necessarily false, but merely, stories that run akin to history, but do not meet standards of evidence and factual accuracy. Myths are anecdotal reflections of lived events retold over and over again for the public to understand something of the history of the war. Because they conveyed a brutal imagery of suffering understood widely, the trenches were the most remembered of the war's many experiences.

War memoirs, because of their autobiographical form, all have elements of mythology: they are personal stories meant to make sense of events that are chaotic and difficult to communicate. It is easy to see how the mythology of the trenches, the retelling of an experience both mundane and terrible at the front, became the dominant perception of World War I. The war's personal tragedy, defined in scores of memoirs, reduced what was a complex and fragmented narrative into a series of digestible personal stories. The popularity of trench books – of authors like Edmund Blunden, Siegfried Sassoon and Robert Graves – gave many the idea that this what the war 'was really like'. These authors' experiences, however different than those of most who served, were appropriated over time as the central tragedy of the war. The western front was the most easily understood experience of the war for the public because it was familiar: its landscape understood by those who served and their friends and relatives, an easily communicated and shared cultural mythology based on sensory images commonly understood as the war's story. If there was one thing that people in the 1930s thought they knew about the war, it was the mud.

This chapter examines the western front trench memoir. As the most common experience shared by veterans of World War I, this body of literature is incredibly important not only because of its familiarity, but also because it created the narrative of the trenches. In some ways trench books have had more impact on the history of the war as it is commonly understood than any other medium. In the 1920s and 1930s the trenches were nearer in the public mind – the war's physical hardship was more familiar – and the war's brutality represented widely in commercial memoirs of difficult service. The literature of the trenches is the means by which most understand the experience of World War I.

Though western front narratives share certain similarities in their imagery, the point of view of the authors is important. Memoirs reflect the military and social classism of the British Army's command structure. Accounts by junior officers, or subalterns, were by far the most common published and have become the most famous accounts of the war. In part, this is because young officers wrote of a British war experience defined by middle-class values: benign heroism and the plucky endurance of the public school boy in the face of personal trials beyond his control. The junior officer's story has come to dominate our perception of the war, for good or bad, because it framed the war's awfulness in moral ways that could be understood and that were of social value. Junior officers' accounts, however, were not the only ones released in the interwar period. They were joined by a limited number of memoirs written by common soldiers, men who wrote of a war lived without batmen, baths and comfortable billets. For other ranks, the war's representations were different and reflected a spirit and camaraderie that was not found in the educated and carefully constructed stoic tragedy of the subaltern's tale.

Creating the trenches

As his troopship approached the French coast, E.C. Matthews recalled the feeling of anticipation as being like 'the schoolboy who swallowed his watch'.[6] It was June 1916. Four months of great battles along the Somme loomed ahead. The speculation of combat weighed upon his mind and played on his imagination. Beginning with his nervous embarkation to France and then moving to the front, Matthew's short memoir of service is set amidst the destructive landscape of the western front. The book follows a familiar format: embarkation, training, movement and finally battle. Trepidation – the ticking of the watch – fear and excitement mixed well with the scene unfolding around him as he moved from his ship to the front, the landscape changing from the pastoral to purgatorial. The road ahead was different than that behind; it was broken by shells and littered by the debris of weary battalions passing. The sound on the air was different too: artillery batteries, distant as he marched but growing nearer, range-finding targets beyond their sights, the staccato thumping of shells in time with the watch, no doubt, still beating inside his gut.

No section of the landscape around Matthews appeared unaffected by war: indeed, even the sky itself was militarised: 'sausage balloons, aeroplanes and shell-bursts dotted the sky around, which bore witness that war in the air was not negligible.'[7] Onwards his battalion moved up and into the vast network of confusing trenches. Like all new battalions, his was led up the line by guides through labyrinthine trails cut from farmland and now fortified with redoubts, wire and thousands of bits of splintered wood makeshiftily holding up the walls. On his first night in the trenches, Matthews recalled huddling in a dugout staring at the candlewicks flickering with each 5.9-inch shell falling amongst them. A familiar image – the candlelight's waver, recalled in many memoirs to show the ground's vibration and the flinching focus of the soldier's gaze upon it, dislocating and unnatural. Daylight brought no shortage of horrors for this *Subaltern in the Field*, who now only a few weeks after leaving England, looked out 'over the parapet and gazed at the mutilated bodies of the fallen who once engaged life, the tragedy of war loomed up in ghastly reality'.[8] There before him was another world so different than the one he inhabited a few days before.

In a mere four pages of his memoir, Matthews moved his reader from the trepidation of a troopship in the English Channel to the terror facing a subaltern in the trenches. His journey from home to front was recognisable: it was taken by millions of men on both sides as they crossed from one world to the next. Matthews's journey is a common one in war literature: the unveiling of the war's panoramic like a curtain rising for a new act in a theatrical *Bildungsroman* where the naive parade ground soldier has his debutante moment seeing the war and its manifold dangers. This unveiling moment is an essential part of war writing, an essential anecdote of experience to remember, because it juxtaposes the notion of before and after, ignorance and innocence contrasted with knowledge and experience gained through hard service. Matthews demonstrated this journey through stages: the landscape itself paralleled his emotional transformation as he moved forward, coming to grips with his own fears, dutifully walking towards the possibility of his own mutilation or death. The landscape before him was broken, crudely turned over, and painfully corrupted by shells and cordite that had destroyed the men who came before. The human metaphor of foreshadowed destruction is all too apparent.

The ubiquitous trench is the great setting of the human drama of World War I. Defensive lines carved into a complex network spanning 475 miles, the trenches came to symbolise more than just the idea of combat; they became a symbol of the war's terribleness. There is a paradox to the horrors of the trenches. As Hew Strachan argues, trenches were dug to protect soldiers from artillery and machine guns and not to harm them.[9] The difficulties of trench life, though, made men remember the physical hardships of wet cold and the seemingly random terror wrought by artillery barrages much more than the protection provided by such discomfort. We have forgotten the protective aspect of the trench because war writers made the idea of the trenches the central aspect of their war experiences. Though action in battle drives many war books, in World War I memoirs the domesticated boredom of trench life was remembered in fact more than assaults or raids, which were considerably less common than just being in the trenches – surviving – in conditions that were not easily forgotten. In memoirs trenches lost their more defensive pragmatic purpose and instead became a space of personal trial and, to some degree, a space of generational transformation, one that contrasted civilian feelings of comfort with the social degradation of a war raging with many cruelties, none so significant or so dramatic as the corrupted farmlands and villages of the western front.

As Matthews's book demonstrates, the metaphor of the trenches was felt personally. The journey up the line was a painful rite of passage, important in memoirs and demonstrative of a consciousness towards the impact of the war on individual masculinity. Traditionally, courage in battle has been seen as an important part of the transition between youth and adulthood. The nature of World War I combat and the democratisation of armies meant that the idea of a trial by battle, or a trial by war, was felt generationally. Though this trial could create bonds of comradeship with men in the line, it also led to dislocation, in particular as the experiences of World War I soldiers were so foreign from any conceptions of warfare they previously had. Eric Leed defines the trial of battle in World War I as being one that was 'disjunctive' instead of an experience that integrated men within a particular set in two ways: war experience set men apart from those who did not share those experiences; war experiences also set men apart from social ideas formed both before and after.[10] The landscape of the western front with its otherworldliness can be seen as the set dressing for the personal, even psychological, break between soldier and society before the war and afterwards.

Memoirists were certainly conscious of the disjunctive nature of the trenches; however, the notion of the rite of passage was important to emphasise specifically because trench service made men different than they were before. Llewelyn Wyn Griffith wrote of 'Those who have been in the trenches, and the rest.'[11] Griffith saw the transformation of those who had passed through this trial as one of rebirth, a spiritual scourging for young men, immature boys according to Carrington, who went to battle 'before their characters had been formed', under the age of 25, most of them, who passed in and out of trench lines that tested their youthful spirit of optimism and endurance to the limits of human physical and psychological resilience.[12] Trenches both made and broke men; subterranean service left its mark on all who felt it because, in part, it signified a clear break between one world and the next, the civilian and soldier, a life before and a life afterwards forever changed.

The difficult task of the World War I memoirist was to reconstruct this landscape for their readers and to make the war's destruction a backdrop for the idea of personal transformation. The destruction of the western front was so otherworldly and so complete in its misery that it created a paradox with the idea of an emergent and redemptive humanity that could come from it. With often little fighting to show, memoirists wrote of the intricacies of daily life on campaign, in this case, surviving the challenges of life beneath the parapet to demonstrate a sense of human agency and individual spirit that transcended the landscape. So much narrative space is devoted to trench aesthetics and the kitsch of kit that it is difficult to not see a greater significance to what it frequently overlooked: that the mundane difficulties of life in the trenches were written about in all their grotesque realities to demonstrate a type of martial competency, if not heroism, in a soldier's ability to adapt and carry on. The suffering of the mud-soaked, shell-shocked British soldier can be seen as being linked to that of the soggy, hungry and equally terrified soldiers of previous wars. Rather than forming squares as at Waterloo, men at the Somme crouched against muddy walls and waited for the shelling to stop. Blunden was conscious of this historical link to the suffering of Britons in past wars. He likened his trench, the Old British Line at Festubert with its many horrors, to that of Troy.[13] Carrington wrote more forcefully: 'All wars fought to a finish between well-matched combatants are equally cruel, whether they are fought with bows and arrows or with poison gas.'[14] Hardship, in soldier literature, often demonstrates trial and resiliency as well as suffering. In order to be a considered a survivor, war memoirists had to construct the backdrop of their trial; they had to write their own epics with the scenery they possessed – in this case the desolation of the western front.

The process of narrating the front formed a significant challenge for writers. For many, narration took the form of an arduous journey from the peaceful home in England to the trenches in France. Along the way, there were many ordeals, minor rites of passage to even get up the line. For Max Plowman the journey to the front was a trial of confusion: days spent speculating on what he would see at the Somme, foretellings of death and terror by old veterans in dark dugouts along the way, and then, finally, walking through the morbid detritus of battles fought only weeks before. Like Matthews before him, Plowman's trek took him across a landscape littered with debris: broken rifles, discarded food tins, webbing, shredded trees, ammunition and helmets whose owners were presumably missing or dead.[15] 'We can only move slowly over this confusion of forsaken trenches,' he wrote of the journey forward.[16] Reaching his destination – a former German trench reversed – offered his company no respite. The landscape, in fact, became more gruesome, the men seemingly more rat-like as they darted in and out of holes in the ground.[17] His platoon's first task was to clean up the remains of two soldiers blown up in a latrine.

The immediate and jarring realities of trench life compared to what came before it was something noticed by all. Plowman's cleaning up of a latrine covered with human remains is one of many anecdotes of the dislocation felt for men arriving for the first time at the trenches, a moment when they were welcomed to the war. Often, it is a soldier's first encounter with danger that is a defining moment. For American Civil War soldiers, this moment was called 'seeing the elephant', when one's civilian life was replaced by their new violent martial existence, emotions heightened and lives altered as a result of combat.[18] For nineteenth-century armies, seeing the elephant came through open order battle lines or fighting columns, combat that even in the age of the rifle musket was close enough for men to see their opponents, in some cases their faces, clearly.[19] The realities of combat in World War I meant that the first exposure a soldier had to a similar form of danger was often going up the line, danger being not that of an enemy soldier, but artillery fire while they were moving through trenches. There was a distinct difference between the trial by battle in nineteenth-century warfare and the more passive trial of endurance found in going up the line in World War I. In the trenches seeing the elephant became not seeing anything but mud walls and the remnants of men, both living and dead, underground. The enemy was artillery fire coming from miles away; the enemy was the mud under one's feet.

As a narrative device, the first trench memory often served as seeing the elephant. Men arrived at the end of their arduous journey across territory destroyed by industrial war through dark corridors of communication trenches where they confronted danger and death, or dead bodies, often anecdotes that foreshadowed later experiences and ironies of service. Graves recalled making way for a stretcher carrying a wounded man who blew off his own face; an accident the result of a ricochet of a percussion bomb aimed too low, his mutilated head covered merely with a sandbag.[20] General Frank Crozier's first impression of the line was of making into a 'quiet' trench, a realisation juxtaposed by the terror of witnessing his first casualty, a 19-year-old Tommy hit by a random shell. 'Constant training for a whole year and then just one day in the line! This is attrition!' he recalled ironically of the poor teenager facing amputation and evacuation immediately after his arrival at the war.[21] Anecdotes like these were remembered to call attention to the war's random terror, its indiscriminate violence, and the fact that no man was safe even in trenches specifically dug for safety. Trial by combat for men was replaced by trial by endurance: mere survival itself an act of minor heroism.

Once in the trenches, men had to adapt to their new existence. Edmund Blunden described this as 'trench education', the title of the second chapter of his memoir *Undertones of War*. Reluctant to go to war as Blunden was, and having no illusions about its awfulness, he was still ignorant of war's discomforts, the trenches leading to eventual desensitisation to brutality. Like that of Plowman and many others before him, Blunden's journey to the trenches was exhausting: he slept for nearly ten hours in a dugout after coming up the line in darkness. When he woke he saw for the first time the 'cramped, tattered, and dingy' life in the Old British Line.[22] He toured his new home taking notice of occasional bones and skulls sticking out 'like mushrooms' from the walls. For Blunden it was a new type of mental and physical conditioning that led eventually to a regularity of duties. He recalled that 'in the trenches a subaltern's business was rather general than particular.'[23] He learned quickly to be proficient in the many 'domestic details' of command, like censoring letters, looking after stores and inspecting rifles.[24] These details took on a certain comfortable routine that helped mitigate the terror around with feelings of domestic and professional agency. Subalterns and their men adapted to the world around out of necessity, making the best out of bad situations.

Though partaking of the hardships of soldiers since time immemorial, the new warfare was distinctly different and it took a different toll on men's bodies, their very senses now overwhelmed by the destruction around. In *A Schoolmaster at War* R.T. Rees recalled that the trenches were both a 'new' and 'loathsome form of fighting', the former not strictly, but the latter certainly, true. Rather than going into winter quarters, he wrote, 'we had to fight in all sorts of seasons, and, when not fighting, to spend most of our time in a stinking ditch.'[25] Rees contrasted what he knew of warfare from his books as a schoolmaster before the war, with what he lived through, the hard life of an infantry officer manning the firestep day and night in all kinds of weather. Walking from intact and pastoral earth – the farms of France and Belgium – to broken landscape was itself a jarring sensory experience: soldiers went from open and limitless spaces to one of confinement where their arms outstretched touched retaining walls, their feet clopping on duckboards instead of earth. They walked with shoulders slumped and eyes glued on boots, to prevent falling. Walking into a trench for the first time, Griffith recalled, 'Sound, sight and smell were all challenged at once, and they must in concert submit to the degrading slavery of war... Sense and soul were of no account [...] we had cast sanity to the winds.'[26] There was something illogical about living underground even if it made perfect logical military sense to do so: the men drawn into trenches and adapting to their unnatural existence, but still recalling its mad otherworldliness.

Adaptation did not mean that men became immune to the trials of their new existence. Sensory discomfort led to continued discord and derision. Certain memoirists fixated on particular things. For Griffith, it was largely smell. For Rees, it was horror of rats, the pernicious vermin the subject of much of Philip Gosse's memoir of his time as a rat control officer on the western front.[27] Memoirs are full of smells and tastes: cooking food; dirty water or tea smelling of petrol; lice; and the ubiquitous wetness of tunics, boots and puttees.[28]

Sound, too, in particular the sounds of shells that came with a whole new invented nomenclature that had its effects on men's minds and bodies. Shells caused men to get windy, to crouch in fear and embrace the walls of their loathsome defensive homes; their constant presence made sense of the trenches, men adopting a reluctant acceptance of their purpose. One former officer wrote of enduring a bombardment, 'The manhood's gone completely out of you.'[29] Nearly all combat memoirs of the western front labour to describe the sound and feel of concussions. Artillery fire is described as too much for the understanding of readers, often referred to as something impossible to believe or convey into words, the absolute terror caused by random death. Despite the impossibility of description, so many memoirists try to describe that feeling, to convey their helplessness, or to construct narratives of discomfort that are essential to understanding the western front's physicality.

The trench itself, then, became the metaphor for the war: for men's psychological and physical transformation on the western front. Men who came up the line eventually learned to adapt to their new homes and wrote about the discomfort to impart a sense of martial trial for their readers. The jarring realities of trench service proved to be just as formative for soldiers as any experience of combat before and after. Moving up the line, adapting to service and confronting dangers both real and imagined were harrowing learning experiences that were related later as a means of defining what the experience of war was like for a generation that served and survived a war waged under cover between two muddy walls.

A subaltern's war

As Blunden indicated, hundreds of miles of trenches were left in the hands of thousands of subalterns, junior officers, whose job was to command platoons and companies of infantry. These officers – under the rank of captain and mostly born into middle-class families – wrote of their experiences in abundance. The very word 'subaltern' defined the experiences of so many soldiers who were temporary gentlemen in the British Army: E.M. Channing-Renton's *A Subaltern in the Field*, Carrington's *A Subaltern's War*, Plowman's *A Subaltern on the Somme*, Matthews's *A Subaltern in the Field* and Richard Skilbeck Smith's *A Subaltern in Macedonea and Judea* were books in which the title reflected the ubiquity of the junior officer's story. The subaltern's memoir was the most common, and likely most popular, type of war book released by publishers and read by Britons. Certainly, the most lasting and popular memoirs to come out of the war – Sassoon's *Complete Memoirs of George Sherston*, Graves's *Good-bye to All That* and Blunden's *Undertones of War* – were three amongst many others that helped define this typology in the minds of readers. Many others who wrote both memoirs and novels of their war experiences serving on the western front joined these iconic writers, all junior officers.[30]

Subalterns' accounts came in many varieties. They were written from every theatre of war and contain a multitude of specific military occupations and experiences. Junior officers wrote of service in Palestine and Mesopotamia, Greece, Gallipoli, Italy, Africa, and the omnipresent France and Flanders. They were trained as gunners, pilots, chaplains, medical officers, logisticians, staff officers and infantry officers. Some were taken captive and a few escaped from prison to write harrowing accounts of their POW adventures. In truth, there were many different subalterns' tales written and sold to the British public in the 20 years after the war. Yet despite the many differences, the 'subaltern's war', as a typology, became one depicting the young middle-class junior officer serving in the trenches on the western front. It is no overstatement to write that the western front officer memoir has become the most iconic representation of the war's literary memory in Britain.

Why did the junior officer's experience become such a powerful trope in the minds of Britons? The reasons for this narrative predominance are complex but important to understanding the war's legacy, the book market and middle-class readership. One factor was certainly the sheer number of demobilised officers who had both the time to write and the talent to do so. Many of these authors had the necessary literary connections to see their books published. Junior officers simply wrote and published their accounts in greater numbers than both generals and privates. Some junior officers were up-and-coming poets or had conceived literary ambitions before the war, which meant that their wartime experiences became one of many subjects to write about. Blunden, Graves and Sassoon were clearly of this type, as were Llwelyn Wyn Griffith, Alfred Pollard, Guy Chapman, Herbert Reed, Ralph Mottram and Frederic Manning, amongst others. These writers went on to establish careers as authors, or in Chapman's case, in the publishing industry, their reputations being established, in part, by their war books. The quality of books from this theatre and their reception by critics helped determine the way the war has been remembered. In part, the disproportionate emphasis in the interwar period on literary elites and junior officer war books reflects their popularity with publishers, men whose firms contracted this type of book in abundance because they told stories that appealed to middle-class readers.

There is another reason the subaltern's tale reverberated within British culture so strongly, one that goes to the heart of the way Britons have conceptualised the war's memory. The junior officer story is one that not only has been written about in abundance, but is an experience that has also resonated. Subalterns' tales emphasise a sense of personal tragedy that is easily visited on the war generation as a whole. Robert Wohl defined the 'lost legions of youth' as a trope within English interpretations on the war, one that privileged a romantic image of the war generation's lost innocence through iconic poets like Siegfried Sassoon and Rupert Brooke.[31] According to Wohl, Britons have perceived the war largely through its literary legacy, one defined by elite junior officers who were deeply disillusioned by the war's tragedy. Trench life proved deeply disillusioning for men of middle-class sensibilities and when it came time to write of that experience, junior officers fell into a cultural stream that privileged the cataclysmic disjunction of the war.

The popularity of the idea of generational tragedy is certainly part of the reason subaltern stories have proved so lasting. In them, there is an element of the coming-of-age story, except instead of romantically discussing life in public school or university, loves and losses, the subaltern's tale focused on the tragic impacts of war on men's minds and bodies. This is an unmistakably romantic narrative: it is easy to see the appeal in the idea of youth tarnished by battle, or what Wohl defined as 'doomed youth led blindly to the slaughter by a cruel age'.[32] Those subalterns who carried on, endured the trenches and came out of the war scathed but alive had a story after the war that fell into a cultural narrative of idealism and innocence, both pastoral and personal, which were irrecoverably lost to the war.

The myth of the subaltern's war cut both ways: it represented both horror and tragedy but also courage and heroism.[33] Junior officers' memoirs discuss notions of fear, suffering and human reactions to these emotions in abundance. They do so in ways that changed how heroism was perceived. Jessica Meyer writes that memoirs 'were also spaces in which men were able to reconstruct their masculine identities as soldier through redefinitions of the masculine ideals that warfare challenged. Courage and cowardice were redefined retrospectively to accommodate the fact that all men felt fear and were perilously close to showing it'.[34] In an age of mechanised warfare, especially of conscript armies, traditional displays of bravery in personal combat were rare. On the western front, the practicalities of survival amidst high-explosive shellfire changed the imagery of heroics from that of great physical skill in combat to a more basic definition of courage: endurance. The ability to survive the western front became a masculine rite of passage for some postwar memoirists to depict. Meyer describes this new heroic mythology as that 'Myth of the Soldier-Hero', which was reinvented as a result of the war, to accommodate notions of endurance, duty, and courage under fire.[35] On this theme, Michael Adams writes, 'the memoirs of the men who survived [trench warfare] often suggest that the war experience had many compensations and that, again, it is only fighting that makes true men and places them in an elite company above and beyond the touch of ordinary mortals.'[36]

Just as the nature of heroism changed because of modern war, the figure of the hero changed as well to accommodate temporary officers from the middle classes. This new type of hero, the youthful and fatigued subaltern, was a temporary officer enduring the conditions of the western front and keeping his composure in front of the men under shellfire. Describing such an event was difficult, but not impossible. Arthur Hanbury-Sparrow, author of *The Land-Locked Lake* (1932), wrote of the difficulty of maintaining his composure while being shelled, 'screaming steel, tearing the veil of the spirit, sweeping aside illusion, disillusion, and showing what we are, slaving, trembling, cowering cowards'.[37] His internal monologue continues: 'For shame's sake pull yourself together, man. Light your pipe.'[38] Something as ordinary as lighting a pipe in front of the men, who were cowering, too, in fear, became an expression of setting an example of courage under fire.

An important fact was the voluntary nature of their service: junior officers were mostly volunteers who were educated for Oxbridge and not to confront carnage. Hastily trained for war, these young officers learned command by commanding: leadership skills developed by trial and error in environments that were as different from comfortable suburban middle-class England as possible. Their stories of braving the barbarism of war and returning to civilisation afterwards became about a sense of fated agency, war enthusiasm changing to dogged persistence with each shell falling. For those who survived the western front it became a generational rite of passage. The historical realities of service for junior officers reaffirm this more passive form of heroic virtue.

Virtue came in the ways subalterns responded to their new environment. Martial virtue in the trenches came in ways that are not always readily apparent: the day-to-day details of life in the trenches were inglorious. Junior officers were battalion workhorses, their leadership skills developed through hundreds of petty tasks learned on the job essentially as they matured into their roles of command. As Blunden indicated, trench education became about developing competency in front of one's men. Rees, a schoolmaster before the war, understood well the types of fellow officers around him: he was used to middle-class public schoolboys. In his memoir he described the type of work subalterns did on a day-to-day basis:

> I always thought that the hardest-worked man in the army was the Subaltern. He had his tour of duty by day and night during one of the four watches [...] he had to see that his men stood-to in the morning, and then that they had their breakfasts, shaved and washed. Then came rifle-inspection and foot inspection, completed by 9 o'clock. All morning there would be work, e.g., repairing trenches and making wire entanglement. After dinner perhaps an hour or two of rest, unless he happened to be on duty. Stand-to again at dusk, after which a three-hour tour of duty and probably a patrol as well.[39]

Junior officers, by his description, were conscientious in their looking-after of the men, sacrificing their sleep to watch over their section of the line to make sure it was in fighting condition. Rees's occupation likely meant he found value in the routines of service and the paternalism of a good officer who, by his description, was similar to being a schoolmaster. Heroism is something far more ordinary in this type of description: the young officer performing his basic duties in the dark gloom of the trenches became a figure of virtue simply by doing his job. Courage could be demonstrated through basic courtesy and conscientiousness toward one's men.

Llewelyn Wyn Griffith reiterated the characteristics of the ideal subaltern: hard work, attention to duty, and endurance of hardship. Originally published at the end of the war books boom in 1931, Griffith's *Up to Mametz* is a gritty account of brutal service and suffering. Throughout the book his men endure the war's conditions largely without questioning the war. Absent in *Up to Mametz* is any sense of fatalism in the spirit of the men even though they are surrounded by the imagery of death.[40] Griffith recalled their being constantly overworked yet unbroken in their spirit. He writes, 'to most of us who served in the infantry the thought of a trench brings back that long span of damnable tiredness, broken here and there by a sudden dry-tongued spasm of fear [...] [N]othing can efface the memory of that all-conquering fatigue.'[41] Griffith often reflects on the familiar images of the trench scene, here recalled later while listening to music, to demonstrate the romantic melancholia of the junior officer's dugout:

> A shuttered room, an oil lamp throwing dingy shadows of a bottle of wine and loaf on a table covered with yellow varnished American cloth; maps and typewritten orders, a Sam Browne belt hanging over the back of a chair, Billy sitting down with unbuttoned tunic, brooding silently, his young face clouded and morose, hearing in the simple time a world of things he could not say; other good men who shared the hard days of war but did not live to look back on them with a profound and unending feeling of miraculous deliverance.[42]

Griffith recalled images that by 1931 were a distinctive part of British culture and life. Plays like *Journey's End* had dramatised the subaltern's mess, with its mud-soaked cynicism and youthful courage, for thousands of theatregoers. The images associated with the officer dugout, such as that of the tired junior officer Billy, burdened by his duties, had become a popular metaphor for the British experience of war on the western front. The young subaltern doing his part was an image that by 1929 had already been romanticised. The war might have been seen as folly by some, but the men who fought it were remembered kindly by their former officers who memorialised their comrades-in-arms, fellow subalterns working tirelessly to survive the war with their dignity intact.

In his study of middlebrow and middle-class war novelists, Hugh Cecil writes that though his subjects were certainly haunted by the war, remembering helped writers cope with their memories. In his words: 'Writing the war was their way of holding on to life and hope.'[43] Certainly, for subalterns confronting their war memories, these impulses were equally important as they struggled to contextualise their life at war with their lives at peace afterwards. By depicting the trench as a rite of passage for young middle-class officers, former subalterns created a tragic mythology that helped frame the way Britons have seen the war generation since.

The 'Poor Bloody Infantry'

Though the subaltern's tale was the predominant published memoir of the Great War experience in British literature, this does not mean that voices from the ranks were silent. Published works by common soldiers were rare but treated as welcome diversions by critics who had grown tired of books by officers.[44] To some degree, officer accounts made those by men in the ranks more distinctive; after all, theirs was the more common experience for Britons who served in the war. Most of the accounts by rankers were written by men who had connections within literary circles or with patrons who could help them write their stories and find a publisher. Perhaps the most famous common soldier experience of World War I published in Britain – Remarque's *All Quiet on the Western Front* – was written from the point of view of a young German soldier. Certainly, there was no great British equivalent in terms of sales, though there were works of quality released by those in the ranks.

Most of the published accounts by other ranks were by men who would be considered exceptional in barracks. The British Army, particularly in 1914, was an institution drawing its volunteers largely from the working class. Voluntary enlistment and conscription widened this traditional pool of servicemen to include men from the middle classes. Though some middle-class soldiers sought commissions, many served with distinction in the ranks. In his autobiographical novel, Frederic Manning drew his protagonist, Bourne, an educated Australian who was officer material, from this type of person: the quintessential temporary gentleman who, as the war of attrition wore on, became the backbone of regimental replacement officers. Manning was this type of soldier and his novel, *The Middle Parts of Fortune* (1929), has been justly praised, since the time it first appeared, as one of the best books on World War I. It should be added that Manning's own biography suggests more ambiguity than his fictionalised portrayal; though he served in the ranks he was later a commissioned officer.[45] Like his protagonist he was alienated from the common soldier by his education and social class, but, a writer with exceptional imagination and ability, he was able to reconstruct the British common soldier's mess in ways that other writers were unable to. Manning's fictionalised portrait of his own experiences is one of the best memory sources for understanding small unit life published in this period.

There are several important memoirs written by men who served in the ranks. Stephen Graham's *A Private in the Guards* (1919) and William Linton Andrews's *Haunting Years: Commentaries of a War Territorial* (1930) are similar accounts. Graham and Andrews were professional writers before the war who enlisted out of patriotism and served on the western front. Both men fought in elite regiments: Graham was in the Scots Guards and Andrews a soldier in a territorial battalion of the Black Watch. Graham's book was released quickly in 1919. The work was published by Macmillan, a firm that also published Rudyard Kipling's *Irish Guards in the Great War* but few other war books in the interwar period. Graham's work details the difficult transition for a mature civilian soldier in an elite regiment.

Graham enlisted in his early thirties. He was a professional writer with travel books to his credit. His occupation, age and sensibilities made him atypical in the ranks. He acknowledged this himself, and many of his colleagues, whom he called 'hard cases', would have never made it into the Guards had it not been for the war, in which drafts of lower quality were required to replenish the ranks from attrition as the war went on.[46] He found the army to be crass and its discipline cruel, but overall necessary, as he partially credited the rigid and harsh training at 'Little Sparta' for winning the war. The personal transformation between a man of artistic temperament, a fervent individualist as he characterised himself, and a soldier, a part in the 'machinery' of war, was an essential part of his memoir. 'An immense gulf seems to separate the man who wrote from the man who shoulders a rifle. It is as if he had died, as if I who write had once been he and died, and then been born again as a soldier.'[47] Graham was a religious man who saw the army in its training within the same paradigm of rebirth as evangelical religion, though this transformation he found far less wholesome. The army encouraged foul language and vice, which disturbed Graham, who found barrack room life to be decidedly 'impure'.[48] Graham's approach was essentially an anthropological investigation of the barrack room by a professional writer who would go back to living by his pen after the war was over.

Similarly, William Linton Andrews wrote of barrack life in the Black Watch from the perspective of a Dundee newspaperman with a public school education. In 1914, Andrews was a 28-year-old vegetarian and teetotaller from Yorkshire who worked as an editor for the *Dundee Advertiser*.[49] He largely found his comrades in the training barracks to be dirty, drunken and prone to violence.[50] His sense of alienation from the men was based on his education and refinement, magnified no doubt by his 'journalistic curiosity about human nature'.[51] This curiosity was a trait that did not endear him to his fellow soldiers. Eventually, other newspapermen joined his company and he felt more comfortable in the ranks with them.[52] As a writer, Andrews never lost his journalistic approach, and his memoir is a compelling chronicle of life in the ranks from the perspective of someone who spent the war thinking in terms of using the experience for potential copy. He liked most of his officers and he found the men heroic in their endurance of poor conditions. He was 'amazed that they stood it all with such heroism'.[53] In 1918, Andrews left the front for officer training, the Armistice coming before he had the opportunity to command. Like Graham, he would return to his profession of writing after the war, eventually gaining a knighthood for his journalism in 1954. *Haunting*

Years, despite its title, is not a disillusioned book, but one that maintains a detached balance towards the war. The book foregrounds Andrews's frustration at the loss of so many of his companions and friends in the ranks who died as a result of failed offensives. This was a common frustration of both officers and men in the ranks who often wrote of hardships with a sense of stoic endurance, but had a hard time justifying the loss of so many comrades in battle.

Giles Eyre's memoir, *Somme Harvest: Memories of a P.B.I. in the Summer of 1916* (1938), is very close to Manning's *The Middle Parts of Fortune* in its subject and in the author's point of view. Eyre was a competent writer who chose to limit his account to three months over the summer of 1916, on the Somme front, from the perspective of a soldier in the 'Poor Bloody Infantry'. Eyre served as a rifleman in the King's Royal Rifle Corps and was captured late in 1916. He wrote and published his memoir 22 years after the events depicted. As is common for many memoirs, his former commanding officer Major-General Sir Hereward Wake wrote the foreword:

> The reader will find that the British soldier is an odd mixture altogether. He will hear him grousing and cursing, with pet names unprintable for spades and everything else. But behind all that he will discover a type of whimsical philosophy, a sort of cheerful pessimism, very hard to beat anywhere; a sturdy shrewd insight; a sympathy that even includes the enemy; a judgement not much disturbed by the curse of war-time propaganda. It will be noticed that he makes no claim to heroism or immunity from ordinary human failings.[54]

Much of the book reinforces this view of the common soldier. Eyre's account, like so much of Great War literature, is about the randomness of war and the irrationality of fate and survival. During an unexpected barrage he notes, 'There is no romantic glamour in such scenes. Fate descends suddenly from nowhere, and its sweeping scythe brings death, agony and terror. There is nothing to hit back at, all man can do is to grit teeth, wait in suspense and curse impotently!'[55]

Eyre's book describes the practical considerations of men in the line. In *Somme Harvest* soldiers drink, pursue women and play hands of rummy. As in Manning's novel, liquor is a principal comfort. 'It [the rum ration] undoubtedly prevented thousands of men from breaking down through sheer hopelessness, and instilled new warmth and courage in chilled, desolate bodies.'[56] Action was sometimes a relief from the monotony of unpleasant trench life.[57] Though Eyre spoke only for himself or, at the most, for the men of his squad, to commanders like General Wake these texts represented the qualities which they wanted their soldiers to have just as much as those which some of them undoubtedly did have.

Eyre had a gift for characterisation and wrote of his squad like a novelist. There was Barty, the Oxford-educated subaltern, a former schoolmaster in a Burberry raincoat.[58] O'Donnell was an Irishman who wrote poetry during bombardments, while his squad-mate Rodwell was fiercely anti-American and sharp-tongued, the latter eventually killed at the Somme.[59] Eyre's eye for interesting characters benefited what was, in essence, a small unit history and differentiated it from others. By focusing on the squad and its *esprit de corps*, the book demonstrates deep feelings of comradeship, the close bond of front-line troops to each other. Though officers were certainly apt to speak of the comradeship of the trenches, in *Somme Harvest* the men speak with their own voices about the subject. Here there was comradeship-in-arms from the men who bore the arms themselves, yet the book remains a composite piece of enlisted and officer stereotypes undoubtedly familiar to readers of war literature by 1938.

Both Frank Richards and John Lucy published their books with Faber in the 1930s. Richards's *Old Soldiers Never Die* (1933) was famously rewritten by Robert Graves after the author sent the war poet a copy of his manuscript hoping for his assistance.[60] Richards's account was of a pre-war soldier who volunteered as a reservist with his old battalion, the 2nd Royal Welch Fusiliers, in August 1914 and served throughout the war. Faber published the book in September 1933 and it was on its third impression by October. Following this success he wrote a second book, *Old Soldier Sahib*, about his experiences in the pre-war regular army. Though there is debate as to how much Graves contributed to the writing, the fact that he took an interest in Richards, particularly in 1933 as war books were again falling out of favour, likely was a reason the book was published by such a distinguished firm. It also demonstrates the difficulties for a working-class author trying to break into the publishing industry. In 1933, Richards was a coal miner with no other publications to his name and Graves helped him compositionally, but also professionally, to find a publisher for an account he thought had great merit.

John Lucy's *There's A Devil in the Drum* (1938) was one of the last books of its type before World War II. It is a wholly unique account of a young Irish Catholic boy who served in the pre-war British Army. Lucy was an Old Contemptible who survived the retreat from Mons in 1914 and fought on the western front as a non-commissioned officer. He was later commissioned an officer and severely wounded at Cambrai. Cyril Falls, the indomitable critic of war books for *The Times Literary Supplement*, described Lucy's book as 'an exceptionally good War book, not only because the author's experiences are interesting, but because he is also an interesting character'.[61] As Falls noted, enlisted accounts of 1914 were exceedingly rare, even by 1938, as were accounts of men who had served as combatants on both sides of the commission divide. As an Irish soldier, the element of loyalty in the face of rebellion and insecurity on the home front became a major theme of the text. By 1938, the war had been chronicled in many different personal accounts, but Lucy demonstrated that it was still possible for a war memoir to be distinctive for its content and narrative point of view.

Like those of their officers, published ranker accounts of the western front demonstrated a certain similarity. Common soldiers were concerned with basic amenities and trench comforts. To some degree, they were more forthright in their vices and direct in language than their officers. These books also demonstrate a little of the ribald humour of life in the ranks. There is a caveat in this characterisation in that men's accounts were all projections of life in the ranks within a paradigm that contrasted these accounts with those of commissioned officers. Critics like Falls were aware of this and throughout the period praised books by rankers as being a rare tonic contrast to the conventional officer memoir. By being written in this context, the texts invariably became juxtapositional and certainly so in their reception. However, there are limitations to ranker memoirs in terms of their authenticity, just as there are limitations within the representation of officer poets. In the case of Andrews and Graham, who were professional writers, the view from the ranks is essentially from men of the officer class observing their colleagues, but not exactly being one of them. Additionally, for Frank Richards, the helping hand of Robert Graves influences our perception of the text. John Lucy's account is exceptional for the reasons stated above, but as an exceptional account it too deserves a caveat. It was the experience of an Irish volunteer who became an officer and was not typical of most Kitchener Army volunteers. There were certainly enlisted accounts published in the interwar period, but few that were representational of the army as a whole, and these were almost entirely usurped in the war's memory by the subaltern's tale.

***

The western front created a dominant perception of war for Britons in the interwar period. This perception was framed by the lived metaphor of destruction witnessed on the western front by individual writers. The experience of war in the trenches, by far the dominant theatre for British soldiers to be deployed in, meant that this experience was shared by millions who had lived through a similar landscape, served in similar locales and even within the same regiments or battalions. Crucially for publishers, this theatre was marketable not only to survivors of combat, who had an interest in war stories applicable to their own experience, but to family members of servicemen who had been killed or severely wounded. Stories from the western front became the most standardised, or the dominant cultural narrative, of World War I. Their appeal was widespread.

Mechanised war changed the nature of the twentieth-century battlefield. In turn, it also changed the nature of war writing. Modern war emphasised survival, rather than gallant action in battle. The subaltern narrative changed the dimensions of the British war book, but did not significantly alter the war book's traditional role as a text meant to convey the meaning of conflict through individual experience. For officers this is manifested in reoccurring themes important to middle-class readers: endurance, friendship, loyalty and duty being paramount. For other ranks, their emphasis was on endurance first and foremost and the usual soldier stories concerning complaints over food, drink, women and pals. Class, then, contributed to the construction of narratives about combat so much that these memoirs largely fall into stereotypes of the classes which they represented. Officers like Sassoon and Blunden were more contemplative, whereas men like Richards or Eyre were more pragmatic, in their reflections. This narrative division according to class took place starkly along the commission divide. What is clear is that the publishing industry sought wide representation of the war in narrative non-fiction, but mostly did so in ways that would appeal to the middle classes, who were the lifeblood of the publishing industry and literary culture that mostly produced the trench tale, the foremost mythology to emerge from the literature of World War I in Britain.

CHAPTER 4

WAR MEMORIES: THE EAST

The experiences of the men who served in the Near and Middle East were distinctly different than those of their comrades in Europe. Eastern memoirs, those on the periphery of the war referred to as 'side shows', dwell on the notion of a very different war fought under contrasting conditions to those of the western front. Fighting in the side shows went together with cultural factors that made the serving British soldier an alien, one who fought in and wrote of a narrative space popularly conceptualised as exotic and dangerous. The Middle East, in particular, conjured romantic reflections, demonstrative of a British culture that was accustomed to narratives of imperial exoticism. The sense of romance attached to war in the East was reinforced through the production of literary and film representations of adventures in Arabia. Of course, some war writers sought to refute these stereotypes, but many more embraced them, and wrote for an audience that was familiar with adventurous imperial literature.[1] The exotic locales, the perception of victory, and the agency found through active above-ground campaigning, make the literature of the East very different than the mud-soaked war books traditionally associated with World War I.

In the broader scheme, memoirs of service in the side shows of the British war effort reflect a literary legacy in the 1920s and 1930s that was far from culturally exclusive to the western front. Indeed, as readers went to bookshops and perused war books in these decades, there were plenty of stories that came from spaces outside the gloom of the trenches.

Despite recent interest in British activities in the Middle East by military and cultural historians, there has been comparably little attention to war literature outside of the western front. In part this is because few prominent literary figures served in these theatres and survived to write their accounts.[2] Those who did write their tales were largely amateur authors, with some notable exceptions. Though there is a lack of critical literature on eastern authors, this is not to say that these books have gone entirely unnoticed. Priya Satia's *Spies in Arabia* is a thorough work of cultural history that weaves together many Great War memoirs from this theatre, mostly by social, literary or political elites, into an overall cultural history of British infatuation with the Middle East. Satia's work is broad in scope, richly detailed and provocative.[3] Her emphasis is on the British intelligence system and the liberal political dream of re-making the Middle East using imperial expansion as a stage of national development. Literature became a key part of the discussion of that expansion.[4] By contrast, historian James Kitchen has engaged with the military history found in memoirs of soldiers who served in Palestine and Mesopotamia. He contests the religious or ideological motivations of participant 'crusaders' as being a postwar construction placed on what was, rather, the cultural tourism of soldiers serving at the time.[5] His research is a reminder that war experiences are often clouded by the memoirist's story-telling zeal and that writers rely on cliché and pre-existing narrative techniques to tell their stories and attract readership. Though valuable for this study, Kitchen's work is more concerned with the deconstruction of imagination than the production, publication and perpetration of these myths after war, which is the purview of this chapter. In addition to Satia and Kitchen's work, historian Justin Fantauzzo has also written on the literature of the Egyptian Expeditionary Force, its prominence in the interwar period and how 'war books provided men of the EEF a direct avenue to respond to their perceived absence and correct the campaign's popular image.'[6] For soldiers serving in a marginalised theatre of war, a war book could be a means of public exposition of deeds both witnessed and performed in the war. Of course, there has also been no shortage of scholarship regarding T.E. Lawrence, who has elicited interest since the war itself, but it should be remembered that Lawrence was one of many authors writing about the Middle East in the 1920s, though his work was exceptionally important in the memory of the war in this theatre.

This chapter examines the literature produced by participants in sideshow campaigns. This wide geographic swath of literature is not meant to 'lump' all side-show accounts together, but instead to demonstrate that literature from outside of the western front, particularly from the eastern theatres, was a prominent part of the non-fiction war book market in this period and created an alternative view of the world war for British readers. As the British and Indian Armies sought to protect the strategic route to India, or British assets in Mesopotamia, or to open a second front directed at the Ottoman Empire, the deployment of soldiers to these theatres was an integral part of the British Empire's strategic war. In their own way eastern authors were attempting to globalise World War I history at a time when publishers' catalogues were drowning in the mud of the western front.

Authors, theatres, and books

Nearly a quarter of non-fiction war books published between 1919 and 1928 were written about campaigns outside of the western front. These memoirs represented principally three geographical swaths: Palestine and Mesopotamia, the Dardanelles, and the Balkans (Serbia, Salonika and Greece).[7] Of these, accounts of service in the Middle East (Palestine and Mesopotamia) were by far the largest group.[8] Accounts were also published of wartime service in Persia and a few of life in Imperial and later Bolshevik Russia. A diverse pool of authors wrote 'eastern' books, including prisoners of war, pilots, female nurses and doctors, generals, intelligence operatives, and irregular fighters attached to 'native' armies. The most common experience represented was that of the junior officer, similar to western front accounts. Civilian women and other ranks did publish books, but not in the same numbers as military officers.

Nearly every major British publisher released war books from these theatres, and a number of prominent publishers contracted several. Thirty-three publishers released books about the side shows, representing a large cross-section of the industry. John Murray, John Lane/The Bodley Head, William Blackwood, Hutchinson, and Edward Arnold each contracted three or more titles. Lane and Blackwood were particularly interested in books featuring adventure, captivity and escape. Edward Arnold released eight titles between 1919 and 1924, mostly concerning the Balkans, East Persia and Gallipoli.

Side-show books represent significant diversity in authorship and depictions of the war. The majority of books were written by social elites – officers, spies, doctors, etc. – but the range of duties performed by participants varies widely. Ranks of authors vary considerably, from major-generals to a few accounts by privates. Even accounts from single campaigns, such as those from Mesopotamia, differ widely depending upon the point of view of the author.

The difference between the two narrative positions, elites on one hand and non-elites on the other, was one of scope. Professional soldiers, diplomats, or intelligence agents such as Lawrence, Aubrey Herbert and Sir Hubert Young were engaged with imperial policy which extended the war for strategic gain into these territories. Imperial agents, diplomats or staff officers knew, and believed in, the importance of their actions in the context of the wider war. For the average soldier or officer writing about the campaigns in Palestine and Mesopotamia, these 'geopolitical' concerns were usually unimportant parts of their narratives. Instead, their accounts were more concerned with their duties and conduct on campaign: they were soldiers assigned the role of winning the war and wrote from this limited perspective. Afterwards, these soldiers came home to write about a victorious experience in the war, but generally did not ruminate on the fallout in the region. Accounts by more common soldiers – infantry officers and other ranks – make a particularly interesting comparison with the point of view of their comrades in Western Europe because they have a vastly different outlook towards the war's conduct than those serving in the trenches.

The Arab Revolt

Perhaps the most distinctive literature to emerge from the side shows was from the Arab Revolt of 1916–18. The Arab Revolt and the campaign in Palestine were a major media event famously covered by the American Lowell Thomas and the British and American presses during the war. When most of the BEF was preparing for, and later fighting in, attritional battles on the western front, the image of horse cavalry and cameleers charging across the desert was starkly contrasted to the very limited gains in that theatre. T.E. Lawrence's story contributed to the popular interest in the revolt, his books having lasting appeal. There were others like Lawrence: imperial agents turned authors, who targeted their works for an audience hungry for stories of eastern adventure. Historian Priya Satia writes, 'The construction of the explorer as author is especially important in this case, for unlike their forerunners elsewhere, many of these agents travelled in Arabia with the intention of fulfilling their dream to become writers 'first and foremost' or with the preconceived notion that travel in Arabia was *primarily* of literary interest.'[9] Lawrence certainly fitted the mould of the explorer/adventurer and he appealed to many because of his biographical exoticism and the adventurousness of his story. His social circle after the war included writers, editors, academics and publishers interested in Lawrence as a heroic personality.

Lawrence's books were bestsellers for publisher Jonathan Cape and are important to understanding the war in the Middle East as it was remembered in the 1920s and 1930s. His *Seven Pillars of Wisdom* caused him no small degree of personal trouble: he lost manuscripts and frequently laboured over and worried about the quality of the prose.[10] Lawrence's biographer Basil Liddell Hart wrote: 'Rarely has a great piece of literature been produced under stress of so many distractions.'[11] Lawrence originally intended the book for a limited audience of his close friends. Upon the encouragement of Gertrude Bell, he decided to publish it in a small, but expensive, private printing.[12] In 1927, Cape encouraged Lawrence to release an abridged version of *Seven Pillars of Wisdom* to earn the revenue necessary to pay the costs of the longer work.[13] *Revolt in the Desert* (1927) was the abridged version, a bestseller which sold 30,000 copies in three months.[14] Lawrence's literary success, in part, was what made him, in Satia's words, 'the only unanimously adored action-hero of the war'.[15]

The Arab Revolt helped to inspire films and further literature about the Middle East. Lawrence was part of a small cadre of friends who published their accounts of the revolt, while his biographers included Robert Graves and Basil Liddell Hart, both of whom published their books with Jonathan Cape.[16] Cape could be said to have created a small literary industry around his bestselling author. Lawrence wrote to Cape, 'You make me a figure of fun with all these pompous biographies. I only hope the public go sick, all over the other three sides of Bedford Square.'[17] For Cape, though, the Lawrence name was good for business. After his death in 1935, *Seven Pillars of Wisdom* was released in full for the first time to the public and has never since been out of print. Between his works and those of his comrades and biographers, Lawrence inspired a lucrative publishing phenomenon essentially devoted to his own story.

This type of idiosyncrasy and celebrity was unheard of from most authors of accounts from the western front.

One of Lawrence's admirers was Sir Hubert Young, one of his comrades thanked in *The Seven Pillars of Wisdom*. Young fought with Lawrence in the Arab Revolt and was a distinguished British political officer and diplomat. He wrote his own account of the Arab Revolt, *The Independent Arab*, and used Lawrence, then Aircraftman T.E. Shaw, as a reader for it. John Murray published the book in 1933.[18] Young had an attractive story: he was an informal intelligence agent in the Middle East before the war who reported to the government on Ottoman affairs. As an Indian Army officer, under the guise of learning about Arab culture, he travelled throughout the Ottoman Empire, learning language and culture, while casually gaining intelligence on the Young Arab movement in 1913.[19] He was instructed in Constantinople 'that the only precautions necessary for travel in the wildest parts of Turkey in Asia were a solar topee and a Union Jack', items he carried through Mesopotamia while gathering information about Turkish military capabilities.[20] On his travels he met and befriended Lawrence, then an English archaeologist, assumed by local German railroad officials to be a spy. Young, like Lawrence, understood that the political situation there was precarious: 'In those early days I assumed, with everyone else out there, that Mesopotamia would be annexed to the British Empire, the only doubt being whether it would come under India or not.'[21] Young saw an opportunity as a young officer to gain experience and influence in the new territory. Later, he was chosen by Lawrence to be one of the leaders of the Arab Revolt. Young was not an adventurer of the same ilk as Lawrence, but was instead a dependable professional officer and administrator with knowledge of the strategic importance of the region to British interests. He intended his memoir to be a plain record of his role in a famous campaign.[22]

Of course, not all who served in the Middle East were enamoured of Lawrence. As the spotlight narrowed on his story, as his success grew in the interwar period, Lawrence's fame alienated others who had served in this theatre. Major Norman Bray's *Shifting Sands* (1934) was inspired by what he believed to be the myth-making of the Arab Revolt that had been accepted by Britons. Bray claimed he was motivated to write the book by his close friends so he could challenge the 'distorted view of the Arab revolt which has been presented to the world. They [his friends] resented the false glamour which had surrounded a movement which called for supreme sacrifice; and condemned the Arabian Nights aspect which did an injustice to the Arab and to the British peoples.'[23] He believed Lawrence's exploits were largely inconsequential to winning the war in the Middle East and that they were exaggerated to the point where they shadowed all other accounts of the theatre.[24] Bray promoted another British officer in Arab robes, Gerard Leachman, whom he believed to be a forgotten hero of British exploits in Arabia. Leachman was described by Bray as a man of modesty, and his death in 1920 left Bray feeling a responsibility of commemorating his life.[25]

Bray had important and powerful friends, both during the war in the figure of Sir Mark Sykes, and afterwards in Austen Chamberlain, who wrote the preface to his book.[26] Furthermore, like Young, he served as a pre-war Indian Army agent in Syria, and was officially sent to the region to learn Arab culture and gather information.[27] Perhaps more important than his criticism of Lawrence was Bray's description of the violence in Mesopotamia in 1919–20 when the British faced an insurgency against their occupation. After the war Bray was made an administrator in Mesopotamia. He was deeply concerned with the British mission to liberate people whom he described as 'long enslaved' from years of Turkish oppression.[28] For men like Bray, the war memoir was a genre that could propagate political statements about imperial life and liberal values; in particular his memoir was a platform to critique Lawrence and emphasise his own small role in postwar British policy. Bray, Young and Lawrence were all agents working toward political goals; each experienced disillusionment with British policy towards events unfolding in territories where they were operating. Their memoirs demonstrated greater political experience and geopolitical perception than most war writers in this period.

Gallipoli memories and Aegean intrigue

One of the more idiosyncratic figures to write of the war in the side shows was a friend of Lawrence and a fellow specialist in eastern affairs, Aubrey Herbert. Herbert's contribution to Great War literature was a hurriedly prepared memoir for publisher Edward Arnold in 1919 entitled *Mons, Anzac and Kut*. The book was a hybrid memoir/diary released soon after the war, not an uncommon form of writing, that depicted three fronts – France in August 1914, Gallipoli, and the Siege of Kut in Mesopotamia.

Herbert was a pre-war independent conservative Member of Parliament from Somerset who made Balkan and Turkish affairs his speciality. He was deeply committed to the Albanian national cause and was instrumental in that nation's gaining its independence. He had friends in high places, being close to the Prime Minister's daughter Violet Asquith as well as John Buchan, Sir Mark Sykes and T.E. Lawrence. At the outbreak of war, Herbert forced his way into the Irish Guards as a stowaway aboard their troopship, and was somewhat reluctantly granted a commission upon his arrival in France. Herbert was wounded in the Retreat from Mons. Upon his recovery, he was deployed to Gallipoli as an intelligence officer with the Anzac Division and later joined Lawrence as a negotiator, attempting to bribe the Turkish army to free the Sixth Indian Division besieged at Kut. Herbert kept a diary and actively wrote home to friends and family during the war.[29] His poor eyesight made the typing of both his letters and his diary a necessity. These entries formed the basis of his later book, in which he spliced narrative commentary with his diary. Herbert's work demonstrates the diplomatic and intelligence frustrations of the British mission in the East.

Mons, Anzac and Kut was published anonymously 'By an M.P.' in a limited run by Edward Arnold in 1919. It sold out its first edition, but quickly lost popularity after an initially favourable reception. It was re-released by Hutchinson in 1930 in the war book boom that year. Herbert, was by now dead; the book's reprint was introduced by his friend the literary critic Desmond MacCarthy, describing it as an excellent account largely ignored in its first printing.[30] MacCarthy was only partly correct: the book had not sold terribly well but had been widely reviewed in Herbert's lifetime, partly due to the author's self-disguise.[31] The *Daily News* indicated that Herbert's anonymity was something of a public joke in London: 'the writer's anonymity is not very anonymous.'[32] This was not surprising as Herbert's war experiences were so idiosyncratic. The book's limited sales were not necessarily an indication of the author's abilities but more of public demand. Upon publication, Herbert received kind words from his friends but was disappointed with his sales, a likely result of the downturn in interest in war books.[33]

Known to Aubrey Herbert was General Sir Ian Hamilton, the commander of the Gallipoli campaign, who published his war diaries in 1920. Hamilton was a career officer who had written two pre-war books about his service. *Gallipoli Diary* (1920) sold nearly four times as many copies as Herbert's *Mons, Anzac and Kut*. Hamilton was the commanding general of a failed military campaign, but already had a reputation as a lively and popular writer. Hamilton reflected upon the aspects of self-justification and command in his preface:

> The tendency of every diary is towards self-justification and complaint; yet, today, personally, I have 'no complaints'. Would it not be wiser, then, as well as more dignified, to let the Dardanelles R.I.P.? [...] A man has only one life on earth. The rest is silence. Whether God will approve of my actions at a moment when the destinies of hundreds of millions of human beings hung on them, God alone knows. But before I go I want to have the verdict of my comrades of all ranks at the Dardanelles, and until they know the truth, as it appeared to me at the time, how can they give that verdict?[34]

Hamilton hoped to answer his critics while he was still alive by revealing his own thoughts on the campaign as it was unfolding. He did so in over 700 pages of text, in two volumes, for Edward Arnold.

Serving under Hamilton and writing from a vastly different point of view, was the novelist Compton Mackenzie. Mackenzie was commissioned in the Royal Marines and attached to Hamilton's staff at Gallipoli. Mackenzie, too, knew Aubrey Herbert and wrote an eccentric portrait of him in his first war memoir, *Gallipoli Memories* (1929), which was followed by three other books on his wartime service in Greece and the Aegean.[35] Mackenzie's tenure as an intelligence officer began because Hamilton admired his writing, specifically his novel *Sinister Street* (1914), and was not based on any experience he had in intelligence or counter-espionage, which eventually became his wartime occupation in Greece.[36] Mackenzie's entertaining *Gallipoli Memories* was a unique war book for its comic observations; the author applied his abilities as a novelist to the panoramic tragedy of the campaign in the Dardanelles. Cyril Falls, reviewing it for *The Times Literary Supplement*, wrote: 'What makes Mr Mackenzie's book novel among reminiscences of the War is that, while most of them are tragic with comic incidents in the background, his is comic with tragedy always looming behind.'[37] Mackenzie's abilities as a novelist meant that he could write humour well, but also he was not in a position at the front where he was subjected to sustained danger. When he was deployed to a forward position, he was again under the protection of GHQ, where he had a batman and even wore silk pyjamas to sleep in his tent. Mackenzie's war was one in which a comic romp was possible, whereas those who were subjected to the daily terror of the trenches, were not in such a privileged position.

Mackenzie's subsequent war books, *First Athenian Memories* (1931), *Greek Memories* (1932/1939) and *Aegean Memories* (1940), depicted his intelligence work in Greece. The publication of *Greek Memories* caused significant controversy. Mackenzie's publisher, Collins, was scheduled to release the book in 1932; however, Mackenzie faced prosecution under the Official Secrets Act (1911) for reproducing official documents in the volume. Mackenzie claimed the charges were malicious and personal. He wrote that the Act was being used as a 'convenient weapon for tyranny'.[38] The publication of *Greek Memories* was delayed until 1939 and the author faced significant fines, which he had to sell personal items and book manuscripts to pay.[39] The final version of *Greek Memories* was reviewed well by *The Times* which noted, 'The author's skill as a novelist enables him to characterise members of his staff, colleagues, superiors, and opponents in ways that make him the envy of less happily inspired historians.'[40] Whatever his point of view, Mackenzie had an idiosyncratic eye for writing war.

Mackenzie's was not the only account of Greek intrigue to be written after the war. Indeed, though Greece remained very much a side show, the issue of neutrality or belligerency of the state, to British intelligence officials, was of supreme importance in the eastern Mediterranean. Mackenzie's somewhat light-hearted memoirs reflected the absurdities of intelligence work with the long gaze of hindsight. Intelligence officer John Cuthbert Lawson published his own account, *Tales of Aegean Intrigue,* in 1920. Lawson was a Cambridge don who specialised in modern Greek folklore. He was recruited and assigned to Naval Intelligence on account of his travels and his research. He also had language skills much needed by the Royal Navy in that theatre. Like Mackenzie he neither had military training nor had he ever worked in intelligence. He described his work at counter-espionage as follows:

> Our politicians and journalists assure us from time to time that the British Secret Service is the best in the world. I do not know

whether that is true any more than, I imagine, do they; but, if it is true, it must be the outcome of some natural genius in our people for such work, and not of training or organization; for the secret-service work of the Aegean – a difficult enough area – was conducted by amateurs, and I for one never received any guidance.[41]

Intelligence work during the war as depicted by Lawson and Mackenzie was an amateur business. Lawson's account lacks Mackenzie's wit but is a more straightforward narrative of his 'adventure' in the Mediterranean.[42] Concerned with matters of national prestige and convinced of the British role in this theatre as being helpful to the overall war effort, Lawson and Mackenzie both provide accounts of civilian soldiers engaged in espionage for the greater good of national interests, before returning to civilian life after the war and writing of their foibles and adventures.[43] As a narrative form, the amateur spy turned writer was a compelling trope for a war book of the side shows.

Mackenzie and Lawson were not the only British memoirists to write on their war experiences in the Near East. Accounts from the Balkans, Salonika and east Persia were published in the 1920s with varying levels of success.[44] The expedition to Persia under General Lionel Dunsterville generated three books, each published by Edward Arnold, of this campaign. Additionally, there were distinctive books by women on the Serbia/Salonika theatre. Flora Sandes, who fought in the Serbian army, published her memoir *The Autobiography of a Woman Soldier* in 1927. Sandes achieved a degree of celebrity both during the war and afterwards. Three memoirs were published by women who participated in medical aid in this theatre, two of whom were in the Scottish Women's Hospitals. Isabel Hutton's *With A Woman's Unit in Serbia, Salonika, Sebastopol* (1928) was a distinctive memoir of the difficulties of a female physician in wartime.[45] Of the more traditional service accounts by officers, both Donovan Young's *A Subaltern in Serbia* (1922) and Richard Smith's *A Subaltern in Macedonia and Judea* (1930) describe the lives of junior officers fighting along the Serbian front. Both were by authors who served in the Balkan theatre before being dispatched to fight in the more adventurous Palestinian campaign. Though the Balkans did not generate the same interest from publishers as Mesopotamia and Palestine, the Aegean was not an ignored theatre, but one that saw the publication of a characteristic group of texts.

Temporary crusaders

The majority of soldiers serving in the Middle East did not have the literary or political connections of the likes of T.E. Lawrence, Hubert Young, Aubrey Herbert or Compton Mackenzie, imperial agents with political or military access to intelligence and the ability to ascertain the grand strategy of their campaign. Rather, the average soldier, as in all theatres of operations, concentrated on the narrow point of view of their unit's actions. Soldier memoirs of the side shows reflect the same general characteristics of the western front in that they are expressions of small unit cohesiveness and are limited to the battles witnessed. The imagery constructed by the authors depicts military life in its most rudimentary sense. There is one caveat to this depiction: in hindsight, soldiers depicted fighting in the East in heroic language, including the word 'crusader', and frequently using Biblical images to justify the 'liberation' of Palestine from the Ottoman Turks.

Though eventually eclipsed by the output of their comrades on the western front, war books from the Middle East are distinguished by both their number their interpretative point of view. A sense of the exotic and virtuous mission of the war is implied in the titles of some works: five of the books released in this period have a variant of the word 'crusade' in the title.[46] Officers wrote most of these accounts, with three notable exceptions.[47] Differences between the fronts are further accentuated as many of the officers dispatched to the side shows had previously served on the western front, allowing a comparison of the two very different faces of the same war.

Edward John Thomson, father of the future historian E.P. Thompson, served as an army chaplain and was particularly interested in memorialising the experience of the men he served with in Mesopotamia. In the interwar period he became a bestselling author and as an expert on Indian literature at Oxford. He began his literary career as a war memoirist and later became a novelist, fictionalising his experiences of serving in Mesopotamia. In 1919, he wrote his war memoir, *The Leicestershires Beyond Baghdad,* before turning to fiction and writing his first war novel, *These Men, Thy Friends*, which also drew upon his war service.[48] In addition to *The Leicestershires*, he published a second war memoir entitled *Crusader's Coast* (1929). Here he described men serving in Mesopotamia as being infused with Biblical and historical references to the places in which they were fighting. 'Every one in the

52nd Division, from whom we took over, impressed upon us, with the air of men anxious to pass on a vital discovery, that the best "Guide" to the country was the Bible, "especially the Old Testament. The whole army is reading it."[49]

The classically educated chaplain, Thompson, drew inspiration from the Biblical civilisation around him in Mesopotamia. For men who identified themselves as 'temporary crusaders', soldiers charged with defeating the Turks in their own territory, the classical or ancient elements added both mystery and justification. Thompson reflected upon this terminology in 1929: 'We were forbidden to call ourselves Crusaders, but many of us were haunted by an older age, and a phantom of human tide seemed to be beating southward over these gracious downs.'[50] To Thompson, a sense of history came naturally: classical allusions, the connections with the Bible, the moral superiority of an imperial army 'liberating' a land seen as long oppressed by the Turks, these were powerful images to impress upon a reading public. Though he was certainly no ardent imperialist, his words helped to give the narrative space of the desert added meaning to his audience who expected the East to be a certain way in their imaginations. The Biblical and classical imagery, in part, was a narrative device to make Arabia accessible to a wider audience.

Indeed a common theme to these memoirs is the relationship between historical and Biblical allusions to events as they were being perpetrated on the ground. The notion of British forces being a latter-day 'crusade' of liberation in the Holy Land was a common one. John More wrote in his *With Allenby's Crusaders* that references to the Bible were often constructed in memory after the war: 'It was hard to realise at the time that many of the outlandish places we passed through or lived in were so steeped in Biblical or historical interest.'[51] For soldiers at the time, their present duties were such that they could not necessarily reflect upon the broader significance of their work. Images of the Bible or Crusades were themes likely to be adopted afterwards.[52] In almost all instances Biblical depictions were a way to distinguish the author's exceptionalism from other books published at the time.

The notion that soldiers construct grand narratives to distinguish their accounts fits Samuel Hynes's analysis of why men largely write war books to remain historically relevant. Hynes writes that men often write not just to show what they went through in war, 'but simply to be there *in* history'.[53] For those fighting in remote theatres of World War I, the impulse to characterise their works in terms of a greater narrative was even more acute, as their marginalised experience warranted even closer attention to the deeds in which they participated. Former officer Rowlands Coldicott wrote, 'the taking of Jerusalem, inferior as a spectacle of brute energy [...] can be shown in a clear, hard light, historically and romantically the greatest of all the episodes that have flamed on a sudden into public view out of the less regarded spaces of the war.'[54] Given also a culture that appreciated schoolboy adventure literature that emphasised medieval romance, a culture broadly interested in exotic depictions of the East and Middle East, then these memoirs had a context more important than the actual conduct of the war in these theatres. Unlike infantry service on the western front, where it was difficult to romanticise the industrial siege warfare of large armies, war in Arabia lent itself to dramatic depiction by soldiers just being there.

Though accounts from the Middle East represented imperialist attitudes found in British culture generally, most authors were not interested in imperial politics. Though of course intersecting with the politics of their society or national policy, war books are often not overtly political and authors sometimes expressed a complete ignorance of international affairs in order to endear themselves to readers. John More hoped his book would be simply 'an honest account of the Palestinian Campaign, together with short descriptions of the country itself'.[55] Like their counterparts on the western front, some memoirists from the eastern theatres had a desire to record the deeds of their comrades for posterity, even considering the failings of individual memories. Coldicott wrote that the Palestine campaign was:

> an achievement history will not be able to blink at or forget. The drums and trampling of more than three conquests have passed over the city since Titus embattled his legions against it, but no man has ever dreamed that it was destined to be stormed again, on a misty December morning, by the trained-band captains of famous London Town.[56]

Coldicott's likening of the achievements of his battalion to that of the legions of Rome was a narrative device to add dramatic significance to a side-show campaign. But this had more to do with a sense of imperial adventure than imperial ambitions. His motivation for writing, he claimed, was that his friends at Cambridge asked him to write down the stories of his 'adventures' in Palestine that he had told them while he was a student.[57] There was no overt geopolitical significance to his account; rather it is a war story of a victorious campaign witnessed by an officer in no position to influence the political or strategic events around him.

Vivian Gilbert's *The Romance of the Last Crusade* is an obvious example of a memoir that used the crusader motif as a narrative device to draw readers into a fairly ordinary war story. Gilbert was an actor before being commissioned an officer in the war. After his service in Palestine, he returned to America and gave dinner speeches on his military service. He was encouraged to write his book based on his dramatic storytelling.[58] In *The Romance of the Last Crusade*, the crusader motif was used to demonstrate a romantic contrast between what war was supposed to be like, the victorious mobile campaign in Palestine, and what it was like on the western front.

> I wanted to believe that we were all knights dedicating our lives to a great cause, training ourselves to aid France, to free Belgium, to crush Prussianism, and make the world a better place to live in. What did it matter if we wore drab khaki instead of suits of glittering armour. The spirit of the Crusaders was in all these men of mine who worked so cheerfully to prepare for the great adventure! And even if they wore ugly little peaked caps instead of helmets with waving plumes, was not their courage just as great, their idealism just as fine, as that of the knights of old who had set out with such dauntless faith under the leadership of Richard the Lion Hearted to free the Holy Land.[59]

Gilbert's text is littered with images of the Crusades and the Bible, but these references are unsophisticated, and the book demonstrates mostly a casual tourist's interest in the historical landscape through the trope of imperial romanticism.

The title of Cecil Sommers's published diary, *Temporary Crusaders* (1919), perhaps describes accounts from the Middle East best: books written by temporary junior officers distinguished mostly by the scenery they depicted and the type of war they were fighting. They share the same point of view as subalterns' tales from the western front with a different backdrop. For the most part, 'crusaders' were preoccupied with material comforts, limited in their knowledge of the wider war and somewhat distant from the men under their command. Officers continuously searched for cold drink, comfortable sleeping arrangements, tobacco and decent food. In this way the day-to-day depictions of war in this theatre are very similar to those of officers from other fronts. Battle scenes are invariably tragic for their loss of life, offering some degree of realism to the works. There are distinctive conflicts between British soldiers and local villagers, perhaps made more characteristic than their counterparts in France, because of the alien culture represented. An essential difference, however, is the optimism which many of these books convey to the reader that undoubtedly came from mobile fighting in a theatre of war where there was a clear sense of victory. Memoirs by officers in the Middle East provide a contrast between fighting in this theatre and that of the western front, which was a far different war altogether.

East vs. West

The very nature of the East/West binary in war literature insinuates differences between these theatres of operations. Certainly, the campaign in Palestine was viewed as a triumph of logistical and mobile warfare in its time and thus is easily contrasted with the stalemate of the western front. In their narratives, memoirists engaged in this type of comparison, especially as many of them had served on the western front before being deployed eastwards. Some officers, like Vivian Gilbert, had served on both fronts and could juxtapose the fighting. He wrote of France, 'There was so little one could say: it was all unutterably beastly – it wasn't fighting, it wasn't fair play, it was just slaughter.'[60] Additionally, some like E.J. Thompson had family members fighting in Europe, which allowed for further contemplation of their war experience as something to contrast with their siblings'.[61] The war in Europe was the principal theatre of operations for the BEF, and soldiers were cognisant of the nature of their side-show campaigns' marginality from their inception. This peripheral perspective in a larger war fought across continents and seas proved to be a major motivation to write war memoirs from other theatres. Soldiers wanted to tell their distinctive war stories so that their experiences too could be remembered.

The dissimilarity of the fronts was certainly not exaggerated. The climate, conduct and conditions of battle were vastly different. One officer recalled that 'We ate sand, drank sand, breathed sand – and above all was a pitiless sun.'[62] Flies, fleas and heat took their toll on men who were unaccustomed to the discomforts of campaigning in the desert. Yet sheer movement across open ground boosted morale. Lieutenant Colonel Edward Cooke, writing as 'Arnewood' in his memoir *With the Guns West and East*, recalled the excitement of observing an artillery battery moving forward under fire. 'It was a fine sight to see batteries of artillery under heavy shell fire galloping into action in the open, and our infantry under the barrage fire seizing position after position with great gallantry.'[63] He likened charging yeomanry to that of their crusader ancestors, the campaign towards Jerusalem being seen in his eyes as one of 'deliverance from the Turk'.[64] This was a far different war than the one in France.

With the different combat conditions came, for many, a sense of relief at being deployed eastwards, in part, because of the adventure of serving abroad.[65] The Middle East was a welcome diversion for infantrymen who had experienced little romance or exoticism on the western front. However, some degree of caution should be exercised when examining men's positive reflections in their memoirs. Though relief, romance and adventure are certainly themes present, the Middle East was not a 'soft' theatre; indeed soldiers who fought there experienced and wrote about much hardship. Like their counterparts on the western front, soldiers in the Middle East, too, were trying to write accounts of endurance and hard fighting to demonstrate that they had done their part in the war. Some men felt great relief at being assigned to the Middle East, while others depicted great hardship in the harsh conditions of fighting. Especially for Indian Army soldiers at the siege of Kut, their experience in Mesopotamia was of hard fighting, brutal siege, surrender and captivity. Theirs was an experience hardly to be envied.

The East/West binary was one identified by elite writers of the western front who mythologised the East as a romantic contrast to the trenches of France. Lawrence became a hero and a mentor to some of these writers. Robert Graves was a friend of Lawrence and focused on this comparison in his discussion of Lawrence's literary work alongside that of the war poets. For Graves, the individualistic form of warfare in Arabia was something completely alien to the western front. He wrote in his biography of Lawrence, 'He [Lawrence] commented to me once on the anti-war poetry of Siegfried Sassoon [...] that had Sassoon been serving with him in Arabia he would have written in a completely different vein.'[66] Graves continued, 'Lawrence's revolt in the desert was a form of fighting so unlike "civilized"; war, and so romantically appealing, that it is perhaps fortunate that Siegfried Sassoon, Wilfred Owen, Edmund Blunden, and the other poets who got badly involved in the war were all infantrymen in France.'[67] Graves, who certainly counted as one of those 'poets who got badly involved in the war', found romance and freedom in tales of the desert. The individualism and seemingly anti-modern tactics of desert warfare were a tempting muse. They were also one that would have inspired the literary talent of his generation to veneration of combat instead of their repulsion by the war's industrial brutality. The East/West binary was ironically specified by Graves as one of 'civilised' warfare on the western front, where there were high casualties and a brutal landscape of destruction, and barbaric warfare in the East, with open war, heroism and deeds of great personal courage. Graves knew little of desert warfare other than through his close association with Lawrence; he romanticised this theatre because his own experiences were so very different from it.

Certainly, for officers who were transferred to the Middle East, there was an expectation of adventure not found on the western front. Bernard Blaser recalled asking upon learning of his deployment, 'were we not on our way to the East, the mysterious, ever sunny, East? We were filled with that feeling of expectancy which normal mortals experience on approaching a strange land, but which is intensified tremendously in those of artistic temperament.'[68] To the budding war writer, many of whom thought of themselves as men of artistic sensibilities, the romanticism of travel to the exotic Middle East was a relief from war in Europe and came with a distinct hope of adventure. This is not to imply that there was not grave trepidation felt by many about being deployed into another combat theatre, but only that in these memoirs there is often a sense of relief about deployment outside of Europe.

For soldiers who transferred from the western front to Palestine, there was a sense of optimism and adventure in their books, hopes that were often dashed when they got there. Romantic feelings about the desert were often offset by the harsh life on campaign. As on the western front, the realities of war often tempered the romantic impulses of authors.

Cecil Sommers in *Temporary Crusaders* expressed great relief at the climate and open movement of desert warfare compared to his experience on the western front.[69] However, his spirits were quickly dampened by the heavy rains and cold nights of Palestine in winter, a grim irony for a man expecting the desert to be unlike his experience on the western front.[70] Arnewood recalled celebrating Christmas 1917 in Shafat: 'we thought of roast turkey, plum pudding and a roaring fire as we sat shivering under a tarpaulin, soaked to the skin.'[71] Campaigning in the Middle East came with its own unique hardships.

Indeed, memoirists complained about the difficulties of desert warfare in their books specifically to refute the notion of having an easy war in the side shows. Descriptions of insects – especially lice and fleas – and the dirtiness of the towns occupied by the British Army are abundant.[72] Though rats were less common in the desert, flies were more plentiful, as well as scorpions, spiders and the looming threat of diseases like dysentery, typhus and cholera, which were relatively uncommon on the western front. Continual thirst, relentless dust, sun blisters and unpleasant sanitary conditions made war in Mesopotamia and Palestine even more difficult for some soldiers, particularly those used to northern European climates. More wrote:

> The flies became maddening to cope with. They swarmed into one's shelter to get what little shade there was, causing the occupant to avoid even that little comfort. Rifles became hot to touch – water bottles almost boiled. The sand reflected back the fierce heat [...] At this time we were all suffering from septic sores. The slightest scratch turned septic.[73]

For infantrymen, even the daily task of marching could be agonising due to sand and dust, that when combined with strict orders for water rationing became unbearable.[74] Memoirs emphasised the day-to-day difficulties of life on campaign vividly so that the reader understood that war against the Ottoman Empire had its own challenges.

British notions of cultural superiority were part of the frustrations of soldiers in these theatres, and cultural clashes were common. Local Arabs were frequently depicted as opportunistic and untrustworthy. Pilot Alan Bott wrote of a life of comparative luxury in Palestine, flying Nieuports by day and sleeping in a tent in an orange grove at night. 'Those were pleasant days,' he wrote. 'The fruit has just ripened, and by stretching an arm outside of the tent-flap, one could pick full-blooded giant Jaffa oranges.'[75] His idyllic war changed after being shot down and surrounded by a 'band of ragged Arabs'.[76] He found himself 'on the wrong side of the war's looking glass':

> I did not realise that I was directly concerned in the Arabs' intentions and actions, but looked at the motley group from the detached point of view of a cinematograph spectator. They were an unkempt group, with ragged robes and dirty head-dresses and straggling beards and unfriendly eyes, – the sort of nomads who, during the lawless days of war, would – and did – cheerfully kill travellers for the sake of a pair of boots, a dress, or a rifle.[77]

Fellow pilot John Tennant wrote similarly of the Arab population living near him in Mesopotamia in his *In the Clouds Above Baghdad* (1920):

> The Arabs were a continual source of worry; in fact the war was one of British against Turk, the whole surrounded by Arabs. They were like jackals hanging about both camps, and woe betide the Englishman or Turk who was caught alone. All our camps had to be fortified, wired in, and defended, for the marauders were on a foray every night [...] Most of us slept with loaded revolvers in our hands [...][78]

Though both men were pilots and not infantry soldiers, elites within the military and privileged as such, their accounts of the alien culture of Arabia confirm many racial stereotypes held by their brother officers in the infantry. The perceived shifting alliances of the local population between the Ottoman and British Empires played on their sense of paranoia. It should be added that though often disparaging towards local Arabs or towards Turkish soldiers for their brutality and disregard of human life, memoirists could also be complimentary about the excellent fighting abilities of the enemy.[79]

Additionally, there are further peculiarities of this literature that complicate romantic depictions of the Middle East. The men besieged at Kut had a combat experience not entirely different from that of the western front. They were under enemy bombardment in field fortifications, huddling in wet trenches, besieged around the beleaguered city. Their dwindling rations, sickness, and eventual capitulation to the enemy, test the limit of the generalisation that war in the Middle East was a less difficult experience than on the western front. These self-described 'Kuttites' endured siege and starvation before the agony and intense humiliation of surrender to the Turks in 1916. The memoirs of Kut, a small but distinct body of literature, detail enemy capture and captivity and the maltreatment of POWs at the hands of their Turkish captors. These were texts written as expository accounts that were exotic but essentially unromantic in their depictions of captivity and suffering.

The sense of relief at being transferred to the eastern theatres is most apparent in the way some authors describe fighting and the enemy. Victory and a sense of advancing against a poorly supplied, but hardened and brave, foe distinguished many eastern memoirs. Though romanticised, these descriptions refute the notion that war in the side shows was any less difficult than on the western front. Moreover, some memoirs depict capture, maltreatment and humiliation at the hands of the Ottomans. In writings on the Mesopotamian campaign, narratives are punctuated by blunders, defeat, and hostility at the hands of the indigenous populations. It is important not to ignore the contextual situation in the Middle East, especially Mesopotamia, where the British were facing an insurgency when some of these books were being written and published in the early 1920s. Though, in general, British service in the side shows was recalled favourably by veterans, it should not be insinuated that this was because their service was light. It is far more likely that they found a distinct pride in their war service and thus coloured their memoirs with depictions of victory.

The greater war

The crusader motif and the relief to be fighting a mobile war define a far different conflict than that of the western front. With victory came triumphant depictions of the war. But there was also a sense of marginalisation: of men fighting in a remote and neglected theatre, one that fitted with older depictions by imperial officials. John Tennant wrote in his pilot memoir *In the Clouds Above Baghdad*, 'Little did the British public, more immediately affected by the greater wars, realise how forgotten British officers were dying in nameless fights, or rotting with fever in distant outposts.'[80] Tennant's description of the 'greater' war on the western front represents the acute sense of soldiers serving in the side shows that their theatre was simply overlooked.

The idea of fighting a greater war on the margins came with a sense of irony, but one that was understood in terms of its own exoticism. Tennant's description of the lonely colonial official suffering the indignities of disease, isolation, hostility and death was a common one. To a soldier serving in Mesopotamia, particularly those in the Indian Army, this was a familiar theme of their service. Early in his memoir, Tennant described just such a figure whom he recalled meeting at the start of his service in Mesopotamia:

> there appeared a ragged individual in pyjamas and helmet; he had been there all summer and had long since lost all interest in life. The arrival of fresh blood from England, however, cheered him, and talk of London over a warm bottle of beer seemed to awaken further desire to live.[81]

Tennant's 'forgotten' were agents of empire linked to a rich literary tradition of Europeans serving abroad in alien locales. Side-show memoirs, though particular to World War I, were also colonial narratives of intrigue, battle, conquest and occupation.

As with some patriotic memoirists from the western front, the theme of victory and regimental pride in victorious service was common. Vivian Gilbert wrote at the end of *Romance* that 'I had been through the horrors of a great war but had experienced much of its romance and adventure.'[82] He concluded his account by staring out and looking on the fields of Palestine watching Jews, Christians and Muslims all harvesting their crops of grain in harmony. He wrote: 'We had finished our crusade, peace and freedom were in the Holy Land for the first time for five hundred years – and it seemed all worth while.'[83] To Gilbert, the sentiment of a war fought for a greater good was the framework that inspired his account of the 'crusade' in the Holy Land. Arnewood recalled similarly: 'Both Syrians and Jews were very grateful to us for their deliverance from the Turk.'[84] The combination of liberation and victory was seen as justification for the war and the British conquest. This is profoundly different than the sense of futility of many western front books. It demonstrates as well the sense of a legitimate and lasting outcome of peace, which was not as prevalent in works emerging from Europe.

Triumphant themes are easy to find in Palestine. For those who survived the Mesopotamian campaign, especially for the Kuttites, but even for men like Thompson and Tennant who survived General Maud's victorious Mesopotamian campaign of 1917, there was a more mixed depiction of triumph and hardship. This conflicted portrait had similarities with the books of the western front. John More wrote: 'When looking down on the long rows of corpses the thought was involuntarily forced upon one that war is a mad, useless business. The futility of killing, and of being killed by one's fellow-men, seemed so evident.'[85] The exoticism of the East attracted romantic images of battle, but the depictions of the actual conduct of the war, with its results, were similar from theatre to theatre. Memoirists, in general, shared this abhorrence for high casualties and reverence for lost men. Similarly, the sense of comradeship and the soldierly virtues of heroism and honour, though often exaggerated in texts, did little to soothe the sense of generational loss and trial that remained consistent regardless of the theatre of war. Tennant wrote:

> The majority of us who have survived the war are no doubt doomed to die in our beds; when that moment arrives how we shall envy that gay company who went before, sword in hand and faces to the enemy, flower of a generation who with Time are gradually forgotten. Meanwhile we, their old companions, will not forget; we work, play, and make new friends, but we do not forget those old gentlemen of England.[86]

Like their comrades on the western front, the emphasis on being a survivor of a great catastrophe was equally apparent in the side shows. The war dead received praise from writers regardless of where they died.

***

Though the memoirs of the side shows have much to say about the war, they are largely unclouded by the remorseless questioning of the war found in so much of the literature generated by the western front. If we are to consider the side shows as distinctive narrative spaces, then geography becomes a determining factor in any discussion of Great War literature, particularly of non-fiction, where the war's representation took on a different meaning in an alien culture. Somewhat astonishingly, memoirs of service outside of the western front are not, by and large, negative accounts of the war itself or its aims and motivations, especially as these were campaigns for the propagation of imperial war aims, far away from home. Unlike the western front, where debate raged over the war's representation, accounts from the side shows are not reflective in the same way, and are more triumphant in their depictions of victory. Though a decidedly minority body of texts, when collected as a whole, the narrative spaces of the side shows demonstrate that publishers looked to idiosyncratic authors for interesting stories of the war, often exotic thrillers or adventure accounts, and sought to represent the conflict on all fronts and from varying perspectives. They offer evidence against the notion of Great War literary memory being the singular domain of writers from the western front.

CHAPTER 5

WAR EXPERIENCES: SUFFERING

Ten years after returning home, Henry Williamson recalled the powerful grip the experience of war still had over his life. Residing in the English countryside and making a living by his pen, Williamson's life as an author was vastly different than that as a soldier. Though he was long since out of the trenches, the battlefield was never far from his mind, the war manifesting itself in curious ways. Hearing the local village church bells ring, the tower itself a memorial to war dead, caused Williamson to have something of a metaphysical experience, where he felt overcome by his memories. Hearing the bells, he remembered France.

> The wraith of the War, glimmering with this inner vision, bears me to the wide and shattered country of the Somme, to every broken wood and trench and sunken lane, among the broad, straggling belts of rusty wire smashed and twisted in the chalky loam, while the ruddy clouds of brick-dust hang over the shelled villages by day, and at night the eastern horizon roars and bubbles with light.[1]

Entirely destructive, the war, here portrayed as a possessing spirit, resurrected feelings of terror and resentment.[2] Could there be a more moving statement of the jarring nature of traumatic memories than the dislocation caused between a pastoral and idyllic present English countryside and the desolate and violently corrupted landscape of France in his memory?

Williamson's war experiences were distilled down to a powerful draught of disillusionment. Known for his war novel *The Patriot's*

Progress, Williamson was one person in a literary movement that defined the war's suffering as a means of measuring its impact, a type of collective cultural memorialisation of the war's pathos by writers attempting to define its relevance. Part of remembering, for Williamson and many others, was coming up with imaginary ways to show the resurrection of tragic memories to readers, ways that touched upon the dramatic emotional journey he felt when he was reminded of France. To have served and suffered, to have been a youthful victim of circumstances, was the mark of what he interpreted as a generation's rite of passage. These feelings were vividly depicted in trench scenery, often recalled by middle-aged hands touching old letters or pieces of kit, or in Williamson's case, triggered by something as ordinary as the bells ringing in an English village church. Williamson's burdensome memories were morose but perhaps not entirely meaningless, as he continued to revisit and wrestle with them afterwards.

Williamson was not alone in his disillusionment, nor was he in his feelings of victimisation. The war had destroyed forever his conception of its justifications; the memorial bell's tolling served as a reminder not of sacrifice or heroism, but instead, only the material destruction and suffering of the western front. Predictably, he contextualised his memories through the classic paradigm of soldier disillusionment: he saw not 'patriotism and heroism' in his war experience but only 'suffering'.[3]

The war generation is often collectively defined by its conflicted memories of the war, what was vaguely called disillusionment, a feeling that defined a sense of dislocation and disappointment for veterans after the war. It is not an overstatement to claim that by the 1930s the literature of the Great War had changed the way that people perceived returning soldiers, ones who were grappling with and struggling through their lives now begun, in earnest, in peace. Wilfred Owen's 'pity of war' was found in manifold depictions of disillusionment found in published novels and memoirs. In terms of the war's social memory, the cultural perception of the disillusioned war veteran was a literary trope that demonstrated, most clearly, the severity of the war's conduct and its lasting toll.

Disillusionment, suffering, and victimisation: these are words that require a degree of context to understand meaningfully. This chapter will consider the ways in which war memoirs defined the war's inhumanity through depictions of suffering and victimisation. The goal here is not to reinforce old historiographical clichés about the so-called Lost Generation, nor is it to generalise too broadly about soldiers and their memories. Instead, the intention is to address ideas that were culturally important to writers in the 1920s and 1930s – depictions of suffering in war demonstrated through three distinct perspectives: the men who fought and suffered in the trenches; the men and women who cared for the suffering of the wounded; and the men who suffered in captivity as prisoners of war. These three points of view on battle offer distinctive perspectives on the way that suffering was represented for British readers: each offers something unique by their narrative perspectives. Each perspective also demonstrates a way of examining some of the controversial aspects of war literature in this period. For better or worse, war books were debated in the interwar era because their content, either by design or by accident, reinforced a growing public perception of war's social and cultural destructiveness – the reverberations of a generational Armageddon found in war books written by authors who could never say truly 'good-bye to all that'.

Disillusionment, victimisation, and suffering

For centuries soldiers have written about the personal transformation experienced in battle. In twentieth-century literature, soldier stories were often told from the perspective of civilians, who experienced war and then wrote of the dislocation experienced between their lives at war and those at peace. Paul Fussell sees this process as an inherently ironic one, tragic and absurd, one represented widely in soldier literature of the Great War.[4] Disillusionment is a word commonly used to reflect the jarring dislocation felt by soldiers at the front – defined by Fussell as a type of situational irony: somewhere between the naive expectations of new recruits and the painful realities of service felt by hardened veterans came a sense of disenchantment with cause or conduct of war. As a cultural and literary trope, disillusionment has widely contributed to the interwar period being defined as an age of war regret.

There is a paradox to this interpretation. Just as the Great War was depicted by many writers in terms of its horror and brutality – its painful and shocking meaninglessness – in its public memory in the 1920s the war was memorialised through sacred commemorative ceremonies that were anything but ironic and nothing if not meaningful.[5] In the dedication of war memorials and in the yearly ritual of Armistice Day, Britons actively negotiated their war memories for a generation, before World War II led to a redefining of those memories in postwar/post-colonial Britain.[6] In the early 1920s, Britons created a distinct culture of war remembrance that placed emphasis on honouring the sacrifice of the war dead first and foremost. This was necessary for families to come to terms with the loss of loved ones and to create a narrative for understanding their deaths.[7] As George Mosse has argued, Britons were not alone in interpreting the war as a sacred generational event,[8] but they did so within a national culture of mourning and remembrance that placed emphasis on the war's cost, where feelings of loss eventually trumped notions of noble sacrifice. Over time, this emphasis on mourning the war dead contributed to a growing sense of victimisation that defined the way Britons viewed the soldiers of the Great War.[9]

For good or ill, the Great War soldiers' collective traumatisation is part of Britain's war remembrance, its culture of suffering. Just as memorial tablets and crosses were being erected to the noble war dead, war writers in the interwar period were publishing their own interpretations of the war's meaning, often conflicted and grim accounts that emphasised the sordid awfulness of modern warfare.[10] War books provided the visceral imagery of disillusionment for readers. Whether their depictions were intended to be interpreted as disillusioned or not, the dehumanisation felt by those suffering at the front was enough to encourage sympathy towards soldiers and contributed to perceptions of their victimisation. In part, war books reflected a growing culture of war consciousness in the interwar period that emphasised the individual experience of war as tragedy first and foremost: the disputed narrative of disillusionment became a part of the war's story for the British public because of the tragic overtones of war felt by the masses.

The victimised British soldier, as a trope, grew even more powerful in the later twentieth century as war memoirs became quasi-sacred cultural texts for interpreting the war's meaning. After World War II, Britons began to question whether the earlier war had any legacy other than suffering. This was especially true during the period of the 50th anniversary of the conflict in the 1960s. By the time Paul Fussell began writing *The Great War and Modern Memory* in the early 1970s, the victimised Tommy was firmly entrenched in the public perception of the war. Fussell's work gave academic credence to what was already an accepted way of looking at Great War soldiers.[11]

War literature evoking pain and loss has became a part of the soldier-victim narrative and has had a lasting cultural impact on the way that Britons have interpreted the experiences of World War I since. Yet, in the 1920s and 1930s things were less certain: there was an ongoing debate among veterans about the war's representations, and disillusioned war books were often widely criticised by other veterans. No one questioned that the war itself was responsible for mass suffering, but some protested against deeply disillusioned accounts as being tasteless, their depictions insulting to the spirit of soldiers who had fought and died for cause and country.

Since the 1920s, the story of the western front, whether recounted as romantic tragedy or nihilistic horror, has been a central component in the literary myth of the war, which military historians have long criticised for creating stereotypes. Gary Sheffield writes: '"Disillusionment" is capable of such wide interpretation as to become almost meaningless as a concept.'[12] For historians like Sheffield, the Great War's literary legacy polluted traditional postwar notions of victory and defeat by injecting a somewhat poisonous sense of cultural dissatisfaction. He continues: 'Literary specialists and cultural historians are apt to make sweeping statements about this particular phenomenon, often based on the experiences of a small handful of officer-poets.'[13] Both Sheffield and his fellow military historian Brian Bond have argued that disillusionment was not representational of the war generation, nor is it a precise term methodologically.[14] Both are apt to cite the strong morale of soldiers fighting in the BEF during the war and the pride that many veterans felt upon their homecoming as evidence that the predominant critical narrative of the war's legacy is fundamentally wrong.

Disillusionment, it has been argued, was a cultural trope of the late 1920s and was a product of postwar dissatisfaction as much as of anything experienced during the war itself. Soldiers in the line were prone to weariness and complaining, but this did not translate directly into loss of morale or an urge to mutiny.[15] Janet Watson writes, 'widespread acceptance of disillusionment as the soldier's story of the war was itself a post-war phenomenon, which was strongly and vociferously resisted at the time.'[16] There is ample evidence to demonstrate that veterans' disillusionment with the war developed as a reaction to their dissatisfaction with the peace; to the fact that postwar Britain failed to provide a home 'fit for heroes'.

Homecoming was certainly jarring for many. Even as measured an author as Charles Carrington referred to 1919 as the 'maddest year of all'. He wrote: 'This was the moment of disenchantment. The spell which had bound us for so long was broken; the charm failed; and illusion came crashing down about our ears and left us in an unfamiliar world — our fairy gold turned to dust and ashes.'[17] Soldiers like Carrington who had been through so much and demonstrated such profound emotional and physical resilience during the war faced in peace a return to civilian life with a potential host of disappointments. Of course, this sense of disappointment boiled over into postwar writing, where men and women tried to contextualise their experiences by wrestling with the most difficult question for soldiers to confront in the 1920s and 1930s: whether their suffering mattered in a postwar world that seemed to be growing more, and not less, insecure.[18]

If not disillusionment, then what? The study of the experience of violence in warfare is largely about understanding the ordeal of combat. Essential to that ordeal is the way that soldiers frame their experiences within the culture in which they live. Of course, military history, in all its facets, is connected to notions of suffering.[19] However, suffering itself is a culturally constructed notion; it reflects a physical experience that is interpreted in different ways depending upon the social mores of those who live through it. For the Great War generation, suffering was often conceptualised in terms of masculine responses to violence that were adjusted and reinterpreted in response to fear; soldiers endured the war and wrote about their trials to demonstrate not only that they felt terror and witnessed ample battlefield horrors, but also to demonstrate their ability to cope with these feelings.[20] Emotional reticence and resilience of spirit were both hallmarks of the British middle classes, reflecting values culturally important in the 1920s and 1930s, values that are essential to understanding the war literature produced by junior officers. Rather than the British veteran being seen as a disillusioned victim of misguided patriotism, as has been a popular interpretation since the 1990s, many veterans wrote of suffering to convey a different message: emotional strength, resilience and survival in the face of great suffering, the face of generational tragedy.[21]

Suffering at the front

A host of revisionist historians have questioned whether the British experience of World War I should be interpreted through elite writers such as Wilfred Owen, Robert Graves, Siegfried Sassoon and Edmund Blunden. This cadre of 'literati' represent the most popular writers of the war generation, their works culturally dominant and important to understanding the ways in which Britons have internalised the conflict's meaning since the late 1920s.[22] If we consider two of these writers – the memoirists Blunden and Graves – we can understand something of how they framed their narratives around suffering, or the individual struggle to understand combat and its effects on their lives. Both were poets and both were deeply sensitive to the impact of war upon their writing, each author using his war experiences as a lifelong muse. Part of their lasting appeal as agents of tragedy, undoubtedly, stems from the coming-of-age themes of both texts: young men when they were commissioned, each went through a preparatory school of hard combat before coming to maturity as a writer.

Neither Graves nor Blunden had patriotic or heroic illusions about the prospects of war in 1914. Blunden, indeed, began his war memoir *Undertones of War* by discrediting his own sense of disenchantment: 'I was not anxious to go [. . .] There was something about France in those days which seemed to me, despite all journalistic enchanters, to be dangerous.'[23] The mildly ironic use of the word dangerous is telling; Blunden here is showing his reader both his naivety as to the actual dangers of battle, while also demonstrating something of his later-life ironic humour towards his younger self. The 'enchanters' to Blunden were propagandist newspapermen and not his own boyish sensibility that was, though naive, perceptive of the fact that deployment to France was a foreboding prospect. Blunden never intended *Undertones* to be a generational statement, but instead only a work of individual memory; he was not making an overtly political statement on the nature *of* war by writing his memoir *about* the war.[24] The work's narrative point of view, in fact, resists familiarity. Blunden was an esoteric poet at war, struggling to understand the shattered world around him in terms of his own pastoral sentimentalism, an ongoing reflection on ruination. Blunden was deeply affected by his surroundings – a landscape whose suffering mirrored that of the men who huddled beneath its earth.

Yet, Blunden was very much removed from the common soldier by his education, perception of the war and profession as a writer.

For Robert Graves disillusionment, too, is a difficult moniker. His nephew and biographer Richard Perceval Graves writes that Graves had conflicted feelings about his embarkation to France in October 1914. Graves joined the army not out of 'sentiment or patriotism' but instead because he believed it was his duty as a gentleman; he volunteered despite the pacifist leanings which he harboured at the time.[25] Graves's story is well known but his sense of duty is sometimes overlooked: he served and suffered through the duration of the war with the Royal Welch Fusiliers and remained a lifelong devotee of his regiment despite any ill-feelings he bore toward the war's brutality. Even though he had cynicism towards patriotism in an abstract sense, the young Graves had a significant, even a heroic, sense of duty to his regiment and certainly towards his comrades-in-arms.

The controversy surrounding the publication of *Good-bye to All That* (1929) has shadowed the work as being interpreted as a *Bildungsroman*, where Graves sought to demonstrate the war's importance, but also his upbringing, schooling and postwar domestic life and travels. The memoir was written hurriedly for publication while Graves was in the midst of 'a complicated domestic crisis'.[26] His first marriage had ended and he was in love with another woman.[27] In the spring of 1929, he largely dictated the work in just over a month, and then revised it for publication in November.[28] The work became a major commercial success but faced much criticism, including from close quarters. Both Edmund Blunden and Siegfried Sassoon attacked *Good-bye* for its many inaccuracies and famously disputed its content.[29] In particular, Blunden took issue with Graves's tone, believing that the author's tenor was tasteless. He wrote of *Good-bye* that it was a 'distortion' that was 'like using the cemeteries which crowd the old line of battle from north to south as latrines.'[30]

Good-bye to All That found new publishing life in the 1960s and 1970s during the 50th anniversary of the war. The book's revival was, in part, due to the cultural issues surrounding the Vietnam conflict and widespread anti-war sentiment. Within that context, the literary scholar Paul Fussell lauded Graves in *The Great War and Modern Memory*.[31] Seen through Fussell's eyes, Graves is distinctly anti-everything: he's anti-war, anti-army and anti-modern, a similar writer to Joseph Heller and Evelyn

Waugh in his grasp of the absurdity of war.[32] Jay Winter writes that Graves's 'ironic detachment, his status as a "trickster", subverts the notion that any kind of history can be written about the war'.[33] Graves was unlike many other memoirists because he rejected the notion of truth from the start, using his cutting perception of events as a tool rather than a liability.

In 1929, Graves wrote his autobiography based on feelings he had harboured since the war. Rather than rashly lashing out against the war in 1929, instead Graves had long contemplated writing a war book. As a young officer and aspiring poet, he used the war as a literary muse while he was serving: he published a book of poems, *Fairies and Fusiliers,* in 1918, which he notably dedicated to his regiment. As early as 1917, he was contemplating writing more directly about the war. At the time he was a young captain, friends with Siegfried Sassoon who was embroiled in a scandal over his famous anti-war protest. Graves wrote a detailed letter to Edmund Gosse the poet, a close friend and sometimes mentor to Sassoon, concerning the strain of the war and its impact on his friend. He wrote:

> He [Sassoon] thinks he is best employed by writing poems which will make people find the war so hateful that they'll stop it at once at whatever cost. I don't. I think that I'll do more good by keeping up my brother soldiers' morale as far as I can. This conflagration of War must, I think, burn itself out, whatever I might write about the wickedness & horror of war; & who knows? but that I might help on a decent peace by cheering up my friends & encouraging them to fight more happily. I suffer all that S.S. suffers, or nearly all, only I'm hiding it till after the war: now I have to laugh & make merry, however much it hurts.[34]

Graves in 1917 was dutiful to his regiment, his nation and, most importantly, to his comrades. This is consistent with his motivation for enlisting in 1914. He was also saving his own critique of the war for a later date, forestalling the eventual publication of his thoughts until afterwards, 'however much it hurts'. The combination here of laughter and horror, the dichotomy of the western front seen ironically through the eyes of a young subaltern clever enough to recognise the tragi-comic faces of war, is present in an early form. The fact that he remained consistent about his overall war experience in both 1917 and 1929 indicates that this work was more than just a hurried 'exorcism' of the war's demons.[35] Though Fussell believed Graves to be the ultimate creator of the theatre of war, a farce-master with an impish sense of humour, as a young officer he felt a distinct loyalty toward his men and regiment, a sense that did not leave him with age. For Graves, publishing a critique of the war as it was going on was antithetical to to fighting and serving with his men.

The depictions of combat in *Good-bye* are largely those consistent with the futility myth of the Great War.[36] Instead of jarring disillusionment – Graves depicts no illusions to start with – there is grimness and irony, both common to many books about the western front. The elements of fabrication in the text, disputed since the time it was published, suggest both psychological trauma and impishness. These are common traits of other war books. In Graves's case, the humour is keener. It is difficult to say that *Good-bye to All That* is a polemic against war, as the book is more ambiguous on warfare as a condition. The heroic qualities which Graves did possess, loyalty to his regiment and pride in his men and their service, were just as apparent after the war as during it. Andrew Rutherford describes the 'ethic' of Graves's memoir to be a 'bleakly heroic code which insists on courage in battle regardless of the cause or the prospect of success'.[37] Here, the author confirmed a more traditionally masculine heroic vision – one that would have been familiar to the generation that venerated Robert Scott's polar exploration – than that of the broken idealist found in the disillusionment tome.[38] Graves's sense of suffering was more romantic than existential.

It is beyond doubt that Graves and Blunden were both traumatically changed by the war. Their books are classics of Great War literature, but neither author was a typical officer in the trenches. Neither *Undertones* nor *Good-bye* was meant to be this in its inception: their suffering was that of elite middle-class men with literary aspirations, the prose story of the coming-of-age war poet.[39] At the core of both memoirs is the notion that the war was tragic, often futile, but also a personally meaningful experience, albeit one that lingered in traumatic memory for years afterwards. Both authors were important generational voices, especially Blunden, who was an inspiration to Charles Carrington, Guy Chapman and other memoirists.[40] Graves was influential in a different way: he caused controversy with soldiers of his own generation, but was eventually accepted by subsequent generations as a spokesperson for those who fought in the war. In their hands, the Great War thus became a terrible malady of modernisation, ironically expressed, by two former subalterns who identified very little with modernism, army life or their fellow soldiers.

Yet, there were hundreds of officers who wrote of their experiences in World War I and to understand something of the war generation's views towards suffering we need to widen the circle from elite poets to more middlebrow memoirists.[41] If we consider three authors whose works were popular at the time but that have not proved iconic – those who had literary ambitions and access to distinguished publishers but who have not shared the same lasting fame as Blunden or Graves – we can understand something of the way other officers on the western front conceptualised the war as a personal trial. Charles Carrington, Guy Chapman and Charles Douie struggled with the war's personal meanings as well as its generational significance. They share much in common: each author served on the same front, each fought in a distinguished battalion/regiment and each survived the same battles. Each man came from a similar background to Blunden and Graves: public school, middle-class and with some elite university education.[42] Though the similarities abound, the way these three authors conceptualised their suffering was somewhat different than that of the war poets; their writings carried with them a distinct memorial connotation that demonstrated suffering as a means of understanding not war's detached irony, but instead the virtue of enduring hardship and surviving. From the mired pathos of serving on the western front, Charles Douie, Guy Chapman and Charles Carrington defined a new type of patriotism through a sense of comradeship found in collective suffering.

Before Charles Carrington came to Passchendaele he had already heard rumours of its desolation. Carrington was no stranger to the war in 1917, but Ypres proved to be unlike anything he had been through at the Somme. Arriving at the front, it was worse than he expected. Referring to the seventeenth-century writer John Bunyan he compared the landscape around him to the Valley of Humiliation from *The Pilgrim's Progress*. It was dispiriting and demoralising to have to fight in such a degenerate space. 'A sort of blank numbness, such as seems to envelop criminals in the condemned cell, settled on my spirits, suggesting to me in many ways which I rationally knew to be impossible that the Valley of the Shadow might be avoided.'[43] He believed that 'this was the end,' that he would 'die or be crushed in the military machine'; his mind and spirit 'could endure no longer postponements of the terror'.[44]

There were no more postponements. His company was sent into action. Carrington commanded his men in the line for days without relief, holding a collection of shell-holes and broken German cement pillboxes, ground captured as part of their assault. His account is one of confusion and terror: he described what it was like to be shelled, the impotence felt due to a complete lack of agency towards one's fate, the psychological process of superstition and compulsion by a man of formerly great nerve, who now was under heavy bombardment. He lost men in his company that he had known for years, including his servant, who had been at his side for 18 months and was killed doing his duty. Carrington emerged from battle confused and emotionally exhausted, struggling to find his billet at Irish Farm. 'Cold, damp and utterly despondent I crept into my valise and slept.'[45] Carrington earned promotion to captain and the Military Cross for this engagement. 'I had expected a court martial,' he wrote ironically.[46]

Charles Carrington's accounts of the Somme and Passchendaele reveal a young officer – he was only 20 when he fought at Ypres – struggling to maintain composure in the face of extreme fear. Near his own limit of endurance in 1917, Carrington was self-effacing, unafraid to show that he was often afraid, representing his suffering by describing fear and loss. Carrington wanted to not only tell his story of the war, but to show readers what he felt as he went through it. He wrote in this vein for a purpose, articulating in his epilogue that soldiers since time immemorial have suffered 'a spiritual experience' comparable to both 'passionate love or passionate religion'.[47] Soldiers, to Carrington, were 'illuminati'. 'If we have known fear and discomfort we have also felt courage and comfort well up in our hearts,' he wrote.[48] Survival brought a unique form of heroism: 'the greater the horror, the nobler the triumph of the man who is not morally ruined by it.'[49]

Guy Chapman's *A Passionate Prodigality* is similar in tone to Carrington's *A Subaltern's War*. Chapman's is a memoir that begins and ends with the notion of fear and the way it plays on a soldier's mind, eventually exhausting even the bravest of men. Like Blunden, Guy

Chapman was 'loath' to be deployed to France, confessing, 'I was very much afraid; and again, afraid of being afraid, anxious lest I should show it.'[50] As a newly commissioned officer, Chapman had no military experience to rely upon, nor did he have any real leadership experience that would prepare him for the ordeal of command on the western front. Like Carrington, he served in France in 1916 and then was posted to Ypres for the summer offensives of 1917. By that point his battalion was nearly spent: 'Our speech has grown coarser; our humour threadbare, at best cruel, met by sardonic laughter.'[51] Attrition was dehumanising. 'We descended to primal man.'[52]

Yet, when he was offered leave in October 1917, at the height of the Third Battle of Ypres, Chapman refused it. He wanted to stay with his battalion because they were in battle and he was part of their struggle. He reflected upon his colonel, R.A. Smith, to whom he in part dedicated the book, writing 'that he enjoyed the war even in its most terrifying aspects. The worse the trial to be faced the more perfect became the balance of his nervous system and the greater the increase of his physical and moral power.'[53] Though war seemed so very dehumanising, in a similar way to Carrington, it also brought out aspects of character that otherwise would never have been tested, men's mettle facing a supreme trial. Chapman reflected mystically that this was the power that the war had over him, both then and afterwards:

> Once you have lain in her arms you can admit no other mistress. You may loathe, you may execrate, but you cannot deny her. No lover can offer you defter caresses, more exquisite tortures, such breaking delights. No wine gives fiercer intoxication, no drug more vivid exaltation. Every writer of imagination who had set down in honesty his experience had confessed it. Even those who hate her most are prisoners to her spell.[54]

Chapman's widow, the novelist Storm Jameson, indicated that his love of his battalion remained lifelong. 'When he lost the companionship of the trenches,' she wrote, 'he lost an integral part of himself, Nothing else, however valued, ever wholly took its place in him.'[55] For a man who was so afraid, but brave enough to write about his fears and confront them, Chapman found something he could extract from the experience of the trenches that touched his soul. His book is a memorial to the dehumanisation of war as well as the reforming of human beings through a rite of passage, a great trial. This form of suffering led to Chapman not necessarily being haunted by his memories so much as he was nostalgic for their power.

Charles Douie's memoir, *The Weary Road*, defines the Great War's suffering in generational terms as a rite of passage. As the title would suggest, Douie found the war necessary, but utterly draining. Like Graves, he was commissioned right from school and was deployed to the western front while still a teenager. Looking back in his late 20s, the adult Douie contextualised his memories of the war, writing, 'War gave us in full measure much that we would wish to forget in the way of sorrow and suffering. But war gave us also in recompense and in as full a measure memories of courage and high fellowship.'[56]

There is nothing particularly exceptional in Douie's reflection that the war brought both suffering and some form of virtue found in comradeship. As long as war has been written about, these traits have been important to soldiers who have chronicled the martial fraternity to those in their audience who likely knew nothing of what it was like to be one of a band of battle-scarred brothers. Yet such reflections seem somewhat anachronistic in 1929, the year of Erich Remarque. Douie was very conscious of his archaic sense of martial virtue, but he also thought that the literature of the war had missed something essential to the story of his war. He wrote:

> For many of us the most important, the formative years of our life were spent under conditions similar to those of primitive man, living in holes and exposed to sun, wind, and rain, surrounded by watchful enemies, for ever in the presence of disaster and death. We learned to hold in high honour some virtues no longer of much account in a protected community – courage, fidelity, loyalty to friends. Death was to us a byword. Our lives were forfeit, and we knew it. Life has never presented itself in this guise to men living in urban communities. The very atmosphere of the battlefield defies description and eludes the imagination.[57]

Describing the battlefield as both 'blended majesty and horror', Douie concerned himself with explaining that the war was a great trial which men lived through, survived, and returned from with purpose. Their purpose was to inform, to gain respect and their fair share of honour, and most certainly, to convey to the next generation the true perils of war and its dire costs, yet also that soldiers could live through such a trial and come away from it with a sense of humanity intact. The trenches for Carrington, Chapman and Douie created conflicted feelings about their own personal courage; but each writer found the rite of passage of war to be important for understanding, however conflictedly, its justification.

Suffering behind the lines: hospitals

Though accounts from the trenches predominated among war books released in the interwar period, some important memoirs were written from behind the lines. Both hospital workers and prisoners of war confronted hardships different than those of junior officers; their accounts demonstrate that their suffering, too, was important to the narrative history coming out of the world war. 'No one survived the Great War unscathed,' writes Emily Mayhew.[58] 'The wounded had their scars, as did the men and women who cared for them – although theirs were less easy to see.'[59] In many ways, it was because of the cultural privileging of combatants that those behind the lines felt a need to write of their own experiences, to demonstrate that their war efforts were of value, that they lived through experiences that were world-shattering and life-changing just like those who survived bombardments and gas attacks in the trenches.

One of the more prominent subgenres of Great War writing came from medical workers who were responsible for mending bodies and minds broken by war. Tragedy and suffering are endemic in this literature: medical accounts depict the struggles of doctors, nurses and orderlies to do their duty under fire, often in impossible situations. Medicos spent their days and nights treating wounded in a 'clammy atmosphere reeking of bloodstained iodine and stale cigarette smoke', desperately trying to save the lives of those who came through their aid stations suffering wounds that defied even the most creative of imaginary descriptions.[60] Representing suffering, for some medical aid workers, was a means of demonstrating agency through the treating of the wounded. In the hands of a politically conscious memoirist, such as Vera Brittain, suffering was a means of both honouring the war generation's fallen and furthering the political cause of pacifism.

During the war itself nearly 50 titles were released that depicted medical caregivers in war.[61] Afterwards, another 20 medical memoirs were published, most famously Vera Brittain's *Testament of Youth*.[62] Medical literature depicts the struggle between civilian doctors, volunteers and nurses functioning within a military hierarchy that was largely alien to them and which they often resented. They were caregivers first and military officers and nurses second, making their role one that sometimes conflicted with the military authorities.

There is a degree of distance found in medical literature. Medicos worked from the front lines to the rear, where their services were employed largely outside the killing zone of the trenches, as they worked at ambulance depots or casualty clearing stations. Whereas battle depictions are common in military memoirs, the action described by medicos takes place after the first shots are fired and often for weeks and months after major battles ended. Their being on the periphery of battle makes these accounts different than those of officers or men fighting for their lives in the lines, as does the perspective of the medical aid worker, in the ways in which they depicted their professional duty to save lives. The job of military medical personnel was to deal with the war's human destruction, the aftermath of battle, which gave medical writers a unique point of view on suffering.

Medical doctors, usually commissioned as Army Medical Officers, were torn between their professional obligations and ethical considerations regarding the health of the 'rank and file' and the requirements of the military. Army doctor Henry Gervis recalled sometimes forgetting his military status as an officer because he believed his duties were distinctly civilian.[63] Repeatedly he had to be reminded that he was a King's commissioned officer as well as a doctor and working in an army hospital. Of course, part of this distinction was to create a sense of separation between doctors and fighters: to distinguish a medical officer's role as a support professional, removed from the carnage on the battlefield by credentials and specialisation. Harold Dearden, in his edited published diary *Medicine and Duty* (1928), in which 'duty' connoted a positive military virtue, confessed complete ignorance of the overall strategy and conduct of the war beyond what he witnessed from the periphery. As in civilian practice, his job was medicine. He wrote, 'For the war itself, of its subtle moves and momentous phases, I know literally nothing. From the beginning to the end I was a mere camp follower.'[64] For civilian doctors in the armed services the sense of being a professional alien in military uniform was an important part of distinguishing their medical books as a different type of war literature.

Doctors often reflected upon their experiences with a degree of professional detachment. Dearden's diary, published in 1928, demonstrates that though doctors witnessed the awful remnants of combat, their memories were not always disillusioned. He wrote, 'in all sincerity, [the war was] one of the happiest periods of my life.'[65] On the same page, he described a soldier who lost both his legs in combat. The notion of physicians fighting a 'happy' war in France was one shared by David Rorie, former commander of the field ambulance for the distinguished 51st (Highland) Division on the western front. Rorie saw both 'joy and sorrows' on active service, but emphasised that 'undue stress [in his book] is laid on the cheerful side of the war.'[66] Rorie's account demonstrates thoughtful recollection about comradeship instead of brash outrage against the horrors of the war.

> And as for cheerfulness, what officer who was *la-bas* can ever forget the extraordinary power of the men to make the best of and magnify any little gleam of sunshine that flashed into their dull, depressing, and often sordid, routine of mud and blood; their ready response to a joke when there was, Heaven knows, little enough to jest over, and their constant good comradeship and good nature?[67]

The desire to record the brave deeds of his fellow doctors, ambulance drivers and, especially, stretcher-bearers, was an important part of his book. Hospital life was so utterly dispiriting that his focus was not on the carnage, but instead on comradeship. The spirit of making the best out of a bad situation pervades the text: his officers kept their mess well-stocked, their flasks full, and found gallows humour in being shelled. Rorie did not gloss over the morbidity of medical service or avoid graphic depictions of his duties at the front, but he did not want his book dominated by bloodiness. To do so would have detracted from his central intention: to pay tribute to his unit's professional competency, sacrifice and conduct.

Dr Isabel Hutton of the Scottish Women's Hospitals (SWH) had similar motivations in paying tribute to her unit. As a female doctor in a field hospital in Serbia, Hutton was one of a minority in a profession dominated by men and had been deployed to a side-show campaign. Her book offers particular insight into the war work of professional women working outside the official military hierarchy. Remarkably, Hutton served in combat zones in France, Serbia and Russia with the SWH. She witnessed the war up-close and treated the wounded over years of service writing:

> I only wish I could set down adequately the story of the everyday patience and heroism of the Allied troops and their leaders, or make you share the sufferings of gallant little Serbia [. . .] I would also like to tell you of the constant war that the doctors, sisters, and V.A.D.'s [Voluntary Aid Detachment nurses] wage against unromantic dirt, death and disease, and of the splendid spirit of unselfishness that was universal – the cheerfulness of service, the good comradeship and charity, the absence of sex antagonism, and, above all, that make-the-best-of-it spirit which was triumphant even in the most trying circumstances [. . .][68]

Hutton's memoir had obvious feminist motivations, but it was also an account by a scientist who found gratification in her professional competency in a war zone, satisfaction with doing a job she knew she could do well. *With a Women's Unit* is not a book about British war aims in the Balkans – politics is not really important – and there is little discussion of victory, defeat or the moral implications of the war. Instead it is a book about hardships faced and overcome, comradeship, and the basic duties of a physician and hospital administrator in war serving with other women who shared her commitment to cause and country. Of course, Hutton saw the ramifications of war as being tragic, but her service was also empowering.

Not all doctors saw the war in such rewarding terms. Arthur Osburn's *Unwilling Passenger* is replete with descriptions of graphic wounds and the futility of modern war.[69] Osburn had served in the South African War and dreaded more of the same.

> It was war again; and I must go cheerfully and perform my duty faithfully and, if Fate should ordain, die (and clearly in the circumstances that was likely, more than likely) as courageously as I could, well aware in my own mind that I was not brave, in fact about as nervous as the proverbial mouse.[70]

Unwilling Passenger depicts the frustrations of a professional officer facing the challenge of mass casualties that overwhelmed his abilities, not to mention his small horse-drawn medical pannier. He described witnessing lancers wounded by artillery barrage in 1914:

> I stared at this heap – a moving mound of death. Then, from all sides of the yard, a chorus of screams, shouts and groans. Around this central heap of dead men the wounded lay on all sides. Some had been blown to the other end of the yard, their backs broken. One sat up dazed and whimpering, his back against a wall, holding part of his intestine in his hand. Those nearest to the heap, with terrible stomach wounds, or with legs and arms torn away, were only moaning and writing; it was those further off, comparatively speaking the least damaged yet terribly injured, who shouted and screamed in agony [. . .][71]

Osburn went from patient to patient with chloroform and morphine attempting to treat their horrible wounds while caked in blood and mud. Graphic depictions like this were written both for expository value as well as for polemical effect, to show just how difficult battlefield surgery was for those who knew little about it.[72] As he worked his way from wounded man to wounded man, he clearly saw his limitations in such conditions: a single medical officer alone and trying to comfort a mass of men and writhing horses blown apart. Chaplain Edward Thompson recalled the lasting effects of witnessing a chaotic aid post full of suffering wounded, writing, 'I saw without seeing, things that are burned into memory.'[73]

The healer's duty in war, the space of rehabilitation somewhere between healing and killing, was rife with contradictions. Osburn wrote, 'To those of us who spent their lives first in urging their fellows to keep fit, and then in binding up their shattered bodies in war, this sense of futility comes inevitably.'[74] He called his service an 'accessory to killing', describing his belief that healing men entailed sending them back to the line, where they risked life and limb again.[75] Osburn's revulsion was not universally shared, but the central irony of military medicine was certainly noted by others.

Nurses faced an equally daunting task in trying to care for men whose bodies were mutilated by the machinery of modern war. Part of the story of the Great War that has come down to us is of the civilian nurse, or more commonly VAD, working hard to allay men's suffering, a story familiar from Vera Brittain's bestselling *Testament of Youth*. Part of Brittain's motivation for writing *Testament* was to tell a story she believed untold: that women's war work was equally important to the history of the war. She wrote:

> before I started finally writing these memories, several war autobiographies came out round about 1928–29, including Edmund Blunden's 'Undertones of War', Robert Graves' 'Goodbye to All That' and Siegfried Sassoon's 'Memoirs of a Fox-Hunting Man' and I thought: 'Why should these young men have the war to themselves? Surely my story is as interesting as theirs?'[76]

Brittain believed her story was as necessary to the lived memory of the Great War as the hundreds of accounts written and published by soldiers. The resounding success of *Testament* indicates that she was correct; the nurse's tale was as interesting to readers as that of the subaltern.

Testament of Youth was the most famous Great War medical memoir published in Britain. Though not the only nurse's account, it has been the most influential, and has had a lasting popular following since 1933. Compositionally, Brittain skilfully crafted her war experience into a tragedy which she wrote on behalf of fellow victims of the war. Margaret Higonnet and Christine Hallett have argued that many women's accounts of the war, including Brittain's and Mary Borden's, were distinct literatures of trauma with 'cynical overtones' toward the war itself and its agents of propaganda.[77] Though this was undoubtedly true of Brittain, it is not true of all women writers. According to Jane Potter, many women writers in their works 'attested to the continuing righteousness of the cause and asserted patriotic values'.[78] Moreover, memories of the war were subject to changes of beliefs in the years after the events were lived: what was believed in 1917 might be very different than what was believed in 1930. As has been noted by historian Janet Watson and literary critic Lynn Layton, differences exist between Brittain's war diaries and letters and how she constructed her memoir later, in the late 1920s.[79] Though she demonstrated a variety of conflicted feelings toward the war when it was ongoing, in later reflection she distilled those complexities into disillusioned catastrophe, a personal tragedy representational of her generation. Her reimagination of the war in memory politicised *Testament* within the context of the British anti-war movement of the early 1930s.

Testament defined the 'tragedy' of war in the minds of many. Brittain described it 'as a memorial to the dead who can now create no memorial for themselves'.[80] Through writing she hoped to mourn the loss of many who could never tell their own stories. To speak for others who could not speak for themselves was an impulse shared by many combat memoirists, particularly those who valued the notion of *esprit de corps*. In Brittain's case, her motivations were more universal, framed generationally and not regimentally. She hoped her book could be a memorial that would honour the dead but also speak against war itself, its futility and inhumanity. The way she hoped to accomplish this goal was through writing about personal suffering.[81]

Interestingly, Brittain had clear opinions as to how she wanted the book to be received. In a letter in 1933 she outlined 12 key points that she wanted emphasised in the marketing of the book by her publisher. Highlighted were the ignorance and innocence of her generation, the claim that those 'who survived the War nevertheless died, psychologically and emotionally, during its progress', that the book was a memorial to the dead, and her own 'indictment of the civilization' that caused the war. Further she wrote, 'Author's conclusions not empty theories but based on personal experience of sorrow, sacrifice and conflict which led her to seek for some philosophy of life that would save future civilization from similar catastrophe'.[82] Brittain wanted her own feelings of suffering and trauma to be the meta-narrative for her generation as a whole.

Few other memoirists sought such a tall order. Though the idea of the 'war generation' was a common one, it was rare for authors to claim to be the voice of it. Most war memoirs of the 1920s and 1930s were carefully commemorative works: paying tribute to comrades, relaying the story of a particular theatre or an individual unit, but not using personal tragedy to promote a political philosophy. Though the 1930s is often portrayed as a period of extreme political opinions, in the words of Richard Overy a 'morbid age', there were few war memoirists like Brittain, and even fewer could articulate their message of pacifism as well as she did.[83]

An interesting book to contrast with *Testament* is Hugh Bayly's *Triple Challenge: War, Whirligigs, and Windmills*. Bayly was a medical doctor and a staunch conservative Northern Irish Unionist before the war. He served as a medical officer in the Guards Division and treated the Prime Minister's son, Raymond Asquith, when he was mortally wounded at the Somme in September 1916. Bayly's memoir is a largely a political tract extolling his opinions on politics, the war and society. He wrote:

> Of the making of books giving their authors' experiences and conclusions concerning the war and afterwards there is no end. But, as the war period of the lives of many of us was the most real and intense portion of our lives, it is not unnatural that those great days should absorb our thoughts, and that on them our memoirs should become concentrated. Some, apparently, saw in the war only evil. To me that great event marked the triumph of good over evil; sacred years [...][84]

Bayly, like Brittain, saw the war as a sacred personal experience, though he viewed its suffering as generationally virtuous, a grand trial met by brave soldiers. Though he certainly was a polemicist advocating military service, Bayly was not a blind patriot – he criticised Third Ypres and Haig's generalship along with the 'needless' loss of life in the war – yet he was determined to show a war experience different than that of the pacifists of his day, for whom he had little regard.[85]

For authors like Brittain who were concerned with the political climate of their age, suffering could reflect those inclinations. For those affected by the trauma of war, such as Arthur Osburn, the memoir could be a useful way of purging their memories. But not every author, even those who witnessed perhaps the greatest amount of human suffering in large contingencies as medical aid workers, sought to demonstrate the war's aftermath in terms of generational catastrophe and universal tragedy. Though naturally physicians' accounts were overtly disillusioned – most were written in the late 1920s and 30s and depict the aftermath of terrible battles – they do not have a uniform political message. The difficulties on the fronts in which physicians served and the overwhelming nature of medical work made these representations even more important in remembrance. However, the story of Great War medicine, in its many forms, was eventually eclipsed by Brittain's *Testament of Youth*, which sold extremely well and was reprinted in large numbers. Brittain's tragedy became an experience adopted in popular culture as the caregiver's in war, though in the 1930s it was one book among many that sought to make sense of the suffering witnessed by medicos in the war.

Peripheral suffering: prisoners

The story of the British prisoner of war was recounted in dozens of published memoirs in the interwar period.[86] In the first six years after the war alone, 20 repatriated British POWs wrote accounts of their captivity for major publishers.[87] Many of these books pertained to the cat-and-mouse adventure of escape from camps in Germany and central Anatolia. Yet for some, the clear focus was for the prisoner to bear witness to the suffering of British soldiers and the survival of their officers in an alien land. Self-identified as 'prisoners of the Sultan', British officers recounted their captivity in the hands of the Ottoman Turks as a trial of human endurance against a hated foe and enemy. Central to their narratives was the notion of suffering, their military service largely defined by their ability to resist hardship and maintain the dignity of their rank and nationality in circumstances that were very different than those at the front.

The men who wrote memoirs of Ottoman captivity were nearly all officers, and many had served in India before being deployed to either the Dardanelles or Mesopotamia. Their memoirs reflect the privileges of this imperial pedigree. Officers had distinct feelings of British racial superiority and were used to being treated in a way that was commensurate with their rank. In their day-to-day lives they were used to having servants to prepare food and do their washing, well-bred horses to ride for both war and recreation, and to a high level of professionalism that meant orders were followed unquestioned. It was within this classist and racial hierarchy that captive officers framed their experiences for readers. When they described suffering and abuse by the Turks, they were doing so within the understood conventions of being both an officer and a gentleman facing trials brought by an enemy deemed as inhumane and barbaric. They recorded their suffering as a means of showing that their war experiences mattered as much as those who suffered from bullets and shells: to preserve, in part, their martial dignity.

The memoirs of Turkish captivity each tell a story of confinement and maltreatment by an eastern other, defined by one author as 'The Terrible Turk'.[88] They were written, largely, to bear witness to a forgotten experience in World War I. The war against the Ottomans was seen as an imperial side show, the experience of being a prisoner an aside to that side show. As such, captivity memoirs were expository; they told a story that audiences were unfamiliar with. Through their distressing memoirs, repatriated POWs depicted the plight of men who forfeited their martial status and spent most of the war confined in Turkey, hundreds of miles from their comrades who were winning the war in the Middle East. The importance of bearing witness to suffering was to demonstrate a sense of agency through a war experience that robbed them of their martial masculinity; their victory was not won on the battlefield, but found in surviving discomfort and disease and living to write their tales.[89] By showing hardship and trial, essentially by demonstrating their suffering as a stoic reaction to humiliation, these writers were able to justify an experience that could be interpreted by some as being, at the very least, unfortunate, and at the most, dishonourable.

POW memoirs begin, in earnest, with surrender. John Still recalled surrendering at Gallipoli, where he served in the East Yorkshire Regiment, his small company of men fighting a futile battle that ended with their being outnumbered and surrounded.[90] His colonel was bayoneted after he gave up, the first of many war crimes he details. Still and his fellow soldiers feared for their lives. He was appalled by the Turkish habit of killing prisoners: 'a wounded soldier behind a ridge, hid from the eye of the world's Press, has about as much chance with the Turks as he would have with a pack of wolves.'[91] He continued, 'There were good Turks; there are good wolves [...] but their rarity was above that of rubies.'[92] By surrendering, Still and his fellow soldiers were entrusting their lives into the hands of soldiers whom they respected for their martial prowess, but did not see as being civilised or respectful of the laws of war. He wrote, 'an order from an Asiatic when you have lived for eighteen years in Asia is a strange experience. I disliked it.'[93]

For Edward Keeling and E.W.C. Sandes, surrender came not as a result of battlefield defeat, but instead as a result of the mass capitulation of the 6th Indian Division at Kut, the worst humiliation for armies in the East in the war. Falling upon the mercy of their

Turkish captors, both Keeling's and Sandes's memoirs are accounts of neglect, ineptitude, and intentional racial humiliation by the Arabs and Turks who mocked and threatened British officers with menacing gestures, eventually parading them through Baghdad in 'Roman triumph'.[94] Officers faced a long trek north to Anatolia, and their Turkish guards provided no comfort, in the form of food or shelter, for soldiers under their care. Sandes wrote bitterly of his captors, 'the Turkish officer of this part of Turkey-in-Asia is after all only a savage at heart, with a thin veneer of civilisation which rubs off with the greatest of ease.'[95] Edward Mousley, who was very ill for most of the trip northwards to Kastamuni camp, saw a metaphor of civilisation in the broken old cart that he was carried on. 'Rattling and loosely bolted and wobbling, they appear to be on the point of breaking down at every minute [...] like Turkey itself, it just goes on.'[96]

The two-month journey for the 'Kuttites' to their respective POW camps revealed a host of atrocities that were chronicled with a purpose: to indict the Ottoman Turkish cruelty towards prisoners of war. Through their neglect, the Ottomans disrespected and demeaned commissioned officers who were conscious of their status and felt entitled to adequate care. Officers had to scrounge for food and relied upon one another for medical care, deprivation uncommon in the pre-war army, which contributed to feelings of humiliation and insecurity. Still wrote:

> In Turkey it has amounted to this – that British officers have been sent to live in places where at least it is very hard to keep body and soul together – have there been put under various restrictions and disadvantages – and have been left to support themselves as best they might.[97]

For officers used to being treated honourably, respectfully, and with material comforts commensurate with their rank, their treatment in captivity with its privations, financial extortion, disease and physical discomfort, was intolerable. Keeling surmised that it was not so much intentional cruelty on the part of the Ottomans, but instead neglect. 'Our own treatment was not brutal; it was merely apathetic.'[98] More problematic was the Turkish decision to have white British officers mess with Indian officers, which was seen as an overtly political act, 'to encourage strife between the Mussulman prisoners and the others'.[99] Keeling agreed and saw the act as one intended to 'rally the Muhammadan officers to the cause of Turkey', noting that 'it certainly had the opposite effect'.[100]

More significant, perhaps, than the feelings officers bore towards their own treatment was the anger they felt towards Turkish treatment of their men. Captured British other ranks were starved, beaten and neglected to death by the Turks. The plight of common soldiers caused British officers anger, their own impotence in the face of these atrocities, much guilt. They sought to bear witness to the suffering of men who could not write their own story.[101] On their way to their camps in Anatolia, which were comparatively comfortable, officers witnessed men dying of starvation and some who were beaten severely by their captors. Sandes wrote that responsibility for the thousands of lives lost was at 'the hands of a barbarous nation. Let us hope they will be avenged when the civilised world learns of the fate of these men.'[102] Undoubtedly part of his motivation for writing was to demonstrate exactly that, as it was for Keeling, who wrote, 'It is doubtful whether any prisoners of war in modern times, not actually massacred, have endured more than the prisoners of Kut.'[103] John Still's memoir, *A Prisoner in Turkey*, begins with extracts of the 1918 Report on the Treatment of British Prisoners of War in Turkey.[104] He uses the report of atrocities and violence as a means of framing his memoir, which is a chronicle, in part, of abuses he witnessed against British officers and men at the hands of the Ottomans who were charged with their care.

Another aspect of suffering depicted in prisoner memoirs is more remote, but still recorded so that the world might know of Turkish atrocities. Mousley, Sandes and Keeling all reported on the massacres of Armenians in Mesopotamia and Anatolia. Keeling reported grimly coming upon a well near Mosul full of the bones of massacred Armenians.[105] As the officers continued their march northwards, they ran into abandoned villages that had been populated by Armenians, now all massacred.[106] Sandes wrote, 'The Young Turk party, backed by the German Government, had much to answer for respecting these atrocities.'[107] For officers whose future was anything but secure, being marched through towns which had been cleared of inhabitants, wells full of the bones of the massacred, the remnants of Turkish killings, confirmed an impression of the cruelty of the Turks which remained with them well after the war. Part of their suffering was witnessing the suffering of others without the ability to do anything about it. Writing became a means of justification for those feelings.

Later when writing their memoirs, British officers sought to demonstrate their own plight in captivity with their pens. In survival, officers were able to demonstrate their preserved sense of dignity in the face of hardships that were uncommon in western Europe, even for those who were captured and held in Germany. For men who had been stripped of their professional sense of agency – that of fighting and command – captivity was a form of hardship that cut deeply into their sense of martial pride. By surviving and bearing witness to their suffering, former prisoners attempted to restore a sense of their martial dignity.

***

All soldiers suffer and all are prone to a sense of disillusionment with cause or country in the face of fear, hardship and death. In Great War memoirs, suffering is endemic, but situationally specific to the duties performed and the 'face of battle' witnessed. For infantry officers, their plight came through moments of intense fear while still commanding men to fight and die for their country. Though at times their duties seemed impossible to perform, their memoirs reveal remarkable endurance and emotional resilience, so much that it questions whether the story of their suffering is one really of disillusionment, or instead, of fortitude under fire, of carrying on. That these memoirs were written some time after the war, makes their message even more poignant, as their authors could easily have polemicised their memories. For medicos, trauma too was endemic – dealing with suffering is literally part of their occupational role in war – but the reactions of doctors and nurses were not uniform in their reflections upon suffering, but instead, incredibly varied. For prisoners, the humiliation of surrender demonstrated a host of emotional issues, but their desire to bear witness to atrocities and suffering as a means of justification after the war was over demonstrates a clear sense of martial duty to their comrades. All three types of war book reflect something similar: the writer's ability to reflect upon difficult circumstances and try to make sense of suffering either borne or witnessed.

In a broader sense, the characterisation of the victimised veteran of World War I is neither a fair representation nor a common one. Though some, like Henry Williamson and Vera Brittain, helped to define disillusionment in their war experiences, many others wrote to refute such sentiments. Soldiers psychologically processed their war memories in individual ways, and their written accounts, though composed for a particular audience and constructed within a particular culture, reflect great varieties that resist convenient stereotypes. Despite their differences of interpretation on the war, all war writers reacted to suffering, a universal trait that was interpreted individually. Rather than as disillusioned victims, perhaps members of the war generation were attempting to write another story: as men and women who had suffered, but who also triumphed in their survival.

CHAPTER 6

WAR EXPERIENCES: HEROISM

In 1929, Ernest Hemingway published his World War I novel *A Farewell to Arms*. In it Hemingway famously wrote about the disconnection felt by combat veterans when confronted by the heroic abstractions prominent in early twentieth-century wartime rhetoric. In a new age of mostly mechanical warfare, the language of heroism seemed trite, empty and archaic compared to the realities experienced by soldiers at the front. Hemingway wrote: 'Abstract words such as glory, honor, courage or hallow were obscene beside the concrete names of villages, the numbers of roads, the names of rivers, the numbers of regiments and the dates.'[1] It is a familiar quotation used to demonstrate the problem of heroism in World War I, indicative of a linguistic turn away from the heroic ideal and towards more cynical expressions in war literature. How could a conflict that upended great heroic expectations with such unforgiving violence be represented by such hollow words?

Hemingway's cynicism towards heroic word play reflected a growing scepticism in postwar culture towards patriotic sentimentalism. Afterwards, the war was thought by some to be a colossal mistake: its inception a product of martial madness, its conduct folly, and its legacy polluted by the postwar political upheaval and violence in Europe. In Britain, this scepticism was the first revision of the predominant wartime patriotism that began to be questioned in light of the war's outcomes as they were popularly understood. In literature, popular feelings of disillusionment were ironically and bitterly expressed in Wilfred Owen's iconic wartime poem 'Dulce et Decorum Est' and in Richard Aldington's novel *Death of a Hero*, works written a dozen years apart, but both focused upon the tragedy of men losing their belief that there was anything heroic in sacrifice. Was there anything redemptive in suffering and dying for one's country? Historian Eric Leed writes that heroic language was particularly painful for returning soldiers, that martial words themselves reminded men of the dislocation between the violence witnessed in war and their return to civilian life. He writes, 'These words illuminated too starkly the victimization of those at the front.'[2] For those whose lives were so altered by the experience of war, civilian notions of heroic idealism were not easily reconciled with their memories of the front.

Rather than dying in the trenches, the heroic ideal survived the war and continued to be defined in somewhat traditional ways by writers who returned from the front and articulated their memories on the page. Perhaps the most significant of the war's forgotten legacies is that which was most common in war memoirs: the desire to memorialise comrades who served, itself a heroic impulse, one extremely common in war literature. Yet honouring heroism, especially of the western front, seems anachronistic for many. 'Even when an heroic reality, imitated realistically in art, can be shown to have existed, biographically or historically,' Andrew Rutherford writes, 'readers may well feel uneasily that it affronts their expectations of both literature and life.'[3] In other words, readers have come to expect certain stereotypes of war literature – cynical portraits of victims surviving amidst the absurdity of war – and books that do not support this preconceived notion are on uneasy ground. Samuel Hynes describes this as 'the war we remember because we want the First World War to be the worst, the cautionary example of war horror'.[4] Yet, the war was not interpreted this way, not always, and not by every survivor.[5] Instead of a collection of cynics, Rutherford writes, British war literature of the twentieth century is full of 'conscious and effective moral agents' who redefined heroism in light of changing definitions of courage that came from men adapting to new battlefield realities.[6]

This chapter considers the moral agents who have been neglected in the war's literary memory: the men who wrote heroic war books. Heroism is an essential part of World War I's story and, rather than heroic depictions diminishing as a result of the war, soldiers who served and then later wrote about their service often did so in terms that reinforced martial ideals of courage, honour and sacrifice. As courage consecrated and socially sanctified, heroism was expressed in tales of suffering and adventure written by authors who memorialised both ordinary and exceptional forms of bravery in their works. Though there are many types of heroism present in war books, three specific and somewhat unique heroic archetypes developed as a response to the war's conduct: the 'unremarkable' heroism, en masse, of the citizen-soldier; the eccentric and plucky heroism of the escaped prisoner of war; and the exceptional chivalric heroism of the fighter pilot. Each of these typologies demonstrated a new perspective on how the heroic ideal continued after World War I. They are variants and reconstructions of what Jessica Meyer and Graham Dawson describe as the 'soldier hero', a masculine ideal defined by traditional traits of martial fortitude, virtue and bearing reimagined by memoirists to meet the challenges of battle in World War I.[7] Each has been influential on the way that Britons have defined heroism since.

Unremarkable heroism

Before he gained fame as Winston Churchill's personal physician, Charles Wilson was a medical officer in the Royal Fusiliers on the western front. In that capacity he kept a diary, later edited as part of his book on combat psychology, *The Anatomy of Courage*, which he wrote during World War II as a guide to understanding the effects of combat stress. Wilson wrote in his diary of looking into the faces of soldiers who had reached the limits of their endurance at the Somme. 'All around me are faces which sleep might not have visited for a week, they have dark shadows under eyes that are older, more serious.'[8] Sleep deprivation and stress had made young men suddenly old. The experience of combat for the citizen-soldiers of his battalion was jarring, unfamiliar and emotionally confusing. Beyond anything else, it was exhausting. He continued, 'boys have lost their freshness in a month [...] The sap has gone out of them. They are dried up.'[9]

All men who serve in combat have to wrestle with physical and emotional fatigue that forces them to either find ways of coping with stress or psychologically break down. Such is the cumulated effect of prolonged fear and anxiety. Yet, the men under Wilson's care were not exactly dried-up victims: they had also fought through a hard campaign and had survived. They had made it through intense combat, bombardment and assaults on the Somme and had not been broken, not entirely. Many of the men in his battalion who lived through their experiences in 1916 would see the next year. Many, if not most, would survive the war. Despite being spent of their courage and at the end of their tether, these men were carrying on and there is stoic heroism in his description, a form of martial heroism found in the courage to risk their lives, to suffer, and to endure battle until the sap had run out of them.

Exhaustion is the great enemy of endurance. Even for men who have significant reservoirs of courage, fatigue from constant exposure to combat stress and campaigning takes its toll. For those who fought in World War I, mostly civilians in uniform facing combat for the first time, the combination of unfamiliar routine and brutal service made life at the front particularly jarring. Most of the civilian-soldiers that were the bulk of the BEF had not been subject to the prolonged exposure to fear experienced on a battlefield; as civilians, their senses were not accustomed to fighting, their bodies unused to living in conditions that were as cold, wet and uncomfortable as the western front or as hot and sickly as the eastern Mediterranean.[10] It is no wonder that so many who wrote about the war afterwards remembered its otherworldliness, service largely reimagined as the surmounting of hundreds of hardships, whether they be septic skin sores in the Palestine or trench foot at Ypres.

New technologies and tactics, not to mention the new armies conducting operations, changed the way that Britons defined heroism. Courage itself had to be reimagined to meet the challenges of the new battlefield, in the face of shifting combat conditions that altered the way that soldiers saw the idea of bravery. As scholars like Jessica Meyer and Edward Madigan have demonstrated, expressions of courage became more passive, less focused on individual heroics and more on the ability to endure battle.[11] For civilian-soldiers fighting industrial war huddled beneath field fortifications and enduring the random terror of bombardment, courage was redefined as emotional resilience in the face of terror.[12] High-explosive bombardments may have stripped men of their sense of agency, but the principal way that soldiers met that loss was with a reinvented sense of courage, defined as ability to stick it out.[13] This was a type of courage that the common citizen-soldier could achieve.

Just as courage became redefined, the notion of the hero too changed, to bring to the fore those who were civilians and fundamentally un-martial beings. Heroism and the idea of the hero changed, in part, because Britain was a nation reconciling itself to mass casualties, death and mourning.[14] As Stephanie Barczewski has argued in her book on Antarctic explorers Robert Scott and Ernest Shackleton, the face of heroism changed throughout the twentieth century, the figure of the hero redefined by different generations that privileged specific heroic attributes. For those who grew up in the shadow of imperial exploration, those attributes included such things as manly determination to overcome personal obstacles, self-sacrifice, athleticism, and stoicism in the face of trial.[15] The challenge of the Great War was that its generation had a perceived notion of what a hero was, but that type of heroism was fundamentally challenged by industrialised war. In response to the emotional responses of men towards the changing battlefield, bravery became more ordinary, defined in terms of good cheer rather than daring, men supporting each other when times got tough. Heroism, in turn, became celebrated en masse in war memoirs published to pay tribute to common expressions of courage. R.T. Rees, a former junior officer on the western front, recalled:

> The real hero, if there is one, is a faithful and old soldier who feared nothing. But even if one is not heroic oneself, it is nevertheless a great experience to have known those who were, men whose heroism was revealed as much in cheerful endurance of hardship as in gallant great feats of arms.[16]

Similarly, journalist Philip Gibbs defined the war as 'appalling in its vastness of sacrifice and suffering, wonderful in its mass-heroism', an apt phrase for what Rees saw as the stoic endurance of common soldiers.[17] Within Britain's first truly mass army came the notion of mass heroics, of men together sharing in the burdens of combat, suffering together, a type of heroic inaction.

The idea of mass-heroism, of men suffering, stressing and surviving together, was an important part of the war's memory. Conscientious memoirists after the war were concerned with memorialising mass heroism through the martial virtue of comradeship, the foundation of soldier relationships.[18] Charles Douie was particularly concerned that soldiers receive their due honours in a postwar period that he believed had robbed them of their martial glory:

The war is regarded as an improper subject for conversation; and all references to it are discouraged except on Armistice Day. One day of the year the dead at least have their meed of honour; the living are without honour even on that day. In our schools every boy and girl learns something of a heroic past. Salamis and Marathon and Thermopylae are familiar names to the boys who have never heard, and never will hear, of the grim and steady ranks who kept the Germans from the sea in the First Battle of Ypres and again in the long agony of the fighting on the Somme and the Lys in the spring of 1918.[19]

For Douie, part of the reason for writing a war memoir was to recapture something of the heroism of men both living and dead who fought for their country, and to memorialise their experience for the public. The first chapter of his war memoir, entitled 'The Soldier', was a tribute to those who he believed had been forgotten in the postwar debates over the war's legacy.

For Ralph Hale Mottram, combat in World War I was abhorrent, his own service at the Ypres Salient described as 'cosmic murder'.[20] He remembered his experiences bleakly in commemorative essays throughout the 1920s and 1930s, the author consciously revisiting the western front over and over again in his writings, as he returned as a tourist to the front. Though he found modern warfare 'dreadful', his service still was meaningful, in part, because he fought alongside brave men.

> My impression was that most men were heroic. It was quite ordinary. Over and over again incidents occurred that would have gained the V.C. they earned in any other war. But with us they were too common, and it is not possible in wars like ours for such things to be witnessed by those who have the dispensing of medals. The behaviour, I will maintain in the face of the whole world, of volunteer amateur infantry in the face of unparalleled dangers was heroic, if you like, but so regular as to become unremarkable.[21]

As a commander of a small unit, Mottram was an intimate witness to the transformation of the men under his command from civilians to soldiers.

He looked after their health and wellbeing, and paid close attention to their ability to function in the line. He knew his men's limitations, but he also knew their courage, and the seemingly unremarkable heroism of their ability to endure.

Former ranker William Linton Andrews concluded his memoir, *Haunting Years,* with a statement of 'Thanksgiving', itself an expression of memorialisation. For him, the heroic ideal was found in the 'spirit' of the battalion in which he served, lauded for their 'courage and good fellowship'.[22] Similar to Douie, Rees and Mottram, his emphasis was on the morale and the good cheer mustered from men in trying times: the banal heroics of survival of spirit. Andrews was not a career soldier – he was a journalist who volunteered and fought as a private in the Black Watch – but his belief in the traditional martial virtue of comradeship is an important key to understanding his memoir. He concluded his book paying tribute to the dead:

> Dear, great-hearted comrades of the Black Watch, no darkness of the grave can keep you from my sight, nothing can dim the light of youth in your friendly eyes [...] The horrors of those years have often haunted my dreams, but I thank God with a humble heart that I came to know and love the spirit of my old battalion.[23]

The war remembered to men like Andrews was one of both heroism and horror; it included both tributes and tribulations. Andrews sought to recapture both, as a means of honouring the dead and the living of his battalion. He found pride in having served with men who had fought and suffered for their nation.

For Rifleman Giles Eyre, who suffered through the Somme and then German captivity, the war certainly had heroic meaning. In the last two pages of his memoir *Somme Harvest,* entitled 'Aftermath', he attempted to contextualise experiences that he had lived through 21 years earlier. Describing those who criticised the war's conduct in print in the 1930s as 'flingers of garbage', Eyre felt that 'the survivors of the ordeal, linger in a new age, bewildered.'[24] Disillusioned with the politics of his day, he chose to memorialise the war dead rather than criticise the war itself. Eyre remembered those who died as a means of making their deaths meaningful. Remembering the war was about recapturing something of the earnest heroism of the common soldier. 'Can we rise to the occasion and recapture our erstwhile spirit and march on shoulder to shoulder – peer and worker, poet and peasant, rich man and beggar man, in our olden spirit of comradeship, and fulfill the reality of the England we fought for?'[25] The war dead were sacred, their memory one that needed to be protected from the cynicism of the age in which the war's survivors were living. Eyre un-ironically invoked Horace as he concluded his book:

> This monument that will remove all the mockery and the ill concealed sneer that a careless and cynical posterity has attached to the soldier's dictum: *Dulce et Decorum Est Pro Patria Mori*.[26]

Plucky heroism: escapers

From the start of World War I, mass captivity became a significant issue for armies. Nearly 200,000 British Empire soldiers were held in POW camps in Germany and Turkish Anatolia. The POW story was part of the war's literary legacy; narratives of prisoners enduring captivity, many of them escaping to return to service, became commonplace in the publishing industry. Rather than focusing on hardship and suffering, which is an essential part of the POW tale, most former prisoners who wrote their accounts were escapees, their books detailing elaborate escape plans and dramatic attempts at freedom. These accounts – daring and adventurous in their telling – were a small subgenre of the heroic war books published in the 1920s and 1930s, one that created an archetype of the plucky British prisoner/escapee.

Surrender and capture brought humiliation and feelings of martial impotence for officers who were trained to fight and lead. Though most British prisoners of war were held idle in camps, their war over, a slim minority sought to escape. Escape was a way to recapture a sense of martial agency; it was a way for men to participate again in the war effort. It was also a means of breaking up the boredom of captivity, which in both Ottoman Turkey and Germany was substantial enough to bring certain men to risk their lives in elaborate escape attempts in the face of great danger. Escapers, with their brashness and bravado, represented a new ingenious form of heroic literature that focused on cleverness, bravery and recaptured martial agency.

The majority of POW memoirs written during the interwar period were by officers who mounted successful escape attempts. Escape literature appealed to publishers because of its excitement: escapees were portrayed as military celebrities, daredevils and courageous adventurers. Historian Michael Moynihan has described escapees as 'a breed apart' from other prisoners.[27] Unquestionably, escapers were an elite. Writing of World War II escapee literature, Samuel Hynes recounts, 'escapers aren't like other war narratives; they're romances.'[28] The romance of escape certainly helped authors attract publishers for their books. Escapee literature had a wider purpose than just entertainment: it helped to redefine the prisoner experience from one of passivity to activity, from the humiliation of surrender to the heroism of escape.

Though many prisoners felt shame in their capture, few decided to risk escape. In part, this was because officers lacked any protocols or extensive training on how to behave if captured.[29] Though the War Office instructed that men should re-join their units 'when able', this was not an explicit order to escape if captured.[30] In camp, senior officers sometimes did not know how to answer their juniors when questioned on the subject: one senior officer even went so far as to give a subordinate a direct written order not to escape until his superiors in London mailed him a ruling from the War Office.[31] The relatively lax security under which prisoners in Anatolia were held made it fairly common for Turkish commandants to demand parole of their internees, which was usually voluntarily given by British officers.[32] One of the ways that escapees distinguished themselves from their fellow captives was in their willingness to incur the risk of escape, a distinction not lost when men later wrote their memoirs. Francis Yeats-Brown recalled the shame of inactivity being greater than the risk involved in attempting escape.[33] What is clear is that out of the shame of capture came the impetus of adventure.

Escapees were adamant about their motivations: to return to the front first and foremost and fight for their country. In most memoirs, the author recalls a type of formulaic escape revelation, usually right after capture.[34] Resolve did not necessarily translate into knowledge, and most officers had no idea how to begin an escape attempt.[35] Cartwright recalls buying a North German Baedeker from a travelling bookseller. He wrote:

> At this time we had no experience of any sort on which to build, and there was a good deal of scepticism shown by the majority of

prisoners as to the possibility of walking several hundred miles through a hostile country without coming into contact with anyone or buying food on the way.[36]

In Anatolia, these fears were compounded by ignorance of the local culture, language and the sparsely populated and difficult terrain in which prisoners would have to walk.[37]

As in World War II POW films, the planning and aesthetics of escape are an essential part of Great War escaper books.[38] Escape planning and the laborious details describing accoutrements offered legitimacy to the escapes themselves, showing the difficulty of procuring supplies, the cleverness of the authors and the length of time it took to plan a successful escape. As the war progressed and men made both successful and unsuccessful attempts, a type of escape culture developed in Germany. Recaptured escapees would share knowledge of techniques and learned from each other's failed attempts: soldiers became better at escaping as the war progressed and shared knowledge with each other.[39] A.J. Evans entitled his memoir *The Escaping Club* because of this sense of an escapee communal identity.[40] Fellow memoirist Walter Duncan recalled:

> There was not one officer who was not imbued with the spirit that I mentioned earlier in this book, of 'Fight the Boche in his own country.' Everyone had two aims continually in view – escape, if possible, and worry the Boche.[41]

Memoirists Grinnell-Milne and Cartwright both met Jocelyn Hardy, perhaps the greatest of the serial-escaper memoirists, in their respective prison camps.[42] Cartwright described Hardy as a 'maniac' for escape and was indebted to him for the knowledge he shared.[43] The fact that prisoners could share techniques and develop plans with each other was an enormous advantage when seeking to escape from camps in Germany. Favourable geography, parcels from Britain and shared knowledge all proved essential to escapes from captivity and provided authors with every opportunity to demonstrate their cleverness and courage to the public.

In Turkey, geography and culture were major deterrents to escape. Escape from Kastamuni or Yozgad camps entailed long marches followed by sea travel to reach an Allied nation. Escape attempts in Germany were sometimes over hundreds of miles, but in Europe the ability to scrounge, purchase or steal food was far greater than in central Turkey. Escape narratives of German captivity have an element of cat-and-mouse play to them; they concern spirited British captives outwitting and tormenting their German captors before eventual success in escape. In the Turkish case, this sense of adventure was present, but it was also mixed with the Orientalist notion of the East as an exotic space, and Turkish culture being distinctly hostile and alien.

Like their counterparts in Germany, officers in Turkey were not trained for escape. The 'learning curve' of the POW was basically non-existent in Turkey, making escape rare. Officers looked at the inhospitable countryside with trepidation and many simply believed, as the Ottomans did, that escape was impossible. Serious deterrents to any attempt were that most men could not speak Turkish and knew very little of local geography. This was in contrast to Germany, which was a popular vacation destination for middle-class Britons before the war, few British officers had spent any time in Turkey to know anything substantial about its language or geography. As implausible as it seems, the genesis of one escape attempt in Turkey came from an American Civil War POW escape story in a magazine.[44] Regional maps were almost impossible to obtain. In one case, an escape party relied upon the 'Public Schools Classical Atlas' sent from England, which had a map of the Black Sea region from 500 BC as their only guide to northern Anatolia.[45] Surprisingly, the party made it to Russia.

As much as geography deterred British officers in Turkey, they did have several advantages over their counterparts in Europe. The Turks believed any escape attempt would fail and thought that no officer would be foolish enough to attempt it. Turkish captors offered freedoms that British officers did not have in Europe. Officers were able to go into bazaars and purchase food supplies, disguises and rope. Guards were careless and some prisoners escaped through their windows. While being held in Istanbul, Francis Yeats-Brown went shopping with his armed guard and bought escape gear, including the fez he used as a disguise. He claimed that he had the audacity to make the guard carry the packages back to prison for him.[46] Of course, this display of bravado accomplished a dual purpose of not only accounting for his eventual escape from prison, but also portraying the Turkish guards as clueless and subordinate to the wits of their English captives. The point remains that Yeats-Brown was given every opportunity to purchase and use equipment for escape.

The major difficulty for escapees was something far more significant than breaking out of the camp, which was relatively easy. Geography was instead the major deterrent. Keeling's ordeal, described in *Adventures in Turkey and Russia*, involved not only a breakout, but also walking through hostile terrain, capture by brigands and then small-boat travel across the Black Sea to the Crimea.[47] When his party arrived in Russia, the nation was in the throes of the 1917 Revolution. Inspired by Keeling's escape attempt, Maurice Johnston and Kenneth Yearsley were part of a mass breakout from Yozgad prison camp that led to a 450-mile cross-country march. The party learned from Keeling how to stockpile food and make rucksacks for their journey. All eight of their party survived to freedom. William Blackwood and Sons published their account in 1919, and it remains one of the most interesting accounts of POW escape and survival of World War I.

Memoirs of Turkish captivity had an exotic appeal lacking in those of German escape. The most well known and profitable of these books was Elias Jones and C.W. Hill's *The Road to En Dor*. Jones and Hill successfully 'spooked' their commandant with a Ouija board and later were transferred to Istanbul because the Turks assumed each man to be insane. Though the tale of Hill and Jones is certainly one of the oddest accounts of escape written by a British officer during the war, the escape attempts made by Yeats-Brown were outright adventure. In his *Caught by the Turks*, he claimed to have intentionally smoked opium until he was hospitalised in Istanbul, in a cunning plot to get transferred to the Turkish capital. For his next attempt, he dyed his hair black and bought a fez to appear Turkish.[48] After escaping from prison, he faced the problem of getting out of Istanbul, as he had no passport or knowledge of Eastern languages. To remedy this, he disguised himself as a convincing German governess, complete with a hat and veil. He wrote of his disguise, 'a veil was advisable, chiefly to tone down my blinding beauty.'[49] After his hopes were dashed as a German woman, he disguised himself as an 'oily' Hungarian mechanic, complete with a false handlebar moustache.[50] Thankfully for the reader, he had his picture taken in each disguise, and included these photographs in his memoir.

It is hard to imagine Yeats-Brown's account as being anything other than an adventure story meant for the popular or boys' market. Fellow captive Alan Bott, a famous Blackwood wartime writer who published under the pseudonym 'Contact', released his escape memoir *Eastern Nights – and Flights* in 1920. Similar to Yeats-Brown, who is featured in it, Bott's is an 'Oriental adventure' book. The author, fearing his book would lose popularity after the Armistice, hoped Blackwood would market it specifically to boys.[51] The juvenile or boys' market was a natural place for these accounts, and even some stories of German captivity contained illustrations geared towards boys and were written in a typically breezy style.[52]

Though some escape accounts are more light-hearted than others, Johnston's *Four-Fifty Miles to Freedom* reminds the reader of just what a difficult and harrowing experience being an escaped prisoner was in an inhospitable landscape with little water or food. German escape attempts often involved the same level of risk and personal hardship, as men averted capture and eventually made it to freedom in a neutral country. These were remarkable stories of endurance and fortitude in an age when popular war books often depicted grim trench warfare. Beyond this, they were individual stories of exceptional masculine heroism that came out of the martial humiliation of captivity.

Knightly heroism: pilots

As celebrated as escapees were for their pluck, ingenuity and heroism, they were surpassed in accolades by the newest of the armed forces, the pilots of the Royal Flying Corps. RFC pilots garnered celebrity status while the war was ongoing, and maintained public interest in the interwar years as the future face of modern heroism. Their memoirs offered a contrast to those by infantry officers and brought a cultural fantasy of romance and honour to a front that seemed to lack either attribute. Maryam Philpott writes, 'Whilst many disillusioned memoirs came from the trenches in the late 1920s, veteran-pilot accounts consistently reinforced the associated notions of glamour, adventure and just war that the public wished to believe in.'[53] Philpott argues that the 'fantasy' of flight created in the 1920s, in part through air war literature, had an important purpose in helping to establish the RAF and cementing in the public mind the myth of the pilot hero.[54]

War Experiences: Heroism

Tales of brave dogfights, harrowing bombing raids and the strafing of balloons and zeppelins filled the pages of wartime newspapers and periodicals. After the war, the so-called modern knights wrote their accounts for major publishers, mythologising a distinctive form of heroic action for readers who were eager to learn about the Great War's more adventurous front, the war in the air. In an age of mud-soaked literature of stalemate on the western front, the freedom and 'clean' fighting of the aerial war piqued the martial fantasies of young boys and helped to recapture a sense of chivalric heroism that many believed to be lost. Brave young pilots intended to create their own mythology of service, or as one former pilot described it, leave behind a 'record of adventures – some grim, some gay'.[55] Flight was the supreme adventure of the war; pilots the supreme authors of the Great War's heroic story.

Fifty-seven years after *Sagittarius Rising* was first published by Peter Davies, Cecil Lewis, who was then in his nineties, recalled the thrill of flight, the skies the last great space for adventure.[56] 'Only the air and all beyond, the greatest master of all, was still unmastered and unsung when I was young.'[57] As an old man remembering the war of his youth, Lewis described the war years somewhat mystically: 'those glorious years when life stretched before me like a landscape from ten thousand feet and there were no shadows in the day'.[58] In his original 1936 foreword, Lewis described the war as also belonging to 'another life', when he was a younger man who 'walked off the playing-fields into the lines'.[59] 'We lived supremely in the moment,' he wrote. 'Our preoccupation was the next patrol, our horizon the next leave [...] We were trained with one object – to kill. We had one hope – to live.'[60] Both nostalgia and romance were elemental parts of Lewis's memories and he referred back to his experiences with the glistening eyes of a survivor who recognised the beautiful exceptionalism of his war experience. In both middle and old age, the former RFC pilot remembered his war as 'a fine introduction to life'.[61]

Unlike the infantry subaltern, the pilot had the luxury of creating a mythology based on individual combat, skill, and active agency against the enemy. Aerial warfare was in its infancy; tactics and technologies were constantly changing. Young pilots were able to participate in something new, adventurous and exceptional compared with their peers in the infantry. From the outside, the pilot seemed to inhabit a different world, accentuated by aerodrome life behind the lines, a comfortable and safe microcosm, and by the openness of the pilot's battlefield, the air, where planes could move freely with unlimited space above the pockmarked landscape. This privilege came with substantial risk: pilots appeared to live a charmed existence, but the realities of their service meant that they faced high casualties and the constant risk of death or capture.

Yet, pilots remembered their war differently, accentuating the adventure, celebrating their own soldier aristocracy, rather than dwelling on risks and horrors. As a skilled and chosen elite, pilots were conscious of their uniqueness, seeing flight as the great escape from a damned life of attritional warfare on the ground. Norman Macmillan recalled being 'lucky' to have left behind the trenches, even despite the great risks of flying.[62] 'Up there', he wrote, 'was Romance, the elemental struggle. But below, in a trench, there was no romance. There was but grim reality, the hidden tragedy of war.'[63] Billy Bishop recalled in simpler terms the feelings of many pilots who had left the trenches for the skies. 'It was the mud, I think, that made me take to flying.'[64]

The great paradox of flight was that the risk of death for RFC officers was marginally higher than if they had stayed in the infantry and the realities of service meant that death could come from mechanical failure as easily as from enemy bullets or anti-aircraft fire.[65] Duncan Grinnell-Milne recalled watching a man burn to death in front of his training class, a teaching moment for all cadets on the risks they were taking by placing their inexperienced lives in the hands of infant technology.[66] Training itself was both dangerous and short, men being deployed to France with only dozens of hours of logged flight time, woefully insufficient by any standards.[67] Despite these perils, memoirists largely remembered their war experiences heroically and not in terms of the trepidation and terror that undoubtedly came with flying. Or rather, fear was considered part of the adventure of flight and their adventurousness stemmed from the belief that they were breaking new ground and engaging with a new technology that made many of their number celebrated elites, despite their youthfulness and inexperience. Surely, part of the heroic ideal of being a pilot was the risk itself: leaving the ground for the skies, in rickety planes made of light-wood and canvas. Each patrol was a risk: each flight an exercise in courage.

Courage came through performing one's duty, which for pilots meant exercising considerable autonomy, intelligence, and creativity in action.

Skill and agency were important attributes.[68] Fighting was likened to sport. Men could engage in 'hunting the Huns in the air', fight a 'great game' against individual German pilots, and be the 'king of all sportsmen, the master of the most daring of man's inventions'.[69] Trench life, observed from above, seemed pitiful compared to the movement over hundreds of open miles aloft, men sharpening their skills with each sortie over enemy lines. This is not to say that men in the RFC portrayed themselves as fearless, but that fear was an enemy met and vanquished. Whitehouse wrote, 'We were afraid, yes; but not of the War itself. We were not afraid of the enemy, or shell-fire, or bullets. We were more afraid of ourselves and our limitations.'[70] Compared to trench warfare, which robbed men of their agency and forced them to adapt their sense of courage to meet their impotence, the pilot was fighting a far different war, one where older conceptions of heroic action, individual martial skill and bravery still applied.

Pilots defined their heroism in terms of duty and honour, sometimes with a type of anachronistic chivalry, no doubt with considerable irony as their mode of warfare consisted of the most modern of technologies. Still, even machine guns and rotary engines did not stop the mythology of the knight taking prominence. One pilot recalled waving to a German before trying to kill him, saluting the enemy 'as it might have been in the days of tilting'.[71] Aces like Albert Ball, Edward Mannock and James McCudden were decorated and celebrated widely as heroes. Samuel Hynes writes that both congratulatory letters from sovereigns and the ritual of dropping flowers over an enemy aerodrome upon the death of an ace were modern incarnations of chivalry and fed into public perceptions of the pilot as a modern knight.[72] Even the less successful pilots were treated like a martial nobility, accentuated by their distinctive uniforms and convivial squadron life which differed so greatly from the war being fought by their colleagues only a matter of miles away from the aerodromes.

Knightly references often appear in RFC memoirs. When they do, they are often forced, an indication that pilots had a self-awareness of the chivalric trope's limitations. Whitehouse, in fact, rejected it, recalling, 'This was war – killing and dying [...] Where was the romance? The ladies who knotted their scarves to the lances of their knights.'[73] Similar to their compatriots fighting in Palestine who likened themselves to crusaders, pilots used romance to emphasise their exceptionalism and mythologise the unique heroism of their peers. Medievalism was a convenient way to demonstrate the central difference between the pilot's war and everyone else's: the individual nature of combat engaged upon a wide-open, indeed almost limitless, space for fighting.[74] Being a knight had less to do with a clear-cut chivalric code and more with skill, agency and autonomy in battle.

Like Cecil Lewis, pilot Duncan Grinnell-Milne came into the RFC from school, only 18 years of age, after first being commissioned as an infantry officer. He received scant flight training before being sent to France where he flew scouting missions before mechanical failure caused him to land his plane behind enemy lines in December 1915. He was taken into captivity for two years. After repeated attempts, Grinnell-Milne escaped from prison in 1918 and rejoined the RFC, where he fought on the western front, firing his last shots on 5 November 1918 from his plane *Schweinhund*, the name brazenly scrawled on his plane in large letters so that the Germans below could read it clearly.[75] He wrote memoirs both of his captivity and escape as well as his adventures as a pilot; his status as both a pilot and escaped prisoner meant that he was a breed apart of a breed apart.

Grinnell-Milne's story is particularly revealing. He wrote two war memoirs, *An Escaper's Log* (1926) about his experiences in prison and *Wind in the Wires* (1933) about flying in the RFC. Each experience was defined as being distinctive, different sides of the same coin.[76] He reflected upon the war romantically: 'We were glad of our youth and the means to use it, not with false heroics but with the spirit of adventure.'[77] He lamented the fact that the war was seen as 'something of a disgrace' in the early 1930s, even a forgotten subject among the youth.[78] He continued, 'Personally, like many another young man, I was proud of having acted as a target to the enemy's practice.'[79] Grinnell-Milne's impressions were also those of a mature man reflecting nostalgically: 'Youth, adventure, high spirits – those wound up for us the mainspring of life. We would have fought just as well without propaganda; we had no need for bitter hatred. So may it have been in the days of chivalry.'[80]

Though Grinnell-Milne's experiences were hardly ordinary, the way he conceptualised the war afterwards was fairly typical of other flight memoirists. His memoir begins with his flight training, describes the technological limitations of early airplanes, climaxes with adventurous descriptions of missions, and ends with his promotion, decoration and survival. Similar to Cecil Lewis, in reflection he approached the war as if it were another life, a youthful adventure, rather than as so many infantry officers did, as a mournful rite of passage. This is not to say that his work was pure gallantry. When Grinnell-Milne returned after two years of captivity, it was as though he rejoined 'another war [...] as though I myself had been killed [...] to be reincarnated, after an uneasy stretch of purgatory, and surrounding familiar enough but amongst men unknown to me'.[81] The air war had changed greatly since 1915 and the men around him were all replacements, a result of attrition. Even with such changes, Grinnell-Milne concluded the 1933 edition of *Wind in the Wires* with a positive postscript on the fighting.[82] 'I have not forgotten the horrors,' he wrote. 'But some of our cleaner fights I can live again, those in which the enemy gave nearly as much as he took.'[83] Few infantry officers described their experiences as ones which they would repeat, however heroic they might have seemed in hindsight. As an older man, Grinnell-Milne prefaced the 1968 reprint of *Wind in the Wires* as such:

> to tell a tale of personal adventure sometimes joyful, occasionally miserable where, as in all warfare, long days of boredom are punctuated by moments of anxiety so intense that [...] I could have wished myself safe in bed and a thousand miles away [...] What I remember is uncomplicated: the haunting thrill of early flying, the skies above Artois and Picardy, the nicknames of old friends and some part of the fortunes of two valiant Squadrons of the old Royal Flying Corps – Number Sixteen and the ever-glorious Number Fifty-Six.[84]

Similar to other pilot-memoirists, Grinnell-Milne remained committed to the idea that service in the RFC was fundamentally noble and adventurous, gallant and heroic, despite its grave costs for so many of his fellow pilots. That he would write of the war's heroism in 1968 and have his book receive a new edition that year, the same year as the Tet Offensive, demonstrates that the RFC's experience of war was seen, even after World War II, romantically, their mythology the only one of the Great War's heroic archetypes to radiate across the decades, unchanged as a result of the conflicted interpretations of the war in British popular memory.

***

To remember the war heroically was to remember it, to some degree, purposefully; to see its suffering as meaningful in a way that helped justify its high costs. To remember the war heroically was also to engage with the war's public memory in a postwar period that was questioning whether Britain's sacrifice was necessary, whether there was any good to come out of such a toll in lives. For the memoirists who wrote about heroism in the 1920s, even those who had no great affinity for fighting, which was most of them, the war had an understood personal meaningfulness, a form of heroic virtue that was not easily communicated and often communicated using abstract language that to many seemed hollow. For a writer like Hemingway, who had great admiration for bravery and expressions of courage, the old heroic words used to describe battle seemed archaic on the modern battlefield. There were many in Britain who did not share his belief, who used these old words to convey feelings that they believed other soldiers would understand, words invested, through trial and comradeship, with a new meanings as a result of the hardship of modern war. If courage was redefined in the trenches, then so too was heroism, reimagined by memoirists who sought to find words for what they witnessed in battle.

World War I created a new heroism to meet a new age of warfare. For the common citizen-soldier, heroism became about endurance, duty, survival and good cheer. It was found in something as uncomplicated as carrying-on despite hardship. Expressions of spirit could be found in hundreds of jokes and bawdy songs about the *trials* of war specifically written about to show that men could *endure* warfare. Courage, thus, was redefined in war books by men like Charles Douie, R.H. Mottram and William Andrews as 'spirit', a ubiquitous trait that average men could attain. This change in the heroic archetype would undoubtedly find new meaning in the second great industrial war fought by the British Empire, when another generation of Tommies had to endure battles in the Western Desert, Burma, Italy and France.

World War I created two heroic archetypes that are well known from cinematic portrayals of courage. We know more about the escapee, perhaps, from his role not in the first war, but in the second. Films like *The Great Escape* and *The Colditz Story* have mythologised the ingenious and plucky escapee as a 'breed apart'. Before there were films depicting escapees, there were war books that mythologised these experiences. Tales of captivity and escape, told to the generation growing up and reading about the adventures of their fathers, undoubtedly had an influence on the next generation of Britons who would look back on their fathers' war and find a heroic narrative legacy that could be adopted for their own purposes.[85]

The story of flight was a romantic dream that was realised in the decade before World War I. The air war would be remembered with that same degree of romance. Beyond all other heroic archetypes, the pilot became the symbol of adventure that came out of a war of attrition. Despite the ironies involved, the men who remembered and mythologised the air war intentionally wrote of daring exploits to define a new sense of a very old form of heroism for a public that was growing tired of accounts of the war of attrition. When men like Duncan Grinnell-Milne and Cecil Lewis wrote their books, in the mid- to late 1930s, Britain was engaged in a debate over the future of war, with rearmament a word on the lips of many. For teenage boys in the 1930s, these works offered a spirit of adventure that accounts from the trenches lacked, a martial ideal that was just as appealing as that of the imperial adventurer or big game hunter was to their fathers and grandfathers. It is no surprise that the great hero to emerge from Britain's next war would be the Spitfire pilot, the new generation of heroic pilot, trained by Great War aces, men who learned their sense of duty, bravery and exceptionalism from those who created that mythology in the first place – the knights of the air.

CONCLUSION

Charles Douie began his war book, *The Weary Road*, describing his attendance at the Menin Gate dedication at Ypres in 1927. He quoted Field Marshal Herbert Plumer, the dedication speaker. 'He is not missing,' the Field Marshal said of the war dead. 'He is here.'[1] From such a poignant sentiment came the genesis of Douie's war memoir, itself an act of public memorialisation for the soldiers of his generation. 'Surely Lord Plumer meant', Douie wrote, 'that the spirit of the soldier is ever present in our midst, that his courage and devotion, his stoic creed of silence and fortitude, inspire the daily life of our generation, have become the heritage of generations yet unborn.'[2]

Courage, devotion, stoicism, fortitude and heritage – these are the words Douie used to describe the qualities of British soldiers in World War I. They are not words that many associate now with the experiences of that war or, more specifically, with the memoirs and novels written and published afterwards. Douie wrote his tribute in 1928, a year before Robert Graves and Erich Remarque published their bestselling books in Britain, and at a time when veterans were questioning the meaning of the war in light of the tenth anniversary of its conclusion. It is understandable that they did so; many could not see any virtuous outcome of the human cost of the war, which seemed by 1928 to be difficult to measure in light of the disappointments of peace. The struggle to understand the meaning of the Great War – one felt by civilians as well as veterans of military service – came with a sense of disillusionment with the idea of war itself, not so much with country or comrades, but with the struggle to see whether any war's suffering was worth it. It is a question that haunts Britons still; it is a question essential to understanding the Great War's history.

Most war writers express a degree of disillusionment in their works. It is a ubiquitous trait of the genre. Young men and women go to war at a formative time in their lives and the realities of combat are always worse than their imaginations will allow.[3] Elements of dissatisfaction and postwar questioning of a war's legacy are a fundamental part of war writing; it is the veterans' prerogative and privilege in societies where war is memorialised and sacrifice venerated that it should also be debated. As veterans write, they confront their memories and come to grips with them, trying to make sense of experiences illogical, traumatic and emotionally conflicting. Memories are often difficult to resurrect, deceptive and socially constructed; they take into account the feelings of the present in the struggle to make sense of the past.[4] For Douie and hundreds of his comrades, the printed word was a way to engage with the memory of the war. It was also a way to leave their stamp on its history.

The great paradox is that out of such an abundance of war writing has come such a limited understanding of how veterans of the Great War interpreted their experiences. Over time, voices like Douie's were gradually forgotten. The question for historians is why some myths of the Great War have held up while others have not. Alon Confino writes that 'the crucial issue in the history of memory is not how a past is represented but why it was received or rejected. For every society sets up images of the past.'[5] Samuel Hynes writes of a process of selection by the public where 'one anecdote is preserved and another is forgotten'.[6] The combined story of the war – an exercise in mythology to Hynes – comes from depictions that resonate with the public, ones that reinforce what people want to know of the war, which myths they find important to understanding the past. Those myths that don't resonate 'sit dustily on library shelves unread partly because they are ill-written and dull, no doubt, but partly because they tell the wrong story, they don't conform to the myth'.[7] Wilfred Owen's pity of war conforms to the myth of tragic innocence; of a talented young poet killed in an imperialist war. His story resonates with the trajectory of the long twentieth century and speaks to readers in the present day because it seems prophetic, prescient and reflective of Europe's own disillusionment with war. Charles Douie's account of weary men enduring and fighting a heroic war that they believed, despite its hardships, to be just has been lost because it doesn't conform to what the public wants the Great War to be. His message of noble sacrifice seems archaic, particularly since World War II, as if belonging to a pre-modern militarism that we simply cannot understand as well as Owen's tragedy. This is not because Douie lacked skill as a writer, or because his work was unpopular in its day, but it is for reasons important to understanding something of the way that war memories are digested, how voices from the past come down to us in the present day.

Literature was important to the war's mythology, ironically, becoming an essential part of its history despite the critical voices of its historians. Reflecting back on the war in 1959, Cyril Falls, who played such an important part in reviewing war books in the 1920s and 1930s, wrote about the way that literature had changed the memory of the war and the perception of its soldiers:

> The flood of anti-militarist literature, for the greater part fiction, which poured from the presses, deriding leadership from top to bottom, treating patriotism as a vice when not as a fraud, as it was bathed in blood and rolled in mud, was astonishing. It was far from being representative but it was assuredly symptomatic of widespread disillusion.[8]

This was an old complaint for Falls who had been criticising sensationalist war literature for decades. But by the 1950s he recognised that the lasting narrative, the most important one, had been born of the disillusioned literature he reviewed so derisively in the 1920s and 1930s. It was disillusionment's unpatriotic element that Falls believed was not reflective of the war generation's feelings towards their service. He felt this personally: Falls had served as a staff officer on the western front and spent the better part of his career writing the history of the Great War. As the cataloguer of the British war book, he spoke from a position of significant authority on not only the war's literature, but also its changing memory, though he would not have called it such. War literature, he believed, had created stereotypes about the men who fought – disillusioned and muddy victims – and ignored the subtleties of service and sacrifice. Literature reduced something that was extremely complex, a global war, to the personal impressions of embittered individuals who had suffered greatly in combat.

CONCLUSION 161

Falls's complaint was one that garnered sympathy from other surviving veterans of the World War I as it approached its 50th anniversary. In 1965, Charles Carrington published a second war memoir, *Soldier from the Wars Returning*. He described it as 'anterior to the pacifist reaction of the nineteen-thirties and [...] untainted by the influence of the later writers who invented the powerful image of "disenchantment" or "disillusion". I go back to an earlier history of ideas.'[9] There was nothing surprising about Carrington's or Falls's reaction to the literature of 'their' war in the 1960s; this had been their position since the 1920s. But by the 1960s their alternative generational narrative was forgotten, the complexities of the war's experiences reduced to tragedy, its memories diluted. The myth of the war poet had surpassed all others; eclipsed were men like Carrington, Falls and Douie. Lost too were the ambiguities found in the war's other experiences: the men and women who remembered the war differently: heroic pilots, POWs, and those who extolled their adventurous tales of fighting in the side shows.

Far from being a legend or something 'invented', disillusionment was a part of the literary reaction to World War I. The great postwar fallacy was not that disillusionment was a legitimate feeling for many veterans, but instead that these feelings were uniform, a generational narrative. For many veterans, there was more to their war experiences than futility, stupid senior officers and 'doomed youth' – the central tenets of the lost generation mythology identified by Robert Wohl and so maligned by historians since.[10] To some, the legend was insulting because it took what was a complex emotional reaction to the war and made it something that anyone could understand on such simple terms. After living a full life, Guy Chapman wrote in the 1970s:

> I am never grateful for comment, however sensible, on that war, from men who were not in it. For the rest I am perpetually conscious of irrecoverable loss, the lost friends I knew for so short a time, the impoverishment of life. The poetry is not the pity. To hell with your generalized pity! What the survivor remembers is not the fears he knew, the pains, but the faces and a few words of the men who were with him, *les pauvres couillons du front*.[11]

Chapman recalled the men he served with, their language and spirit, as being something rich and complex, far more than mere victimisation would allow. This sense of unit loyalty and camaraderie came with tragic undertones; Chapman was perpetually conscious of the dead for the rest of his life. To him and many of his compatriots they were not a generation that should be pitied for serving, but one that should be remembered for their sacrifice, an important distinction that hints at far more than disillusionment's reductiveness allows.

The idea of the war generation referring back on their experiences with widespread regret is one that is easily debunked by examining that generation's writings broadly and reading them carefully. In the 1920s and 1930s the war's memory was anything but uniform. Writers and publishers saw to it that the war was published in all its facets, representations from all its fronts. Each experience brought with it a different side of the war's memory. By fighter pilots, the war in the air was mythologised, not in terms of war regret or generational tragedy, but in terms of heroism, bravery and *esprit de corps*. By infantry officers in Palestine, the war was not depicted the same way as the existentialist hell of attrition, mired in mud, disease and death, of the western front, but instead remembered for its adventurous desert warfare and proud victory against the Turks. For POWs, their guilt of confinement, suffering, and adventure in escape, were opportunities for regaining agency by depicting harrowing acts of courage in the face of suffering and imprisonment. Even on the western front, the narrative space where the canonical war poets first sensed and described the war's great pity, many accounts depicted the nobility of endurance of modern war in the face of terror and death. These too were war experiences remembered and published by survivors.

The varied responses to the Great War came about because the British publishing industry released books about it. Every aspect of the conflict was represented in the many different literatures of the war. Every major publisher (and many minor) released war memoirs to the public, contributing to a literary marketplace where the war was never far from the minds of readers. Complementing this literature were hundreds of novels, collections of poetry, official and unofficial histories, and plays about the war that fictionalised the experience of war for the public in ways never imagined beforehand. This ambiguous literature brought the face of battle to the front parlours of the nation. Often grim and horrific in depictions, war books were also diverse, as individualistic as their authors, causing controversy over their interpretations. Many authors wrote to both warn of the human cost of war but also to honour the sacrifices and heroism of the war generation. Some wrote to prevent future wars. Some wrote to memorialise bravery. Yet, it was the British publishing industry that gave veterans a voice in this debate and in the process changed the British war book by introducing a new author demographic – the mobilised citizen-soldier. The war's story has come down to us because dedicated editors and publishers encouraged and helped war witnesses to write and publish their stories.

The war books catalogue demonstrates an overlooked interpretive breadth on what the war meant in public memory in the period when that memory was most acute: the 1920s and 1930s. Though some bitter war memories were expressed – all war books have tragic undertones – the vast majority of non-fiction that was published came down on the side of meaning over meaninglessness, personal transcendence instead of futility. 'I had seen the travail which God had given the sons of men to be exercised therewith, and at the beginning of life it was proved to me that calamity is man's true touchstone.'[12] Such was how John Lucy concluded his memoir *There's a Devil in the Drum,* 20 years after he was wounded on the western front, reflecting the sentiments of many middle-aged former soldiers who looked at the war as a formative experience. War could make men and women disillusioned – it could certainly make them hate war – but service in the Great War did not destroy the notion of martial virtue, however muddied it became by industrialised warfare.

Most of the authors profiled in this book found the war abhorrent. But they also had a high degree of pride in their military service. Veterans viewed their war experiences with what often appear to be contradictory sentiments, but ones at the heart of military service. Duty, loyalty, courage and pride are all present in Great War memoirs, sentiments often contrasted with hardship, loss and suffering. Interestingly, many authors would volunteer at the beginning of World War II out of duty or patriotism, or because they just thought it was the right thing for an old soldier to do. At the start of World War II, Robert Graves volunteered for service in his old regiment, the Royal Welch Fusiliers, but was turned down. For a man who found war as unpleasant as he described in his memoir, this was a telling statement of loyalty to his former regiment. Edmund Blunden, who deeply hated war, spent part of World War II teaching young officer candidates at Oxford the rudimentary aspects of junior officer command. Similarly, Guy Chapman left a good job as a reader for the publisher Jonathan Cape to take a commission as an officer/lecturer on an army educational training course. Cecil Lewis became a flight instructor for young RAF pilots. Charles Carrington worked as a staff officer at Bomber Command. These are just some of the prominent war writers who volunteered again for military service even though they had witnessed first-hand the sacrifices that came with it. The war might have destroyed some of their idealism, but it certainly didn't destroy their sense of duty to their nation.

It is perhaps the history of sacrifice and commemoration that this book hopes to remember. Writing a war memoir was a commemorative act, a way that an individual could memorialise those whom they served with at the front. With remembrance came an acknowledgement of the sacrifices of the war generation, tributes to bravery and descriptions of suffering. In our contemporary society it seems unthinkable that such a bloody war could be interpreted as meaningful and that there was any great moral to the slaughter of 1914–18. Many of the war generation's memoirists, though, did not see the war this way. They were a haunted generation, but one that continued to write of the war's impact, speculating about what future generations would think of them, and whether we too would remember their sacrifice. Ralph Mottram wrote of gazing upon the Menin Gate and thinking:

> But we must remember that we are a dwindling number. Who will march through that gate in ten and twenty years hence, and with what knowledge? No, the names are well graven up there, on so solid a structure. For the day will come when they will be but names and the arch will be their only memorial.[13]

As long as there are readers interested in the Great War, then Mottram's fear of the dead being forgotten is unwarranted. The Great War generation left behind hundreds of ways to remember the war's experiences through the eyes of those who survived their touchstone and lived to write their stories.

NOTES

Introduction

1. C.S. Lewis, *Surprised by Joy* (London: Geoffrey Bles, 1955), p. 178.
2. Ibid.
3. Ibid., p. 185.
4. For more on Lewis's war experience, see K.J. Gilchrist, *A Morning After War* (New York: Peter Lang, 2005). For an alternative interpretation of Lewis's war service, see Colin Duriez, *Bedeviled: Lewis, Tolkien and the Shadow of Evil* (New York: InterVarsity Press, 2015), pp. 38–40.
5. On changes in World War I historiography, see Jay Winter and Antoine Prost, *The Great War in History* (Cambridge: Cambridge University Press, 2005); Stephen Heathorn, 'The Mnemonic Turn in the Cultural Historiography of Britain's Great War', *The Historical Journal* 48: 4 (2005), pp. 1103–24; and Heather Jones, 'As the Centenary Approaches: The Regeneration of First World War Historiography', *Historical Journal* 56: 3 (2013), pp. 857–78.
6. See Robert Wohl, *The Generation of 1914* (Cambridge, MA: Harvard University Press, 1979), pp. 85–6.
7. Ernest Hemingway, *A Moveable Feast* (New York: Scribner, 2009), p. 61.
8. Rudyard Kipling, *The Irish Guards in the Great War, Volume I* (New York: Doubleday, 1923), p. ix.
9. Charles Douie, *The Weary Road* (London: John Murray, 1929), p. 3.
10. R.H. Mottram, John Easton, and Eric Partridge, *Three Men's War* (New York: Harper Brothers, 1930), p. 5.
11. Jessica Meyer, *Men of War* (New York: Palgrave Macmillan, 2009), pp. 129–30.
12. Studies directly related to the history of the book in this period include Jane Potter, *Boys in Khaki, Girls in Print: Women's Literary Responses to the Great War 1914–1918* (Oxford: Clarendon Press, 2005); Mary Hammond and Shafquat Towheed, eds, *Publishing in the First World War* (London: Palgrave, 2007); Rosa

Maria Bracco, *Merchants of Hope, British Middlebrow Writers and the First World War, 1919–1939* (Oxford: Berg, 1993).
13. For a summary of these interpretations, see Adrian Gregory, *The Last Great War: British Society and the First World War* (Oxford: Oxford University Press, 2008), pp. 271–2.
14. Dan Todman, *The Great War: Myth and Memory* (London: Hambledon, 2005), pp. 153–8.
15. John Keegan, *The Face of Battle* (London: Jonathan Cape, 1976), p. 34.
16. His approach was in line with that of new social historians of his era.
17. John Keegan, *The Face of Battle* (New York: Penguin Books, 1978), p. 34.
18. See Stéphane Audoin-Rouzeau and Annette Becker, *14–18: Understanding the Great War* (New York: Hill and Wang, 2000); Gary Sheffield, *Forgotten Victory* (London: Headline, 2001).
19. See Jay Winter, *Sites of Memory, Sites of Mourning* (Cambridge: Cambridge University Press, 1995) and *Remembering War* (New Haven: Yale University Press, 2006).
20. Winter, *Remembering War*, pp. 3–6.
21. See Robin Prior and Trevor Wilson, 'Paul Fussell at War', *War in History* I (1994), pp. 63–80; Todman, *The Great War*, pp. 158–60; Leonard Smith, 'Paul Fussell's *The Great War and Modern Memory*: Twenty-Five Years Later', *History and Theory* XL (2001), pp. 241–60.
22. Samuel Hynes, *A War Imagined* (London: Pimlico, 1990), pp. 8–9.
23. See Alexander Watson, *Enduring the Great War* (Cambridge: Cambridge University Press, 2008), pp. 72–84. Watson dissects the notion of disillusionment from other, often contributing feelings, such as war-weariness and alienation.
24. For more on the wide social and cultural expanse of the idea of disenchantment – before, during and after the war – see Andrew Frayn, *Writing Disenchantment* (Manchester: Manchester University Press, 2014).
25. Brian Bond, *Survivors of a Kind: Memoirs of the Western Front* (London: Continuum, 2008).
26. Hugh Cecil, *The Flower of Battle: How Britain Wrote the Great War* (South Royalton, VT: Steerforth Press, 1996).
27. Rosa Maria Bracco, *Merchants of Hope* (London: Berg, 1993).
28. Michael Roper, 'Re-remembering the Soldier Hero: The Psychic and Social Construction of Memory in Personal Narratives of the Great War', *History Workshop Journal* 50 (Autumn 2000), p. 183.
29. In addition to the works by Winter, see Adrian Gregory's *The Silence of Memory* (London: Berg, 1994) and Alex King's *Memorials of the Great War in Britain* (London: Berg, 1998) which are invaluable for understanding the culture of mourning and memorialisation in Britain after the war.
30. Joanna Bourke, *Dismembering the Male* (London: Reaktion Books, 1996); Jessica Meyer, *Men of War: Masculinity and the First World War in Britain* (London: Palgrave Macmillan, 2009); Michael Roper, *The Secret Battle* (Manchester: Manchester University Press, 2010).

31. Alexander Watson, *Enduring the Great War* (Cambridge: Cambridge University Press, 2008); Edward Madigan, '"Sticking to a Hateful Task": Resilience, Humour, and British Understandings of Combatant Courage, 1914–1918', *War in History* 20: 1 (2013), pp. 76–98.
32. Todman, *The Great War*, pp. 224–6.
33. See David Reynolds, *The Long Shadow* (London: Simon and Schuster, 2013).
34. Ralph Hale Mottram, *Through the Menin Gate* (London: Chatto & Windus, 1932), p. 233.

Chapter 1   Writing the War

1. NLS, JMA, Acc. 12927/184 Folder B.Q.2, Murray to Buchanan, 5 November 1918.
2. Charles Edmunds, *A Subaltern's War* (London: Peter Davies, 1929), p. 189. Carrington used the pseudonym Charles Edmunds.
3. Ibid.
4. Charles Douie, *The Weary Road*, pp. 203–204.
5. John Keegan, *A History of Warfare* (London: Pimlico, 1993), p. 21.
6. Modris Eksteins, *Rites of Spring* (New York: First Mariner, 2000), p. 253.
7. Yuval Noah Harari, 'Military Memoirs: A Historical Overview of the Genre from the Middle Ages to the Late Modern Era', *War in History* 14:3 (2007), p. 290.
8. Authors like Buchanan had little to say on the war's legacy because the war was still ongoing when they wrote their books, whereas Carrington and Douie had to grapple with the war's legacy in their books to understand its significance.
9. Jay Winter and Emmanuel Sivan, 'Setting the Framework', in Jay Winter and Emmanuel Sivan, eds, *War and Remembrance in the Twentieth Century* (Cambridge: Cambridge University Press, 1999), p. 10.
10. Samuel Hynes makes a distinction between the impulse to report and remember by war writers. He attributes letter collections and diaries to the former category, where in memoirs the emphasis is on remembering. See Hynes, *The Soldiers' Tale: Bearing Witness to Modern War* (New York: Penguin, 1998), p. xiv.
11. Ibid., p. 2.
12. See Yuval Harari's survey of military memoirs, 'Military Memoirs: A Historical Overview of the Genre from the Middle Ages to the Late Modern Era', *War in History* 14: 3 (2007), pp. 289–309.
13. Discussed in greater detail in Chapter 2.
14. Andrew Green, *Writing the Great War: Sir James Edmunds and the Official Histories* (London: Frank Cass, 2003), pp. 1–3.
15. Ibid., p. 44.
16. Ibid., p. 56.

17. Buchan's wartime histories were collected into *Nelson's History of the War*; Arthur Conan Doyle's histories were published as *The British Campaigns in France and Flanders*. For a scholarly survey of the war's early histories, see Keith Grieves, 'Early Historical Responses to the Great War: Fortescue, Conan Doyle, and Buchan', in Brian Bond, ed., *The First World War and British Military History* (Oxford: Clarendon Press, 1991).
18. Yuval Harari has written extensively on this topic. See Yuval Noah Harari, 'Armchairs, Coffee, and Authority: Eye-witnesses and Flesh-witnesses Speak about War, 1100–2000', *The Journal of Military History* 74 (January 2010), pp. 53–78; Yuval Noah Harari, 'Scholars, Eyewitnesses, and Flesh-witnesses of War: A Tense Relationship', *Partial Answers* 7:2 (2009), pp. 213–28.
19. R.H. Mottram's essay 'A Personal Record' offers some explanation as to how many felt about their war memoirs and history. See R.H. Mottram, John Easton and Eric Partridge, *Three Men's War* (London: Harper, 1930), p. 4.
20. Edmunds, *A Subaltern's War*, p. 7.
21. His compositional files are found in his papers: IWM, Papers of C.E. Carrington, M.C., Box 81/11/2.
22. E.J. Thompson, M.C., *The Leicestershires Beyond Baghdad* (London: The Epworth Press, J. Alfred Sharp, 1919), pp. 9–10.
23. Ibid.
24. Ibid., pp. 8–9.
25. E.C. Matthews, *A Subaltern in the Field* (London: Heath Cranton, 1920), p. 10.
26. Ibid.
27. Arthur Osburn, *Unwilling Passenger* (London: Faber & Faber, 1932), p. 13.
28. Ibid.
29. Harari, 'Scholars, Eyewitnesses, and Flesh-witnesses of War: A Tense Relationship', p. 222.
30. Osburn, *Unwilling Passenger*, p. 13.
31. Stephen Graham, *A Private in the Guards* (New York: Macmillan, 1919), p. v.
32. Jay Winter, *The Great War and the British People* (New York: Palgrave Macmillan, 2003), p. 284.
33. Llewelyn Wyn Griffith, *Up to Mametz and Beyond* (Barnsley: Pen and Sword, 2010), p. 108.
34. Graham, *A Private in the Guards*, p. 331.
35. Harari, 'Military Memoirs', p. 290.
36. Hynes, *Soldiers' Tale*, p. 9.
37. John More, *With Allenby's Crusaders* (London: Heath Cranton, 1923), p. 9.
38. Eksteins indicates a type of mass cultural repression after the war. In published memoirs, there seems just as much remembrance as repression by veterans interested in telling their stories. See Eksteins, *Rites of Spring*, pp. 252–8.
39. Major R.T. Rees, *A Schoolmaster at War* (London: Haycock Press, 1935), Preface.
40. Ibid.
41. See Robert Graves, *Good-bye to All That* (London: Jonathan Cape, 1929), chapter XI.

42. Robert Graves, *Good-bye to All That* (New York: Viking, 1998), p. 89.
43. Lieut. Col. Neil Fraser-Tytler, DSO, TD, RA (TA), *Field Guns in France* (London: Hutchinson, 1922), p. 15.
44. Ardern Beaman, *The Squadroon* (London: John Lane, 1920), pp. vii–viii.
45. Ibid.
46. William Linton Andrews, *Haunting Years: The Commentaries of a War Territorial* (London: Hutchinson, 1930), p. 6.
47. Ibid., pp. 6–7.
48. H.C.W. Bishop, *A Kut Prisoner* (London: John Lane, 1920), p. ix.
49. Ibid.
50. Graves, *But It Still Goes On* (London: Jonathan Cape, 1930), p. 42.
51. Ibid.
52. David Rorie, *A Medico's Luck in the War* (Aberdeen: Milne and Hutchinson, 1929), p. 4.
53. M.C.C. Harrison and H.A. Cartwright, *Within Four Walls* (London: Edward Arnold, 1930), pp. vii–viii.
54. Mark VII (Max Plowman), *A Subaltern on the Somme* (New York: E.P. Dutton, 1928), p. vii.
55. A.L. Pollard, *Fire-Eater: Memoirs of a V.C.* (London: Hutchinson, 1932), p. 13.
56. Guy Chapman, *Vain Glory: A Miscellany of the Great War 1914–1918 written by those who fought in it on each side and on all fronts* (London: Cassell, 1937), p. x.
57. Philip Gosse, *Memoirs of a Camp Follower: A Naturalist Goes to War* (London: Longmans, Green and Co., 1934), p. xii.
58. John Still, *A Prisoner in Turkey* (London: John Lane, 1920), p. vii.
59. H.G. Durnford, *The Tunnellers of Holzminden* (Cambridge: Cambridge University Press, 1930), p. viii. Plainness is also noted by Ardern Beaman who described his work as being 'to paint in plain and faithful colours the life and sentiment' of the men in which he served. Ardern Beaman, *The Squadroon* (London: John Lane, 1920), p. xiii.
60. David Rorie, *A Medico's Luck in the War: Being the reminiscences of R.A.M.C. work with the 51st (Highland) Division* (Aberdeen: Milne and Hutchinson, 1929), p. 264.
61. Kate McLoughlin defines this as 'autopsy' in her *Authoring War* (Cambridge: Cambridge University Press, 2011), pp. 42–3. See also Yuval Noah Harari's two essays on the idea of the 'flesh-witness': 'Armchairs, Coffee, and Authority: Eye-witnesses and Flesh-witnesses Speak about War, 1100–2000', pp. 53–78 and 'Scholars, Eyewitnesses, and Flesh-witnesses of War: A Tense Relationship', pp. 213–28.
62. Chapman, *Vain Glory*, p. vii.
63. Harari, 'Military Memoirs', pp. 306–308. Harari problematises the 'cultural approach' to military writings and their interpretative value.
64. Rowlands Coldicott, *London Men in Palestine* (New York: Longmans, Green & Co., 1919), p. viii.

65. Thomas Hope Floyd, *At Ypres with Best-Dunkley* (London: John Lane, 1920), p. vii.
66. Ibid.
67. Hynes, *The Soldiers' Tale*, p. 25.
68. Kalí Tal, *Worlds of Hurt* (Cambridge: Cambridge University Press, 1996), p. 7.
69. Ibid.
70. Gregory, *The Last Great War*, pp. 272–3.
71. Vera Brittain, *Testament of Youth* (London: Gollancz, 1933), p. 11.
72. Ibid., p. 12.
73. Mottram, Easton and Partridge, *Three Men's War*, p. 3.
74. Captain Geoffrey Dugdale, MC, *Langemarck and Cambrai* (Uckfield, East Sussex: The Naval and Military Press, Ltd, 2009), Introduction. Reprint.
75. Pollard, *Fire-Eater*, p. 10.
76. Bernard Blaser, *Kilts Across the Jordan: Being the Experiences and Impressions with the Second Battalion "London Scottish" in Palestine* (London: H.F. & G. Witherby, 1926), Preface.
77. Douie, *The Weary Road*, p. xiii.
78. Captain J.L. Hardy, *I Escape!* (London: John Lane, 1927), Preface.
79. Major Vivian Gilbert, *The Romance of the Last Crusade: With Allenby in Jerusalem* (New York/London: D. Appleton and Company, 1923), Preface.
80. Major Hamilton Gibbs, *The Grey Wave* (London: Hutchinson, 1920), p. x.
81. Carrol Carstairs, *A Generation Missing* (London: Heinemann, 1930), pp. ix–xi.
82. Rees, *A Schoolmaster at War*, Foreword. Hay did not actually read the book before writing the foreword, claiming that he wished to show 'detachment' of mind towards the book.
83. Ibid.
84. Edmunds, *A Subaltern's War*, pp. 192–3.
85. It should be noted that Carrington had great admiration for many war writers of his generation including Edmund Blunden, but disliked sensationalism.
86. Hynes, *The Soldiers' Tale*, p. 26. The term 'battlefield gothic' is his.
87. Dugdale, *Langemarck and Cambrai*, Author's Preface.
88. Ibid.
89. Thomas Hope Floyd, *At Ypres with Best-Dunkley* (London: John Lane, 1920), p. 146.
90. H.G. Durnford, MC, MA, *The Tunnellers*, p. viii. He was persuaded to re-issue the book by his publishers.
91. Pollard, *Fire-Eater*, pp. 11–12.
92. Ibid.
93. Ibid., p. 12.
94. Todman, *Great War*, chapter 4.
95. Winter and Sivan, 'Setting the Framework', p. 18.
96. John Gibbons, *Roll On, Next War! The Common Man's Guide to Army Life* (London: Muller, Ltd. 1935), p. 6.

97. Hugh Bayly, *Triple Challenge or War, Whirligigs and Windmills: A Doctor's Memoirs of the Years 1914–1929* (London: Hutchinson, 1935), Dedication.
98. "Arnewood", *With the Guns West and East* (Plymouth: Mayflower Press, 1923), p. 96.
99. Douie, *The Weary Road*, p. 23.
100. Paul Edwards, 'British War Memoirs', in Vincent Sherry, ed., *The Cambridge Companion to the Literature of the First World War* (Cambridge: Cambridge University Press, 2005), p. 31.

Chapter 2 Publishing the War

1. A.G. MacDonnell, *England, their England* (London: Picador, 1983), p. 7
2. Rees, *A Schoolmaster at War*, Foreword.
3. Cecil, *Flower of Battle*, p. 10; and Bracco, *Merchants of Hope*, pp. 12–13.
4. The website *www.greatwardustjackets.co.uk* is a magnificent resource for understanding the types of cover art from the period.
5. See Harari, 'Military Memoirs', pp. 289–309.
6. Harari, 'Scholars, Eyewitnesses, and Flesh-witnesses of War: A Tense Relationship', pp. 213–28. See also Hynes, *The Soldiers' Tale*, chapter 1.
7. John Feather, *A History of British Publishing* (London: Croom Helm, 1988), pp. 183–94.
8. Ibid., pp. 195–7. Both material and manpower shortages were significant problems during the war.
9. Arthur Waugh, 'Literature and the War', *Fortnightly Review* 96: 575 (November 1914). See also Jane Potter, 'For Country, Conscience and Commerce: Publishers and Publishing, 1914–1918', in Mary Hammond and Shafquat Towheed, eds, *Publishing in the First World War: Essays in Book History* (London: Palgrave Macmillan, 2007), p. 11.
10. See Jane Potter, *Boys in Khaki, Girls in Print: Women's Literary Responses to the Great War 1914–1918* (Oxford: Clarendon Press, 2005); Angela Smith, *Women's Writing of the First World War: An Anthology* (Manchester: Manchester University Press, 2000); Margaret Higonnet, *Lines of Fire: Women Writers of WWI* (New York: Plume, 1999).
11. See Michael Paris, *Over the Top: The Great War and Juvenile Literature in Britain* (Westport, CT: Praeger, 2004).
12. See Jane Potter's excellent essay, 'For Country, Conscience and Commerce: Publishers and Publishing, 1914–1918', in Hammond and Towheed, eds, *Publishing in the First World War*.
13. NLS, JMA, Acc: 12927/187, folder: 'The Secret of the Navy', letter from John Murray to F. Harcourt Kitchin (Bennett Copplestone), 1 February 1918.
14. Feather, *A History of British Publishing*, p. 196.

15. Ian Norrie, *Mumby's Publishing and Bookselling in the Twentieth Century* (London: Bell & Hyman, 1982), p. 20. Norrie provides the following figures for titles released by year: 1913 – 12,379; 1918 – 7,716.
16. Potter, 'For Country', p. 13.
17. Arthur Waugh, *A Hundred Years of Publishing: Being the Story of Chapman & Hall, Ltd.* (London: Chapman & Hall, 1930), p. 286.
18. There were 57 non-fiction war books released in 1919 by 32 different publishers. In 1920, another 57 non-fiction war books were released. Publishers like John Lane, Edward Arnold, John Murray and Chatto & Windus released multiple titles.
19. NLS, WBC, MS 30591, letter from George Blackwood to Alan Bott, 12 October 1920.
20. 'Prospects of the Season', *The Bookseller* (October 1920).
21. Twenty-one new non-fiction war book titles were released in 1921.
22. NLS, WBC, MS 30591, letter from George Blackwood to Captain Douglas Browne, 23 September 1920.
23. Hugh Walpole, 'The Best Books of 1929', *Saturday Review of Politics, Literature, Science and Art* (December 1929), p. 747.
24. Ibid. On this point Walpole wrote, 'I suppose, the distance is just sufficient for the war to be bearable for those who shared in it and exciting for those who did not.'
25. Feather, *A History of British Publishing*, p. 197.
26. NLS, WBC, MS 30591, Correspondence between George Blackwood and Douglas Brown, letter from Blackwood to Brown, 25 July 1919.
27. John Murray interview, *The Bookseller* (May 1920), p. 316.
28. Jacob Omnium, 'Under Cover', *The Bookseller* (February 1920).
29. Henrietta Tayler, *A Scottish Nurse at Work* (London: John Lane, 1920), p. 15.
30. NLS, WBC, MS 30591. Correspondence between Blackwood and Alan Bott, Blackwood to Bott, 1 July 1920, 12 October 1920 and Bott to Blackwood, 28 July 1920; NLS, JMA, Acc: 12927/184, folder BR 18, letter from John Murray to Commander Bingham, 27 February 1919.
31. 'Best-Sellers of January', *The Bookseller and Stationery Trades' Journal* (February 1922), p. 85.
32. 'Best-Sellers of March', *The Bookseller and Stationery Trades' Journal* (April 1922), p. 93. Included in the list were *The Road to En-Dor*, *Way of Revelation*, *Disenchantment* and *Tell England* – two memoirs and two novels.
33. Cecil, *The Flower of Battle*, p. 177. Hugh Cecil indicates that Raymond's popularity lasted well into the 1950s.
34. URSC, RHA, John Lane Collection, J.L 9/29 File E.H. Jones, correspondence between E.H. Jones and John Lane (publisher) regarding contract and editions, 27 June 1919 to 27 May 1930.
35. For a succinct summary of *Disenchantment*'s writing and publication history, see Keith Grieves, 'C.E. Montagu and the Making of *Disenchantment*, 1914–1921', *War in History* 4:35 (1997), pp. 35–59.

36. Anonymous, 'Review of Waiting for Daylight', *Saturday Review of Politics, Literature, Science and Art*, 133:3471 (May 1922), p. 470.
37. Ibid.
38. 'Notices of Books: The Romance of the Last Crusade by Vivian Gilbert', *The Bookseller and Stationery Trades' Journal* (June 1924), p. 79.
39. Gerald Gould, 'The Natural Man', *Saturday Review of Politics, Literature, Science and Art*, 133:3591 (August 1924), p. 195.
40. 'Trade and Literary Gossip', *The Bookseller and Stationery Trades' Journal* (January 1921), p. 6; and 'Best Selling Books in March', *The Bookseller and Stationery Trades' Journal* (April 1924), p. 68.
41. Mottram, *The Spanish Farm Trilogy* (1924–6); F.M. Ford, *Parade's End* Tetralogy (1924–8); Montague, *Disenchantment* (1922), *Fiery Particles* (1923), *Rough Justice* (1926), *Action* (1928).
42. Stephen Trout, 'R.H. Mottram: The Great War, and Europa's Beast', in Patrick Quinn, ed., *Recharting the Thirties* (Cranbury, NJ: Associated University Presses, 1996), pp. 51–2.
43. Anonymous, 'Tales of Three Campaigns', *Saturday Review of Politics, Literature, Science and Art*, 142:3708 (November 1926), p. 620.
44. 'Industry Statistics', *The Publisher and Bookseller* (3 January 1930), p. 11. Of overall titles printed in 1929, there was an increase in novels and a decrease in non-fiction generally.
45. Richard Overy, *The Morbid Age*, p. 175.
46. Ibid., p. 177.
47. Robert Graves and Alan Hodge, *The Long Week End* (New York: Norton, 1994), p. 205.
48. Reynolds, *The Long Shadow*, p. 201.
49. Jacob Omnium, 'Under Cover', *The Publisher and Bookseller* (20 September 1929), pp. 520–1.
50. Advertisement 'A War Book that Does Not Repel', *The Publisher and Bookseller* (11 October 1929), p. 728.
51. Though advertisements for the book are present in *The Bookseller*, the book's success appears to have evaded the editors until May, two months after its release.
52. 'Notes and News', *The Publisher and Bookseller* (10 May 1929), p. 905.
53. Advertisement for *All Quiet on the Western Front*, *The Publisher and Bookseller* (2 August 1929), p. 211.
54. Many of these books were contracted in 1929.
55. Eksteins, *Rites of Spring*, p. 282.
56. Ibid., p. 277. Eksteins believes that Remarque spawned the revival of war books in Britain. It should be noted that the revival was already underway when he was published in March. Additionally, Janet Watson has covered much of the war books debate in this period in her *Fighting Different Wars: Experience, Memory, and the First World War in Britain* (Cambridge: Cambridge University Press, 2004), pp. 185–218.

57. Cecil, *The Flower of Battle*, pp. 8–9.
58. Douglas Jerrold, 'Current Comments', *The English Review* (January 1930), p. 14.
59. Ibid., 15.
60. Ibid.
61. Watson, *Fighting Different Wars*, pp. 219–39.
62. R.V. Dawson, 'Journey's End: A Supplementary Estimate', *The English Review* (November 1929), p. 620.
63. A.C. Ward, *The Nineteen-Twenties: Literature and Ideas in the Post-War Decade* (London: Methuen 1930), p. 12.
64. Frank Richards, *Old Soldiers Never Die* (London: Faber, 1933).
65. 'Best Selling Books During July', *The Bookseller* (2 August 1929), p. 241.
66. Eksteins, *Rites of Spring*, pp. 253–4.
67. Hynes, *A War Imagined*, p. 425.
68. 'The Garlands Wither', *The Times Literary Supplement* (12 June 1930).
69. F.E. Whitton, 'Durat in Extemum', *The Bookman*, 77:461 (February 1930), p. 306.
70. Review of 'Generals Die in Bed', *Saturday Review of Politics, Literature, Science and Art* (August 1930), p. 150.
71. John Brown, 'This War Book Slump', *The Publisher and Bookseller* (1 August 1930), p. 299.
72. Chapman was in infantry officer, Richards an enlisted man, Brittain a VAD, Lewis an RFC pilot and Lucy a working-class Irish 'Old Contemptible' who earned a commission in 1918.
73. F.J. Harvey Darton, 'Books Bought, 1930: A Nine Months' Survey', *The Publisher and Bookseller* (7 November 1930), p. 1071.
74. 'Why a Best Seller?', *The Bookseller and Stationery Trades' Journal* (July 1924), p. 83.
75. 'Notes and News', *The Publisher and Bookseller* (10 May 1929), p. 905.
76. F.J. Harvey Darton, 'Books Bought, 1930: A Nine Months' Survey', *The Publisher and Bookseller* (7 November 1930), p. 1071.
77. Ibid.
78. Ibid., p. 1075.
79. Clive Bloom, *Bestsellers: Popular Fiction Since 1900* (New York: Palgrave, 2002), p. 3.
80. GL, LMA, Edward Arnold and Hodder and Stoughton Collection, Hodder and Stoughton Author's Ledgers, MS 16312. For Buchan, see Vol. 7; for Hay, see Vol. 20; for Sapper, see Vol. 39.
81. NLS, WBC, MS 30588, letter from George Blackwood to Beith, 15 May 1936.
82. Cecil, *The Flower of Battle*; Bracco, *Merchants of Hope*.
83. The price of memoirs was often higher due to illustrations or photographs.
84. GL, LMA, Edward Arnold and Hodder and Stoughton Collection, Trade Catalogues for Edward Arnold, pp. 25, 27, 32, 33, 52. Folder 1920–1, MS

36527/2. See also, Stock Books for Edward Arnold, Ltd. Entry 607. Volume 9049491. Closed Access MS 29076: Item Vol. 5 General, 1903–30. It was not uncommon for non-fiction to be over 10*s.* a title. Novels, in general, were priced either under 6*s.* or at 7*s.* 6*d.*

85. 'Best Selling Books During September', *The Publisher and Bookseller* (3 October 1930), p. 792.
86. Max Egremont, *Siegfried Sassoon: A Life* (New York: Farrar, Straus and Giroux, 2005), p. 361.
87. Advertisement for *Memoirs of an Infantry Officer, The Publisher and Bookseller* (26 September 1930), p. 623.
88. Jean Moorcroft Wilson, *Siegfried Sassoon: The Journey from the Trenches, A Biography* (New York: Routledge, 2003), p. 462, chapter 16, fn. 2.
89. Egremont, *Siegfried Sassoon*, p. 436.
90. URSC, RHA, Jonathan Cape MS 2446, Production Ledger B-H.
91. Ibid.
92. Paul Berry and Mark Bostridge, *Vera Brittain: A Life* (Boston: Northeastern University Press, 2002), p. 264.
93. URSC, RHA, JL 9/29 E.H. Jones, letters from E.H. Jones to John Lane/Bodley Head, 2 May 1930 and 27 May 1930.
94. Ibid.
95. NLS, WBC, MS 30591, letter from Alan Bott to Blackwood, 28 June 1920.
96. NLS, WBC, MS 30591, letter from Alan Bott to Blackwood, 16 October 1926.
97. NLS, WBC, MS 30866, entry for Alan Bott *Eastern Nights – and Flights*, p. 61; entry for Alan Bott *An Airman's Outings*, p. 56.
98. NLS, WBC, MS 30866, entry for Johnston *450 Miles to Freedom*, p. 182.
99. Ibid.
100. GL, LMA, Edward Arnold and Hodder and Stoughton Collection, Hodder and Stoughton Publication Books, Edward Arnold Ltd. v 9049019. MS 29072. Vol. 3 'General' 1923–43, entry for Cartwright/Harrison Within Four Walls, pp. 243–4, p. 270.
101. Ibid.
102. 'Current Topics', *The Bookseller and Stationery Trades' Journal* (March 1924), p. 75.
103. Ibid.
104. 'Summary of Year in Books', *The Publisher and Bookseller* (3 January 1930), p. 11.
105. T.H. Thomas, 'Some War Memoirs', *Journal of Modern History*, 2:4 (1930), p. 629.
106. 'Under Cover', *The Publisher and Bookseller* (28 March 1930), p. 697.
107. Watson, *Fighting Different Wars*, p. 217.
108. Douglas Jerrold, 'Current Comments', *English Review* (January 1930), pp. 13–14.
109. A.R. 'War and Peace: All Our Yesterdays', *The Bookman*, 77:461 (February 1930), p. 299.

110. 'The Patriot's Progress', *Saturday Review of Politics, Literature, Science and Art* (July 1930), p. 92.
111. F.E. Whitton, 'Still They Come', *The Bookman*, 78:463 (April 1930), p. 59; Also, F.E. Whitton, 'Durat in Extremum', *The Bookman* (February 1930), p. 306.
112. Hugh Walpole, 'The Best Books of 1929', *Saturday Review of Politics, Literature, Science and Art* (December 1929), p. 747.
113. Osbert Burdett, 'Flying Corps Headquarters: 1914–1918', *Saturday Review of Politics, Literature, Science and Art* (26 July 1930), p. 117.
114. Falls made this claim in his *War Books*. See Cyril Falls, *War Books: A Critical Guide* (London: Peter Davies, 1929), p. ix.
115. The unfortunate thing was that both were compiled early in 1930 and many excellent war books would be released later in the decade.
116. Edmund Blunden, Cyril Falls, H.M. Tomlinson and R. Wright, *The War: 1914–1918* (London: The Reader, 1930), p. 1.
117. Ibid.
118. Ibid.
119. Ibid., p. 2.
120. Ibid.
121. Ibid.
122. Ibid., p. 4.
123. It should be noted that *War Books: A Critical Guide* was published by Peter Davies who was a veteran of the western front. Davies published two iconic war books, *A Subaltern's War* and *Her Private's We* in 1929–30.
124. Hew Strachan, '"The Real War": Liddell Hart, Cruttwell, and Falls', in Brian Bond, ed., *The First World War and British Military History* (Oxford: Oxford University Press, 1991), pp. 61–4.
125. Ibid.
126. The Blunden list included these genres.
127. Falls, *War Books*, p. xii.
128. Ibid.
129. Ibid., p. xiv.
130. Ibid., p. 180.
131. Ibid., pp. 182–3.
132. Ibid.
133. Ibid., p. 292.
134. Ibid., p. 202.
135. Ibid., p. 292.
136. Hew Strachan 'The Real War', p. 63.

Chapter 3 War Memories: The West

1. Andrew Rutherford, *The Literature of War* (London: Macmillan, 1978), p. 67.
2. Hynes, *A War Imagined*, p. ix.
3. Hynes, *The Soldiers' Tale*, p. 53.

4. Ibid., p. viii. Hynes defines myths as 'the simplified narrative'.
5. Todman, *The Great War*, p. xiii.
6. E.C. Matthews, *A Subaltern in the Field* (London: Heath Cranton, 1920), p. 13.
7. Ibid., p. 15.
8. Ibid., p. 17.
9. Hew Strachan, *The First World War* (New York: Viking, 2003), pp. 163–4.
10. Eric Leed, *No Man's Land: Combat and Identity in World War* (Cambridge: Cambridge University Press, 1979), pp. 74–5.
11. Wyn Griffith, *Up to Mametz* (London: Severn House Ltd, 1981. Reprint), p. 21.
12. Griffith, *Up to Mametz*, p. 21. Edmunds, *A Subaltern's War*, p. 192.
13. Edmund Blunden, *Undertones of War* (Garden City, NY: Doubleday, 1929), p. 14.
14. Edmunds, *A Subaltern's War*, p. 199.
15. Mark VII, *A Subaltern at the Somme*, p. 40.
16. Ibid., p. 41.
17. Ibid., pp. 42–3.
18. Joseph Allen Frank and George Reeves, *"Seeing the Elephant": Raw Recruits at the Battle of Shiloh* (Urbana: University of Illinois Press, 2003), p. 6 fn 2.
19. Paddy Griffith, *Battle Tactics of the Civil War* (New Haven: Yale University Press, 1989), pp. 145–50.
20. Robert Graves, *Good-bye to All That* (Jonathan Cape, 1929), p. 124.
21. Frank Crozier, *A Brass Hat in No Man's Land* (London: Jonathan Cape, 1930), p. 59.
22. Blunden, *Undertones*, p. 13.
23. Ibid., p. 18.
24. Ibid., p. 19.
25. Rees, *A Schoolmaster at War*, p. 27.
26. Griffith, *Up To Mametz and Beyond*, p. 57.
27. Rees, *A Schoolmaster at War*, p. 29. See Gosse's *Memoirs of a Camp Follower* which details his attempts at rat control for the British Second Army on the western front.
28. For an excellent summary of the discomforts of trench life gleaned from memoirs see Denis Winter's *Death's Men* (New York: Penguin, 1979), chapter 6.
29. A.A. Hanbury-Sparrow, *The Land-Locked Lake* (London: A. Barker, 1932), p. 18.
30. Some of the best-known works of fiction include Manning's *Middle Part of Fortune*, Mottram's *Spanish Farm Trilogy*, Aldington's *Death of a Hero*, Wilfred Ewart's *Way of Revelation* and A.P. Herbert's *The Secret Battle*.
31. Robert Wohl, *The Generation of 1914* (Cambridge, MA: Harvard University Press, 1979), chapter 3.
32. Wohl, *Generation of 1914*, p. 105.
33. More on these themes in Chapters 5 and 6.
34. Jessica Meyer, *Men of War: Masculinity and the First World War in Britain* (London: Palgrave Macmillan, 2009), p. 141.

35. Ibid., p. 6.
36. Michael C.C. Adams, '"Anti-War" isn't Always Anti-War', *The Midwest Quarterly* 31:3 (Spring 1990), p. 300.
37. Hanbury-Sparrow, *The Land-Locked Lake*, p. 18.
38. Ibid., 19.
39. Rees, *A Schoolmaster at War*, p. 28.
40. Griffith, *Up To Mametz*, p. 235.
41. Ibid., pp. 59–60.
42. Ibid., pp. 47–8.
43. Cecil, *The Flower of Battle*, pp. 14–15.
44. Frederick Heath, 'A Soldier's Record', *The English Review* (February 1933), pp. 232–3.
45. For details on Manning's biography, see Brian Bond, *Survivors of a Kind*, chapter 6.
46. Stephen Graham, *A Private in the Guards* (New York: The Macmillan Company, 1919), pp. 34–5.
47. Ibid., p. 23.
48. Ibid., pp. 72–3.
49. Andrews, *Haunting Years*, p. 11.
50. Ibid., pp. 15, 19.
51. Ibid., pp. 16–18.
52. Ibid., p. 19.
53. Ibid., p. 202.
54. Giles E.M. Eyre, *Somme Harvest: Memories of a P.B.I. in the Summer of 1916* (London: Jarrolds, 1938), pp. 9–10.
55. Ibid., pp. 25–6.
56. Ibid., p. 34.
57. Ibid., p. 37.
58. Ibid., p. 23.
59. Ibid., pp. 43, 46–7.
60. Brian Bond, *Survivors of a Kind: Memoirs of the Western Front* (London: Continuum Books, 2008), p. 83.
61. Cyril Falls, 'Rankers of the Great War', *The Times Literary Supplement* (2 April 1938), p. 226.

Chapter 4 War Memories: The East

1. Priya Satia, *Spies in Arabia* (Oxford: Oxford University Press, 2008), pp. 60–1.
2. The celebrity poet Rupert Brooke died en route to Gallipoli in 1915.
3. Priya Satia, *Spies in Arabia* (Oxford: Oxford University Press, 2008).
4. Ibid., pp. 31–7.
5. James Kitchen, '"Khaki crusaders": Crusading Rhetoric and the British Imperial Soldier during the Egypt and Palestine Campaigns, 1916–18', *First World War Studies* 1:2 (October 2010), pp. 141–60.

NOTES TO PAGES 87–93   179

6. Justin Fantauzzo, '"Buried Alive": Experience, Memory, and the Interwar Publishing of the Egyptian Expeditionary Force in Postwar Britain, 1915–1939', *Journal of the Canadian Historical Association* 23:2 (2012), p. 241.
7. Of 204 British non-fiction war books compiled for this study covering the years 1919–30, 48 were on these three campaigns (2 on service in Russia). Their numbers dwindle after 1930 as only another eight were released between 1931 and 1938. This makes a total of at least 56 accounts in the interwar period.
8. Twenty-eight of the 204 compiled between 1919 and 1939.
9. Satia, *Spies in Arabia*, pp. 60–1. Italics hers.
10. An interesting account of Lawrence's writing methods can be found in Vyvyan Richards, 'Book Production', in A.W. Lawrence, *T.E. Lawrence: By His Friends* (New York: Doubleday, Doran & Company, 1937), pp. 341–5.
11. B.H. Liddell Hart, *Colonel Lawrence: The Man Behind the Legend* (New York: Dodd, Mead & Company, 1934), p. 323.
12. Ibid., pp. 323–5.
13. Michael Howard, *Jonathan Cape, Publisher* (London: Harmondsworth, 1977), p. 90; Robert Graves, *Lawrence and the Arabs* (London: Jonathan Cape, 1927), pp. 408–409.
14. Howard, *Jonathan Cape*, pp. 90–4.
15. Satia, *Spies in Arabia*, p. 181.
16. Liddell Hart, *Colonel Lawrence: The Man Behind the Legend*; Graves, *Lawrence and the Arabs*.
17. Jonathan Cape, 'T.E. As Author and Translator', in A.W. Lawrence, *T.E. Lawrence: By His Friends*, p. 474.
18. Sir Hubert Young, *The Independent Arab* (London: John Murray, 1933), pp. ix, x.
19. Ibid., pp. 13–21.
20. Ibid., p. 24.
21. Ibid., p. 40.
22. Ibid., pp. ix–x.
23. Major N.N.E. Bray, *Shifting Sands* (London: Unicorn Press, 1934), p. xi.
24. Ibid., p. 158.
25. Ibid., p. 241.
26. Ibid., Preface.
27. Ibid., pp. 15–22.
28. Ibid., p. 169.
29. Margaret Fitzherbert, *The Man Who Was Greenmantle: Biography of Aubrey Herbert* (London: John Murray, 1983), p. 131. When convalescing from his wounds at Mons he began writing the first section of the book in his diary.
30. Desmond MacCarthy, 'Aubrey Herbert', in Aubrey Herbert, *Mons, Anzac and Kut* (London: Hutchinson, 1930), p. 12.
31. SCRO, Herbert Papers, DD DRU 53, News Clipping Album.
32. SCRO, Herbert Papers, DD DRU 53, Daily News clipping, 'A War Diary'.

33. Fitzherbert, *The Man Who Was Greenmantle*, p. 154.
34. General Sir Ian Hamilton, *Gallipoli Diary*, Vol. 1 (London: Edward Arnold, 1920), Preface.
35. Compton Mackenzie, *Gallipoli Memories* (London: Cassell, 1929), p. 62.
36. Ibid., p. 7.
37. 'Gallipoli Memories', *The Times Literary Supplement* (5 December 1929).
38. Compton Mackenzie, *Greek Memories* (London: Cassell, 1939), pp. xii–xiii.
39. Ibid.
40. 'Greece in the War' Review, *The Times* (18 July 1939), p. 9, issue 48360, col. E.
41. John Cuthbert Lawson, *Tales of Aegean Intrigue* (London: Chatto & Windus, 1920), p. 30.
42. Ibid., p. 9. Lawson concludes his introduction with the fact he enjoyed the war service but found the pay very poor.
43. Ibid., pp. 31–4. Lawson was very much concerned with the moral duties of espionage officials and that their conduct not damage British reputation within the region.
44. Included in this list: W.E. Dickson, *East Persia: A Backwater of the Great War* (London: Edward Arnold, 1924); Martin Donohoe, *With the Persian Expedition* (London: Edward Arnold, 1919); L.C. Dunsterville, *The Adventures of Dunsterforce* (London: Edward Arnold, 1920); J.J. Abraham, *My Balkan Log* (London: Chapman and Hall 1921); Albert Barker, *Memories of Macedonia* (London: A.H. Stockwell, 1921); Henry C. Day, *Macedonian Memories* (London: Heath Cranton, 1930); Marguerite Fedden, *Sister's Quarters, Salonika* (London: Grant Richards, 1921); Yvonne Fitzroy, *With the Scottish Nurses in Rumania* (London: John Murray, 1918); Isabel Galloway Hutton, *With a Woman's Unit in Serbia, Salonika and Sebastopol* (London: Williams and Norgate, 1928); Flora Sandes, *The Autobiography of a Woman Soldier* (London: H.F. & G. Witherby, 1927); Vincent Seligman, *The Salonica Side-Show* (London: Allen & Unwin, 1919); Douglas Walshe, *With the Serbs in Macedonia* (London: John Lane, 1920); Donovan Young, *A Subaltern in Serbia* (London: Drane, 1922); Richard Smith, *A Subaltern in Macedonia and Judea* (London: The Mitre Press, 1930).
45. Discussed further in Chapter 5.
46. E.J. Thompson, *Crusader's Coast* (1929); Vivian Gilbert, *Romance of the Last Crusade* (1923); Cecil Sommers, *Temporary Crusaders* (1919); R.E. Adams, *The Modern Crusaders* (1920); John More, *With Allenby's Crusaders* (1923).
47. They are Bernard Blaser, *Kilts Across the Jordan* (London: H.F. & G Witherby, 1926); P.W. Long, *Other Ranks of Kut* (London: Williams and Norgate, 1938); W.J. Blackledge, *The Legion of Marching Madmen* (London: Sampson Low, Marsten & Co., 1936).
48. This novel was dedicated to fellow war memoirist Guy Chapman and his novelist wife Storm Jameson, who helped secure its publication through Alfred Knopf.
49. E.J. Thompson, *Crusader's Coast* (London: Ernest Benn, 1929), p. 11.

50. Ibid., p. 15.
51. John More, *With Allenby's Crusaders* (London: Heath Cranton, Ltd, 1923), pp. 224–5.
52. See Kitchen, "'Khaki Crusaders'".
53. Hynes, *The Soldiers' Tale*, p. 2. Italics his.
54. Coldicott, *London Men in Palestine*, p. viii.
55. More, *With Allenby's Crusaders*, p. 9.
56. Coldicott, *London Men in Palestine*, p. viii.
57. Ibid., p. vii.
58. Gilbert, *The Romance of the Last Crusade*, Preface.
59. Ibid., pp. 36–7
60. Ibid., pp. 43–4.
61. Thompson's brother was killed on the western front.
62. More, *With Allenby's Crusaders*, pp. 37–8.
63. Arnewood, *With the Guns West and East*, p. 63.
64. Ibid., pp. 66, 74.
65. Satia, *Spies in Arabia*, pp. 66–7.
66. Graves, *Lawrence and the Arabs*, p. 417.
67. Ibid.
68. Blaser, *Kilts Across the Jordan*, pp. 11–12.
69. Cecil Sommers, *Temporary Crusaders* (London: John Lane, 1919), p. 1.
70. Ibid., pp. 26–31.
71. Arnewood, *With the Guns West and East*, p. 76.
72. More, *With Allenby's Crusaders*, pp. 9–10; Yeats-Brown, *Caught by the Turks*, pp. 83–4; E.C.W. Sandes, *In Kut and Captivity* (London: John Murray, 1919), p. 338. These are just a few of many references from nearly early every book mentioned regarding the vermin and poor sanitation in the East.
73. More, *With Allenby's Crusaders*, pp. 37–8.
74. Blaser, *Kilts Across the Jordan*, pp. 49–50.
75. Alan Bott, *Eastern Nights – and Flights* (Edinburgh: William Blackwood & Sons, 1920), p. 3.
76. Ibid., p. 10.
77. Ibid., p. 11.
78. J.E. Tennant, *In the Clouds Above Baghdad* (London: Cecil Palmer, 1920), pp. 25–6.
79. More, *With Allenby's Crusaders*, p. 109; Yeats-Brown, *Caught by the Turks*, p. 22; Sandes, *In Kut*, p. 124.
80. Tennant, *In the Clouds*, p. 7.
81. Ibid., p. 17.
82. Gilbert, *The Romance*, p. 235.
83. Ibid.
84. Arnewood, *With the Guns West and East*, p. 74.
85. More, *With Allenby's Crusaders*, pp. 108–109.
86. Tennant, *In the Clouds*, Foreword.

Chapter 5   War Experiences: Suffering

1. Henry Williamson, *The Wet Flanders Plain* (New York: E.P. Dutton, 1929), p. 10.
2. For much of his book he recalls happier times spent in the rear of the fighting.
3. Williamson, *The Wet Flanders Plain*, p. 12.
4. Fussell, *The Great War and Modern Memory*, p. 7.
5. Audoin-Rouzeau and Becker, *14–18*, p. 9.
6. The 1970s saw a new school of historians and literary scholars interested in the experience and trauma of war. See Reynolds, *The Long Shadow*, chapter 10.
7. Gregory, *The Silence of Memory*, p. 23.
8. George Mosse, *Fallen Soldiers: Reshaping the Memory of the World Wars* (Oxford: Oxford University Press, 1990), p. 7.
9. Helen McCartney, 'The First World War Soldier and his Contemporary Image in Britain', *International Affairs* 90:2 (2014), pp. 299–315. McCartney indicates many contemporary trends that help to define the notion of the soldier-victim in British popular culture.
10. Writers engaged in a similar process of memorialisation to those erecting tablets, as both engage with notions of memory and language. Similar to memorials to the war dead, memoirs could be interpreted in different ways See Alex King, *Memorials of the Great War in Britain: The Symbolism and Politics of Remembrance* (London: Bloomsbury, 2014), pp. 2–3.
11. This was accentuated in the 1990s with a publishing boom in World War I fiction that examined this trope further through the works of Sebastian Faulks and Pat Barker.
12. Sheffield, *Forgotten Victory*, p. 158.
13. Ibid., p. 157.
14. Ibid.; also, Bond, *The Unquiet Western Front*, pp. 27–51.
15. Watson, *Enduring the Great War*, pp. 77–84.
16. Watson, *Fighting Different Wars*, p. 217.
17. Edmunds, *A Subaltern's War*, p. 206.
18. William Mulligan's *The Great War for Peace* demonstrates how Allied soldiers and their governments had high hopes for a postwar settlement that led to international peace and that emphasised liberal humanitarianism. Mulligan, *The Great War for Peace* (New Haven, CT: Yale University Press, 2014).
19. Audoin-Rouzeau and Becker, *14–18*, p. 17.
20. See Watson, *Enduring the Great War*, chapter 3.
21. Audoin-Rouzeau and Becker, *14–18*, p. 3.
22. The term is used by Deborah Cohen in her excellent book, *The War Come Home*, p. 8.
23. Blunden, *Undertones*, p. 1.
24. Ibid., pp. vii–viii.

NOTES TO PAGES 117–122   183

25. Richard Perceval Graves, *Robert Graves: The Assault Heroic 1895–1926* (New York: Viking, 1987), pp. 117–18.
26. Robert Graves, *Good-bye to All That* (New York: Doubleday, 1957), Prologue.
27. Bond, *Survivors of a Kind*, p. 2.
28. Graves would discredit his own methods later. See Robert Graves, *Good-bye to All That* (1957), Prologue.
29. Miranda Seymour, *Robert Graves: Life on the Edge* (New York: Henry Holt, 1995), pp. 180–3.
30. Quoted by Robyn Marsack in Edmund Blunden, *Fall In, Ghosts* (Manchester: Carcanet Press, 2014), xii.
31. Fussell, *The Great War*, pp. 203–12.
32. Ibid., p. 220.
33. Winter, *Remembering War*, p. 105; Fussell, *The Great War*, pp. 219–20.
34. ULSC, BC, Gosse Correspondence, folder: 'Letters between Edmund Gosse and Robert Graves', letter from Robert Graves to Edmund Gosse, 24 October 1917.
35. Hynes, *A War Imagined*, p. 425.
36. Todman, *The Great War*, chapter 4.
37. Rutherford, *The Literature of War*, pp. 92–3.
38. Stephanie Barczewski, *Antarctic Destinies* (London: Hambledon Continuum, 2007), pp. 148–50.
39. Indeed, Graves's follow-up to *Good-Bye to All That*, *But it Still Goes On*, was written in part to address the confusion and criticism his book generated.
40. Charles Carrington, *Soldier from the Wars Returning* (Barnsley: Pen and Sword Military Classics, 2006), p. 267; Guy Chapman, *A Kind of Survivor* (London: Gollancz, 1975), p. 118.
41. Rosa Maria Bracco defines the middlebrow as an essentially culturally conservative space between the avant-garde and more popular fiction. See Bracco, *Merchants of Hope*, pp. 12–13.
42. Carrington was privately educated and then attended Oxford. Douie went to Rugby and then Oxford for one year. Chapman attended Westminster and then Christ Church, Oxford where he read law.
43. Edmunds, *A Subaltern's War*, p. 132.
44. Ibid., p. 133.
45. Ibid., p. 185.
46. Ibid.
47. Ibid., p. 194.
48. Ibid.
49. Ibid., p. 200.
50. Guy Chapman, *A Passionate Prodigality* (London: Nicholson & Watson, 1933), p. 3.
51. Ibid., p. 218.
52. Ibid., p. 229.

53. Ibid., p. 226.
54. Ibid., p. 226.
55. Chapman, *A Kind of Survivor*, p. 13.
56. Douie, *The Weary Road*, p. 8.
57. Ibid., p. 12.
58. Emily Mayhew, *Wounded* (Oxford: Oxford University Press, 2014), p. 212.
59. Ibid.
60. Gosse, *Memoirs of a Camp Follower*, p. 108.
61. Accounts were published by both doctors and nurses. See Clair Buck, 'British Women's Writing of the Great War', in Vincent Sherry, ed., *The Cambridge Companion to the Literature of the First World War* (Cambridge: Cambridge University Press, 2005), p. 101. Buck describes nurse memoirs as being particularly important in establishing the relationship of women as eyewitnesses to combat. She writes that wartime accounts by female nurses and VADs demonstrated a sense of the 'adventure' that came with close proximity to combat. See also Jane Potter, *Boys in Khaki, Girls in Print*, pp. 7–8, 154. Potter asserts that nursing memoirs were a type of 'popular romance' published during the war and that they essentially reinforced gender norms rather than challenged them, though some accounts do make a compelling case for their own 'significance'.
62. In America, Ernest Hemingway's *A Farewell to Arms* and Mary Borden's *The Forbidden Zone* remain two of the most critically regarded of books about the medical services during the war.
63. Henry Gervis, *Arms and the Doctor: The Military Experiences of a Middle-aged Medical Man* (London: C.W. Daniel, 1920), p. 10.
64. Harold Dearden, *Medicine and Duty: A War Diary* (London: Heinemann, 1928), p. vi.
65. Ibid., p. xi.
66. David Rorie, *A Medico's Luck in the War: Being the Reminiscences of R.A.M.C. Work with the 51st (Highland) Division* (Aberdeen: Milne and Hutchinson, 1929), pp. 2–3.
67. Ibid., p. 3.
68. Isabel Emslie Hutton, *With A Woman's Unit in Serbia, Salonika and Sebastopol* (London: Williams and Norgate, 1928), pp. 14–15.
69. Osburn, *Unwilling Passenger*, pp. 13–14.
70. Ibid., p. 23.
71. Ibid., pp. 133–5.
72. Other writers, such as Philip Gosse, chose specifically not to put these images in their work, though Gosse felt urged to do so by readers. See Gosse, *Memoirs*, p. xiv.
73. E.J. Thompson, *The Leicestershires Beyond Baghdad* (London: The Epworth Press, J. Alfred Sharp, 1919), p. 93.
74. Osburn, *Unwilling Passenger*, p. 139.
75. Ibid., p. 217.

76. SCL, Vera Brittain/Paul Berry Collection, VB/PB Box 31, 'Origins of Testament of Youth'.
77. Christine Hallett, 'Portrayals of Suffering: Perceptions of Trauma in the Writings of First World War Nurses and Volunteers', *CBMH/BCHM*, 27:1 (2010), pp. 66–7.
78. Potter, *Boys in Khaki, Girls in Print*, p. 223.
79. Watson, *Fighting Different Wars*, pp. 247–59. Lynn Layton, 'Vera Brittain's Testament(s)', in Margaret Higonnet, Jane Jenson, Sonya Michel and Margaret Collons Weitz, eds, *Behind the Lines: Gender and the Two World Wars* (New Haven: Yale University Press, 1987), pp. 70–1.
80. SCL, Vera Brittain/Paul Berry Collection, VB/PB Box 3, letter from Vera Brittain to Phyllis Bentley 29 April 1933 (photocopy of original).
81. Buck, 'British Women's Writing of the Great War', p. 107.
82. SCL, Vera Brittain/Paul Berry Collection, VB/PB Box 31, Enclosed Doc. 'Points Which could be Emphasised in Publicity Work for "Testament of Youth"', Vera Brittain to Miss Hutchinson, 26 July 1933 (Photocopy of original).
83. Brittain became a significant spokesperson for the pacifist movement as the decade went on. See Richard Overy, *The Morbid Age*, pp. 246–7.
84. Bayly, *Triple Challenge*, p. 13.
85. Ibid., pp. 92, 145.
86. See Ian Isherwood, 'Writing the '"ill-managed nursery": British POW Memoirs of the First World War', *First World War Studies*, 5:3 (2014), pp. 267–86.
87. Ibid., p. 269.
88. The expression comes from Francis Yeats-Brown, *Caught by the Turks*, chapter 3.
89. See Isherwood, 'Writing the "ill-managed nursery"', p. 271.
90. John Still, *A Prisoner in Turkey* (London: John Lane, 1920), pp. 27–8.
91. Ibid., p. 39.
92. Ibid., p. 40.
93. Ibid., p. 32.
94. Sandes, *In Kut*, pp. 284–5; Keeling, *Adventures in Turkey and Russia* (London: John Murray, 1924), pp. 8–10.
95. Sandes, *In Kut*, p. 318.
96. Edward Mousley, *Secrets of a Kuttite* (London: John Lane, 1921), p. 201.
97. Still, *A Prisoner*, p. xvii.
98. Keeling, *Adventures*, p. 28.
99. Mousley, *Secrets*, 169; Also, see Sandes, *In Kut*, pp. 286–7.
100. Keeling, *Adventures*, p. 11.
101. Isherwood, 'Writing the "ill-managed nursery"', p. 273.
102. Sandes, *In Kut*, p. 359.
103. Keeling, *Adventures*, p. 19.
104. Still, *Prisoner*, Foreword.
105. Keeling, *Adventures*, p. 34
106. Keeling, *Adventures*, pp. 34–5, 40.
107. Sandes, *In Kut*, p. 325.

Chapter 6 War Experiences: Heroism

1. Ernest Hemingway, *A Farewell to Arms* (New York: Charles Scribner and Sons, 1929), p. 191.
2. Eric Leed, *No Man's Land*, p. 209.
3. Andrew Rutherford, *The Literature of War*, p. 3.
4. Hynes, *Soldiers' Tale*, p. 55.
5. Ibid.
6. Rutherford, *The Literature of War*, p. 3.
7. Jessica Meyer, *Men of War*, p. 6; Graham Dawson, *Soldier Heroes* (London: Routledge, 1994), p. 1.
8. Lord Moran, *The Anatomy of Courage* (London: Constable, 1945), p. 134.
9. Ibid.
10. This is not to say that men who served did not have hard lives before the war, but only that the combination of hard living in the trenches and fear of mutilation and death found at the front was something that no civilian experience could imitate.
11. Jessica Meyer, *Men of War*, p. 141; Edward Madigan, '"Sticking to a Hateful Task": Resilience, Humour, and British Understandings of Combatant Courage, 1914–1918', *War in History* 20: 1, pp. 76–98. Also, see Alex Watson's work on coping mechanisms in battle. Watson, *Enduring the Great War*, chapter 3.
12. Watson, *Enduring*, pp. 34–43.
13. See Madigan, '"Sticking to a Hateful Task"'.
14. See Barczewski, *Antarctic Destinies*, chapter 7.
15. Ibid., pp. 150–3.
16. Rees, *Schoolmaster at War*, Preface.
17. Gibbs, *The Grey Wave*, p. x.
18. Hynes, *Soldiers' Tale*, p. 9.
19. Douie, *The Weary Road*, pp. 3–4.
20. R.H. Mottram, *Through the Menin Gate* (London: Chatto and Windus, 1932), p. 197.
21. Ibid.
22. Andrews, *Haunting Years*, p. 286.
23. Ibid., p. 288.
24. Eyre, *Somme Harvest*, p. 248 (reprint 1991).
25. Ibid., p. 249.
26. Ibid.
27. Michael Moynihan, *Black Bread and Barbed Wire* (London: Leo Cooper, 1978), p. xii.
28. Hynes, *Soldiers' Tale*, p. 237.
29. S.P. MacKenzie, 'The Ethics of Escape: British Officer POWs in the First World War', *War in History* 15:1 (2008), pp. 1–3.
30. Ibid., p. 3.

NOTES TO PAGES 146–151   187

31. ULSC, Liddle Collection, MES 069: Folder Walter Harold Miles, signed order from Colonel Annesley to Harold Miles, 18 October 1917.
32. Keeling, *Adventures in Turkey and Russia*, pp. 72–3. Also, see E.H. Jones and C.W. Hill, *The Road to En-Dor* (London: John Lane, 1919), pp. 114, 160.
33. Yeats-Brown, *Caught by the Turks*, p. 102.
34. Major M.C.C. Harrison and Captain H.A. Cartwright, *Within Four Walls* (London: Edward Arnold, 1930), pp. 14, 28; Geoffrey Harding, *Escape Fever* (London: John Hamilton, 1935), p. 321; Evans, *Escaping Club*, pp. 14–15; and Duncan Grinnell-Milne, *An Escaper's Log* (London: John Lane, 1926), p. 19.
35. Hardy, *I Escape*, p. 22.
36. Harrison and Cartwright, *Within Four Walls*, p. 28.
37. MacKenzie, 'Ethics of Escape', pp. 8–9.
38. For more of this comparison, see ibid., pp. 14–16.
39. Evans, *Escaping Club*, p. 178; Harding, *Escape Fever*, pp. 49, 167; and Hardy, *I Escape!*, p. 22.
40. Evans, *Escaping Club*.
41. Lieutenant Walter Duncan, *How I Escaped from Germany* (private printing, 1919), p. 82.
42. Grinnell-Milne, *An Escaper's Log*, p. 86; and Harrison and Cartwright, *Within Four Walls*, p. 117.
43. Harrison and Cartwright, *Within Four Walls*, p. 117.
44. Captain M.A.B. Johnston and Captain K.D. Yearsley, *Four-Fifty Miles to Freedom* (Edinburgh: William Blackwood & Sons, 1919), pp. 19–20.
45. Keeling, *Adventures in Turkey and Russia*, p. 142.
46. Yeats-Brown, *Caught by the Turks*, p. 206.
47. Keeling, *Adventures*.
48. Yeats-Brown, *Caught by the Turks*, p. 130.
49. Ibid., p. 154.
50. Ibid., p. 160.
51. NLS, WBC, letter from Alan Bott to George Blackwood 12 March 1920. Alan Bott's desire to have his book marketed for boys was shared by K.D. Yearsley, author of *450 Miles to Freedom* from letter, 14 October 1919, Blackwood MS 30618.
52. Harrison and Cartwright, *Within Four Walls*; and Harding, *Escape Fever*.
53. Maryam Philpott, *Air and Sea Power in World War I* (London: I.B.Tauris, 2013), p. 171.
54. Ibid., p. 185.
55. Night Hawke, *Rovers of the Night Sky* (London: Cassell, 1919), pp. v–vi.
56. Davies was the same publisher and Charles Carrington and Frederic Manning.
57. Cecil Lewis, *Sagittarius Rising* (reprint), Foreword, p. vii.
58. Ibid., p. v.
59. Ibid., p. 2.
60. Ibid.
61. Ibid.

62. Norman Macmillan, *Into the Blue* (London: Duckworth, 1929), p. 15.
63. Ibid.
64. Billy Bishop, *Winged Warfare* (London: Hodder and Stoughton, 1918), p. 1.
65. Jay Winter, 'Britain's "Lost Generation" of the First World War', *Population Studies* (November 1977), 31(3), pp. 459–60.
66. Duncan Grinnell-Milne, *Wind in the Wires* (London: Hurst and Blackett, 1933), p. 14.
67. Ibid., pp. 39–40; S.H. Long, *In the Blue* (London: John Lane, 1920), p. 19; Macmillan, *Into the Blue*, pp. 11–12.
68. Philpott, *Air and Sea Power in WWI*, p. 180.
69. 'Hunting the Huns in the Air' was the original subtitle of Billy Bush's Winged Warfare; for 'great game' see Macmillan, *Into the Blue*, p. 14; for 'king of all sportsmen' see Night Hawke, *Rovers of the Night Sky*, p. 77.
70. A.G.J. Whitehouse, *Hell in the Heavens: The Adventures of an Aerial Gunner in the Royal Flying Corps* (London: W & R Chambers, 1938), pp. 116–17.
71. Grinnell-Milne, *Wind in the Wires*, p. 158.
72. Samuel Hynes, *Soldiers' Tale*, p. 87.
73. Whitehouse, *Hell in the Heavens*, p. 26.
74. For more on the medieval trope, see Stefan Goebel, *The Great War and Medieval Memory: War, Remembrance, and Medievalism in Britain and Germany, 1914–1940* (Cambridge: Cambridge University Press, 2006), pp. 223–9.
75. Grinnell-Milne, *Wind in the Wires*, p. 262.
76. Aerial combat was, for him, a great adventure; captivity, largely because of its inaction, a hauntingly dreadful experience
77. Grinnell-Milne, *Wind in the Wires*, p. 136.
78. Ibid.
79. Ibid.
80. Ibid., p. 182.
81. Ibid., p. 226.
82. Interestingly, he reflected upon being more haunted by captivity than battlefield trauma.
83. Grinnell-Milne, *Wind in the Wires*, p. 287.
84. Grinnell-Milne, *Wind in the Wires* (New York: Ace Publishing, 1968), p. 14.
85. S.P. Mackenzie makes this connection as well in his 'The Ethics of Escape' where he writes that World War II POWs learned their craft, in part, from World War I escapers.

Conclusion

1. Douie, *The Weary Road*, p. 1.
2. Ibid., p. 3.
3. Fussell, *The Great War*, p. 7.
4. Jay Winter and Emmanuel Sivan, 'Setting the Framework', in Winter and Sivan, eds, *War and Remembrance in the Twentieth Century*, p. 6.

5. Alon Confino, 'Collective Memory and Cultural History', *American Historical Review* 102:5 (December 1997), p. 1390.
6. Samuel Hynes, 'Personal Narratives and Commemoration', in Winter and Sivan, *War and Remembrance in the Twentieth Century*, p. 207.
7. Ibid., p. 208.
8. Cyril Falls, *The Great War* (New York: Putnam, 1959), p. 421.
9. Charles Carrington, *Soldier from the Wars Returning*, p. 12.
10. Robert Wohl, *The Generation of 1914*, pp. 85–6, 105
11. Guy Chapman, *A Kind of Survivor*, pp. 281–2.
12. John Lucy, *There's a Devil in the Drum*, p. 393.
13. R.H. Mottram, *Through the Menin Gate*, p. 2.

BIBLIOGRAPHY

Archival Sources

Guildhall Library, London Metropolitan Archives (GL, LMA)
    Edward Arnold Ltd. Archive
    Hodder and Stoughton Archive
Imperial War Museum (IWM)
    Department of Documents (DD)
The National Library of Scotland (NLS)
    John Murray Archive (JMA)
    William Blackwood & Sons Collection (WBC)
Somerset Heritage Centre and the South West Heritage Trust (SHC)
    Herbert Family Papers
Somerville College Library, University of Oxford (SCL)
    Vera Brittain/Paul Berry Archive
Special Collections, Leeds University Library (SCLU)
    B.C. Gosse Collection
    Liddle Collection
University of Reading, Special Collections (URSC)
    Random House Archive (RHA)

Periodicals

The Bookseller
The Bookseller and Stationery Trades' Journal
The Bookman
English Review
Fortnightly Review
The Publisher and Bookseller
Saturday Review of Politics, Literature, Science and Art
The Times
The Times Literary Supplement

Primary Sources – Published Non-fiction

Abraham, J. Johnston, *My Balkan Log* (London: Chapman & Hall, 1921).
Adams, Bernard, *Nothing of Importance* (New York: Robert W. McBride & Co., 1918).
Adams, Captain R.E.C., *The Modern Crusaders* (London: Routledge, 1920).
Andrews, W.L., *Haunting Years: The Commentaries of a War Territorial* (London: Hutchinson, 1930).
'Arnewood', *With the Guns West and East* (Plymouth: Mayflower Press, 1923).
Bacon, Capt. Alban F.L., *The Wanderings of a Temporary Warrior* (London: H.F. & G. Witherby, 1922).
Barber, Major Charles H., *Besieged in Kut and After* (Edinburgh: William Blackwood & Sons, 1917).
Baring, Maurice, *R.F.C., H.Q.* (London: Bell, 1920).
Barker, Albert, *Memories of Macedonia* (London: A.H. Stockwell, 1921).
Bayly, Hugh, *Triple Challenge or War, Whirligigs and Windmills: A Doctor's Memoirs of the Years 1914–1929* (London: Hutchinson, 1935).
Beaman, Ardern, *The Squadroon* (London: John Lane, 1920).
Belhaven, The Master of, *The War Diary of the Master of Belhaven* (London: John Murray, 1924).
Bell, Capt. D.H., *A Soldier's Diary of the Great War* (London: Faber & Faber, 1929).
Bewsher, Paul, *"Green Balls" The Adventures of a Night Bomber* (Edinburgh: William Blackwood and Sons, 1919).
Bingham, Edward, *Falklands, Jutland, and the Bight* (London: John Murray, 1919).
Bishop, Billy, *Winged Warfare* (London: Hodder and Stoughton, 1918).
Bishop, H.C.W., *A Kut Prisoner* (London: John Lane, 1920).
Blackham, R.J., *Scalpel, Sword, and Stretcher* (London: Sampson Low, 1931).
Blackledge, W.J., *The Legion of Marching Madmen* (London: Sampson Low, Marsten & Co., 1936).
Blaser, Bernard, *Kilts Across the Jordan: Being the Experiences and Impressions with the Second Battalion "London Scottish" in Palestine* (London: H.F. & G. Witherby, 1926).
Blunden, Edmund, *Undertones of War* (London: Richard Cobden-Sanderson, 1928).
——— *Undertones of War* (Garden City, NY: Doubleday, 1929).
——— *Fall In, Ghosts* (Manchester: Carcanet Press, 2014).
Blunden, Edmund, Cyril Falls, H.M. Tomlinson and R. Wright, *The War: 1914–1918* (London: The Reader, 1930).
Bond, R.C., *Prisoners Grave and Gay* (Edinburgh: Blackwood, 1934).
Bott, Alan, *Eastern Nights – and Flights* (Edinburgh: William Blackwood & Sons, 1920)
Bray, N.N.E., *Shifting Sands* (London: Unicorn Press, 1934).
Brereton, Major C.B., *Tales of Three Campaigns* (London: Selwyn & Blount, 1926).
Brittain, Vera, *Testament of Youth* (London: Gollancz, 1933).
Buchanan, Angus, *Three Years of War in East Africa* (London: John Murray, 1919).
Burrage, A.M., *War is War* (London: Gollancz, 1930).
Carpenter, A.F.B., *The Blocking of Zeebrugge* (London: Herbert Jenkins, 1922).
Carrington, Charles, *Soldier from the Wars Returning* (Barnsley: Naval and Military Press, 2006).
Carstairs, Carroll, *A Generation Missing* (London: Heinemann, 1930).
Channing-Renton, E.M., *A Subaltern in the Field* (London: Heath Cranton, 1920).

Chapman, Guy, *A Kind of Survivor* (London: Gollancz, 1975).
——— *A Passionate Prodigality* (London: Nicholson & Watson, 1933).
——— *Vain Glory: A Miscellany of the Great War 1914–1918 written by those who fought in it on each side and all fronts* (London: Cassell, 1937).
Clayton, P.B., *Plain Tales from Flanders* (London: Longmans, 1929).
Coldicott, Rowlands, *London Men in Palestine* (New York: Longmans, Green & Co., 1919).
Croft, Lt. Colonel W.D., *Three Years With The 9th (Scottish) Division* (London: John Murray, 1919).
Crozier, Frank, *A Brass Hat in No Man's Land* (London: Jonathan Cape, 1930).
Dalton, Hugh, *With British Guns in Italy* (Methuen, 1919).
Day, Henry C., *Macedonian Memories* (London: Heath Cranton, 1930).
Dearden, Harold, *Medicine and Duty: A War Diary* (London: Heinemann, 1928).
Dickson, W.E., *East Persia: A Backwater of the Great War* (London: Edward Arnold, 1924).
Donohoe, Martin, *With the Persian Expedition* (London: Edward Arnold, 1919).
Douie, Charles, *Beyond the Sunset* (London: John Murray, 1935).
——— *The Weary Road: Recollections of a Subaltern of Infantry* (London: John Murray, 1929).
Dugdale, Captain Geoffrey, *Langemarck and Cambrai* (Uckfield, East Sussex: The Naval and Military Press, Ltd, 2009).
Duncan, Lieutenant Walter, *How I Escaped from Germany* (private printing, 1919).
Dunsterville, L.C., *The Adventures of Dunsterforce* (London: Edward Arnold, 1920).
Durnford, H.G., *The Tunnellers of Holzminden* (Cambridge: Cambridge University Press, 1920).
Edmunds, Charles (C.E. Carrington), *A Subaltern's War* (London: Peter Davies, 1929).
Evans, A.J., *The Escaping Club* (London: John Lane, 1921).
Ex-Private X, *War is War* (London: Gollancz, 1930).
Eyre, Giles E.M., *Somme Harvest: Memories of a P.B.I. in the Summer of 1916* (London: Jarrolds, 1938).
Falls, Cyril, *War Books: A Critical Guide* (London: Peter Davies, 1930).
Fedden, Marguerite, *Sister's Quarters, Salonika* (London: Grant Richards, 1921).
Fitzroy, Yvonne, *With the Scottish Nurses in Rumania* (London: John Murray, 1918).
Floyd, Thomas Hope, *At Ypres with Best-Dunkley* (London & New York: John Lane, 1920).
Fraser-Tytler, Lt. Colonel Neil, *Field Guns in France* (London: Hutchinson, 1922).
Fuller, J.F.C., *Memoirs of an Unconventional Soldier* (London: Ivor Nicholson & Watson, 1936).
Fyfe, Hamilton, *The Making of an Optimist* (London: Parsons, 1921).
Gauld, H. Drummond, *The Truth from the Trenches* (London: Arthur Stockwell, 1918).
Gervis, Henry, *Arms and the Doctor: The Military Experiences of a Middle-aged Medical Man* (London: C.W. Daniel, 1920).
Gibbons, John, *Roll On, Next War! The Common Man's Guide to Army Life* (London: Muller, Ltd. 1935).
Gibbs, Major A. Hamilton, *The Grey Wave* (London: Hutchinson, 1920).
Gilbert, Major Vivian, *The Romance of the Last Crusade: With Allenby to Jerusalem* (New York: Appleton, 1924).

Gosse, Philip, *Memoirs of a Camp-Follower: A Naturalist Goes to War* (London: Longmans, 1934).
Graham, Stephen, *A Private in the Guards* (New York: The Macmillan Company, 1919).
——— *The Challenge of the Dead* (London: Cassell, 1921).
Graves, Robert, *Good-Bye to All That* (London: Jonathan Cape, 1929).
——— *Goodbye to All That* (New York: Doubleday, 1957).
——— *But it Still Goes On* (London: Jonathan Cape, 1930).
——— *Lawrence and the Arabs* (London: Jonathan Cape, 1927).
Griffith, Llewelyn Wyn, *Up to Mametz and Beyond* (Barnsley: Pen and Sword, 2010).
——— *Up to Mametz* (London: Severn House, 1981), reprint.
Grinnell-Milne, Duncan, *An Escaper's Log* (London: John Lane, 1926).
——— *Wind in the Wires* (London: Hurst and Blackett, 1933).
——— *Wind in the Wires* (New York: Ace Books, 1968)
'GSO' (Sir Frank Fox), *GHQ (Montreuil-sur-Mer)* (London: Philip Allan, 1920).
Hamilton, General Sir Ian, *Gallipoli Diary* (London: Edward Arnold, 1920).
Hanbury-Sparrow, A.A., *The Land-Locked Lake* (London: A. Barker, 1932).
Harding, Geoffrey, *Escape Fever* (London: John Hamilton, 1935).
Hardy, J.L., *I Escape!* (London: John Lane, 1927).
Harrison, Major M.C.C., and Captain H.A. Cartwright, *Within Four Walls* (London: Edward Arnold, 1930).
Harvey, F.W., *Comrades in Captivity* (London: Sidgwick & Jackson, 1920).
Herbert, Aubrey, *Mons, Anzac and Kut* (London: Hutchinson, 1930).
'By an M.P.' (Aubrey Herbert), *Mons, Anzac, and Kut* (London: Edward Arnold 1919).
Hickey, Capt. D.E., *Rolling into Action – Memoirs of a Tank Corps Section Commander* (London: Hutchinson, 1936).
Howard, Keble, *An Author in Wonderland* (London: Chatto & Windus, 1919).
Hutton, I. Galloway, *With a Woman's Unit in Serbia, Salonika, and Sebastopol* (London: Williams and Norgate, 1929).
Johnston, Captain M.A.B. and Captain K.D. Yearsley, *Four-Fifty Miles to Freedom* (Edinburgh: William Blackwood & Sons, 1919).
Jones, David, *In Parentheses* (New York: Chilmark Press, 1961), reprint.
Jones, E.H. and C.W. Hill, *The Road to En-Dor* (London: John Lane, 1919).
Jones, H.A., *Over the Balkans and South Russia* (London: Edward Arnold, 1923).
Keeling, E.H., *Adventures in Turkey and Russia* (London: John Murray, 1924).
Kipling, Rudyard, *The Irish Guards in the Great War* (Garden City, NY: Doubleday, Page & Co., 1923).
Lawrence, T.E., *Revolt in the Desert* (London: Jonathan Cape, 1927).
——— *The Seven Pillars of Wisdom* (London: Jonathan Cape, 1935).
Lawson, J.C., *Tales of Aegean Intrigue* (London: Chatto & Windus, 1920).
Lewis, Cecil, *Sagittarius Rising* (London: Peter Davies, 1936).
——— *Sagittarius Rising* (Barnsley: Frontline Books, 2009).
Lewis, Wyndham, *Blasting & Bombardiering* (London: Eyre and Spottiswood, 1937).
Lloyd, R.A., *A Trooper in the 'Tins'* (London: Hurst & Blackett, 1938).
Lloyd, T., *The Blazing Trail of Flanders* (London: Heath Cranton, 1933).
Lockhart, Captain J.G., *Palestine Days and Nights* (London: R. Scott, 1920).
Long, P.W., *Other Ranks of Kut* (London: Williams and Norgate, 1938).
Long, S.H., *In The Blue* (London: John Lane, 1920).

Luard, K.E., *Unknown Warriors* (London: Chatto & Windus, 1930).
Lucy, John F., *There's a Devil in the Drum* (London: Faber & Faber, 1938).
Mackenzie, Compton, *Aegean Memories* (London: Cassell, 1939).
―――― *Athenian Memories* (London: Cassell, 1931).
―――― *Gallipoli Memories* (London: Cassell, 1929).
―――― *Greek Memories* (London: Cassell, 1932).
Macmillan, Norman, *Into the Blue* (London: Duckworth, 1929).
Mark VII (Max Plowman), *A Subaltern on the Somme in 1916* (New York: E.P. Dutton, 1928).
Marson, Bertrand, *Scarlet and Khaki* (London: Jonathan Cape, 1930).
Matthews, E.C., *A Subaltern in the Field* (London: Heath Cranton, 1920).
Maxwell, Frank, *Frank Maxwell, V.C., A Memoir and Some Letters* (London: John Murray, 1921).
McCudden, James Thomas Byford, *Five Years in the R.F.C.* (London: Aeroplane Publishing Co., 1918).
'McScotch' (W. McLanachan), *Fighter Pilot* (London: Routledge & Son Ltd., 1936).
Montague, C.E., *Disenchantment* (London: Chatto & Windus, 1922).
Moran, Lord, *The Anatomy of Courage* (New York: Carroll & Graf, 2007).
More, John, *With Allenby's Crusaders* (London: Heath Cranton, 1923).
Mottram, R.H., *Ten Years Ago* (London: Chatto & Windus, 1928).
―――― *Through the Menin Gate* (London: Chatto & Windus, 1932).
Mottram, R.H., John Easton and Eric Partridge, *Three Men's War: The Personal Records of Active Service* (New York and London: Harper Brothers, 1930).
Mousley, Captain E.O., *The Secrets of a Kuttite* (London: John Lane, 1921).
'Night Hawke', M.C. (W.J. Harvey), *Rovers of the Night Sky* (London: Cassell, 1919).
Osburn, Arthur, *Unwilling Passenger* (London: Faber & Faber, 1932).
Pollard, Captain A.O., *Fire-eater: The Memoirs of a VC* (London: Hutchinson, 1932).
Purdom, C.B., ed., *Everyman at War* (London: Dent, 1930).
Quigley, Hugh, *Passchendaele and the Somme* (London: Methuen, 1928).
Read, Herbert, *In Retreat* (London: Hogarth Press, 1925).
Rees, R.T., *A Schoolmaster at War* (London: Haycock Press, 1935).
Richards, Frank, *Old Soldiers Never Die* (London: Faber & Faber, 1933).
Rorie, David, *A Medico's Luck in the War: Reminiscences of R.A.M.C. Work with the 51st (Highland) Division* (Aberdeen: Milne & Hutchinson, 1929).
Sandes, E.W.C., *In Kut and Captivity* (London: John Murray, 1919).
―――― *Tales from Turkey* (London: John Murray, 1924).
Sandes, Flora, *The Autobiography of a Woman Soldier* (London: H.F. & G. Witherby, 1927).
Seligman, V.J., *The Salonica Side-Show* (London: Allen & Unwin, 1919).
Smith, Lesley, *Four Years Out of Life* (London: Philip Allan, 1931).
Smith, Richard, *A Subaltern in Macedonia and Judea* (London: The Mitre Press, 1930).
Sommers, Cecil, *Temporary Crusaders* (London: John Lane, 1919).
Stansgate, William, *In Side Shows* (London: Hodder and Stoughton, 1919).
Still, John, *A Prisoner in Turkey* (London: John Lane, 1920).
Tayler, Henrietta, *A Scottish Nurse at Work* (London: John Lane, 1920).
Teichman, Oskar, *The Diary of a Yeoman M.O.* (London: Fisher & Unwin, 1921).
Tennant, Lt. Colonel J.E., *In the Clouds Above Baghdad* (London: Cecil Palmer, 1920).
Thompson, E.J., *The Leicestershires Beyond Baghdad* (London: Epworth Press, 1919).
―――― *Crusader's Coast* (London: Ernest Benn, 1929).

BIBLIOGRAPHY   195

Townshend, General Charles, *My Campaign in Mesopotamia* (London: T. Butterworth, 1920).
Walshe, Douglas, *With the Serbs in Macedonia* (London: John Lane, 1920).
Warburton, Ernest, *Behind Boche Bars* (London: John Lane, 1920).
Waugh, Alec, *The Prisoners of Mainz* (London: Chapman & Hall, 1919).
Weldon, Captain L.B., *"Hard Lying." Eastern Mediterranean, 1914–1919* (London: Herbert Jenkins, 1925).
West, Arthur Graeme, *Diary of a Dead Officer* (London: Allen & Unwin, 1919).
Whitehouse, A.G.J., *Hell in the Heavens: The Adventures of an Aerial Gunner in the Royal Flying Corps* (London: W & R Chambers, 1938).
Whitsed, Juliet De Key, *Come to the Cook-House Door! A V.A.D. in Salonika* (London: Herbert Joseph, 1932).
Williamson, Benedict, *Happy Days in France & Flanders* (London: Harding More, 1921).
Williamson, Henry, *The Wet Flanders Plain* (New York: E.P. Dutton, 1929).
Yeats-Brown, Francis, *Caught by the Turks* (London: Edward Arnold, 1919).
Young, Captain A. Donovan, *A Subaltern in Serbia* (London: Drane, 1922).
Young, Sir Hubert, *The Independent Arab* (London: John Murray, 1933).

Primary Sources: Fiction

Aldington, Richard, *Death of a Hero* (London: Chatto & Windus, 1929).
Bartlett, Vernon, *No Man's Land* (London: Allen & Unwin, 1930).
Bertrum, Anthony, *The Sword Falls* (London: Allen & Unwin, 1929).
Blaker, Richard, *Medal Without Bar* (London: Hodder and Stoughton, 1930).
Borden, Mary, *The Forbidden Zone* (London: Heinemann, 1929).
Brophy, John, ed., *The Soldier's War* (London: J.M. Dent, 1929).
Ewart, Wilfrid, *Way of Revelation* (London: Putman, 1921).
Ford, Ford Madox, *Some Do Not* (London: Duckworth, 1924).
―――― *No More Parades* (London: Duckworth, 1925).
―――― *A Man Could Stand Up* (London: Duckworth, 1926).
―――― *Last Post* (London: Duckworth, 1928).
Gristwood, A.D., *The Somme including The Coward* (London: Jonathan Cape, 1927).
Gurner, Ronald, *Pass Guard at Ypres* (London: Dent, 1930).
Hemingway, Ernest, *A Farewell to Arms*, (New York: Charles Scribner and Sons, 1929).
Macdonnell, A.G., *England, their England* (London: Picador, 1983).
Manning, Frederick, *Her Privates We* (London, Peter Davies, 1930).
Mottram, R.H., *The Spanish Farm Trilogy* (London: Chatto & Windus, 1927).
O'Flaherty, Liam, *The Return of the Brute* (London: Mandrake 1929).
Raymond Ernest, *Tell England* (London: Cassell, 1928, orig. 1922).
Sassoon, Siegfried, *Memoirs of a Fox-hunting Man* (London: Faber & Faber, 1928).
―――― *Memoirs of an Infantry Officer* (London: Faber & Faber, 1930).
―――― *Sherston's Progress* (London: Faber & Faber, 1936).
Sherriff, R.C. and Vernon Bartlett, *Journey's End* (London: Gollancz, 1930).
Smith, Helen Zenna, *Not So Quiet* (London: Marriott, 1929).
Thompson, Edward, *In Araby Orion* (London: Ernest Benn, 1930).
―――― *These Men, Thy Friends* (London: Afred Knopf, 1928).

Tomlinson, H.M., *All Our Yesterdays* (London: Heinemann, 1930).
Williamson, Henry, *Patriot's Progress* (London: E.P. Dutton, 1930).
Yeates, V.M., *Winged Victory* (London: Jonathan Cape, 1934).

Secondary Sources: Books

Audoin-Rouseau, Stephane (trans. Helen McPhail), *Men At War, 1914–1918: National Sentiment and Trench Journalism in France during the First World War* (Oxford: Berg, 1992).

Audoin-Rouseau, Stephane and Annette Becker, *14–18: Understanding the Great War* (New York: Hill and Wang, 2002).

Barczewski, Stephanie, *Antarctic Destinies* (London: Hambledon Continuum, 2007).

Bates, H.E., *Edward Garnett* (London: Parrish, 1950).

Bergonzi, Bernard, *Heroes Twilight: A Study of the Literature of the Great War* (London: Constable, 1965).

Berry, Paul and Mark Bostridge, *Vera Brittain: A Life* (Boston: Northeastern University Press, 2002).

Bloom, Clive, *Bestsellers: Popular Fiction Since 1900* (New York: Palgrave, 2002).

Bond, Brian, ed., *The First World War and British Military History* (Oxford: Clarendon Press, 1991).

────── *Survivors of a Kind: Memoirs of the Western Front* (London: Continuum Books, 2008).

────── *The Unquiet Western Front: Britain's Role in Literature and History* (New York: Oxford University Press, 2002).

Bourke, Joanna, *Dismembering the Male: Men's Bodies, Britain and the Great War* (London: Reaktion Books, 1999).

────── *Killing: An Intimate History* (London: Basic Books, 1999).

Bourne, J.M., *Britain and the Great War* (London: Arnold, 1989).

Bourne, John, Peter Liddle and Ian Whitehead, eds, *The Great World War 1914–1945, Vol. 1: Lightning Strikes Twice* (London: Harper Collins, 2000).

────── *The Great World War 1914–1945, Vol 2: The People's Experience* (London: Harper Collins, 2001).

Bracco, Rosa Maria, *Merchants of Hope: British Middlebrow Writers and the First World War, 1919–1939* (Oxford: Berg, 1993).

Braybon, Gail, ed., *Evidence, History and the Great War: Historians and the Impact of 1914–1918* (Oxford: Berghahn Books, 2003).

Caesar, Adrian, *Taking It Like a Man: Suffering, Sexuality and the War Poets* (Manchester: Manchester University Press, 1993).

Carpenter, Humphrey, *The Seven Lives of John Murray: The Story of a Publishing Dynasty* (London: John Murray, 2008).

Cecil, Hugh, *The Flower of Battle* (South Royalton, VT: Steerforth Press, 1996).

Clarke, Peter, *Hope and Glory: Britain 1900–2000* (London: Penguin, 2004).

Coetzee, Frans and Marilyn Shevin Coetzee, eds, *Authority, Identity and the Social History of the Great War* (Providence, RI: Berghahn, 1995).

Cohen, Deborah, *War Come Home: Disabled Veterans in Britain and Germany, 1914–1939* (Berkeley, CA: University of California Press, 2001).

Colley, Linda, *Captives: Britain, Empire and the World 1600–1850* (London: Jonathan Cape, 2002).

Cruttwell, C.R.M.F., *A History of the Great War, 1914–1918* (Oxford: Oxford University Press, 1934).
Das, Santanu, *Touch and Intimacy in First World War Literature* (Cambridge: Cambridge University Press, 2005).
Dawson, Graham, *Soldier Heroes: British Adventure, Empire, and the Imagining of Masculinities* (London: Routledge, 1994).
Duriez, Colin, *Bedeviled* (New York: InterVarsity Press, 2015).
Egremont, Max, *Siegfried Sassoon: A Life* (New York: Farrar, Straus and Giroux, 2005).
Eichenberg, Julia and John Paul Newman, eds, *The Great War and Veterans' Internationalism* (New York: Palgrave Macmillan, 2013).
Eksteins, Modris, *Rites of Spring: The Great War and the Birth of the Modern Age* (New York: Mariner Books, 2000).
Enser, A.G.S., *A Subject Bibliography of the First World War: Books in English 1914–1978* (London: André Deutsch, 1979).
Falls, Cyril, *A History of the 36th (Ulster) Division* (London: Constable, 1996).
——— *The Great War* (New York: Putnam, 1959).
Feather, John, *A History of British Publishing* (London: Croom Helm, 1988).
Ferguson, Niall, *The Pity of War* (New York: Basic Books, 1999).
Finkelstein, David and Alistair McCleary, *An Introduction to Book History* (New York: Routledge, 2005).
Fitzherbert, Margaret, *The Man Who Was Greenmantle: Biography of Aubrey Herbert* (London: John Murray, 1983).
Flower, Desmond, *A Century of Best-Sellers, 1830–1930* (London: National Book Council, 1934).
Frank, Joseph Allen and George Reeves, *"Seeing the Elephant": Raw Recruits at the Battle of Shiloh* (Urbana: University of Illinois Press, 2003).
Frayn, Andrew, *Writing Disenchantment: British First World War Prose, 1914–1930* (Manchester: Manchester University Press, 2014).
Fuller, J.G., *Troop Morale and Popular Culture in the British and Dominion Armies 1914–1918* (Oxford: Clarendon Press, 1991).
Fussell, Paul, *The Great War and Modern Memory* (Oxford: Oxford University Press, 1975).
Garnett, David, ed., *The Letters of T.E. Lawrence* (New York: Doubleday, 1939).
Gilchrist, K.J., *A Morning After War* (New York: Peter Lang, 2005).
Glover, Jon and Jon Silkin, eds, *The Penguin Book of First World War Prose* (London: Viking, 1989).
Goebel, Stefan, *The Great War and Medieval Memory: War, Remembrance, and Medievalism in Britain and Germany, 1914–1940* (Cambridge: Cambridge University Press, 2006).
Graves, Richard Perceval, *Robert Graves: The Assault Heroic 1895–1926* (New York: Viking, 1987).
Graves, Robert, *In Broken Images: Selected Correspondence*, ed. Paul O'Prey (Mt. Kisco, NY: Moyer Bell, 1988).
Graves, Robert and Alan Hodge, *The Long Week-End: A Social History of Great Britain 1918–1939* (New York: Norton, 1994).
Green, Andrew, *Writing the Great War: Sir James Edmonds and the Official Histories* (London: Frank Cass, 2003).

Gregory, Adrian, *The Last Great War: British Society and the First World War* (Cambridge: Cambridge University Press, 2010).
——— *The Silence of Memory: Armistice Day 1919–1946* (Oxford: Berg, 1994).
Griffith, Paddy, *Battle Tactics of the Civil War* (New Haven: Yale University Press, 1989).
——— *Battle Tactics of the Western Front* (London: St. Edmundbury Press, 1994).
Gullance, Nicoletta, *"Blood of Our Sons": Men, Women and the Renegotiation of British Citizenship during the Great War* (London: Palgrave, 2002).
Hager, Philip E. and Desmond Taylor, *The Novels of World War I: An Annotated Bibliography* (New York: Garland Publishing Inc., 1981).
Hammond, Mary, *Reading, Publishing and the Formation of Literary Taste in England, 1880–1914* (London: Ashgate, 2006).
Hammond, Mary and Shafquat Towheed, eds, *Publishing in the First World War* (London: Palgrave Macmillan, 2007).
Hart, B.H. Liddell, *Colonel Lawrence: The Man Behind the Legend* (New York: Dodd, Mead & Company, 1934).
Harvey, A.D., *A Muse of Fire: Literature, Art and War* (London: Hambledon Press, 1998).
Higham, Robin and Dennis E. Showalter, eds, *Researching World War I: A Handbook* (Westport CT: Greenwood Press, 2003).
Higonnet, Margaret, *Lines of Fire: Women Writers of WWI* (New York: Plume, 1999).
Higonnet, Margaret, Jane Jenson, Sonya Michel and Margaret Collons Weitz, eds, *Behind the Lines: Gender and the Two World Wars* (New Haven: Yale University Press, 1987).
Holman, Valerie, *Print for Victory: Book Publishing in England 1939–1945* (London: The British Library, 2008).
Holmes, Richard, *Acts of War* (New York: The Free Press, 1985).
——— *Tommy* (London: Harper Perennial, 2005).
Horne, John, ed., *A Companion to World War I* (Chichester: Blackwell, 2012).
Howard, Michael S., *Jonathan Cape, Publisher* (London: Harmondsworth, 1977).
Howsam, Leslie, *Old Books and New Histories: An Orientation to Studies in Book and Print Culture* (Toronto: University of Toronto Press, 2006).
Hynes, Samuel, *The Soldiers' Tale: Bearing Witness to Modern War* (New York: Penguin, 1998).
——— *The Edwardian Turn of Mind* (London: Pimlico, 1991).
——— *A War Imagined: The First World War in English Culture* (London: Pimlico, 1990).
Keegan, John, *The Face of Battle* (London: Viking, 1976).
——— *The First World War* (London: Pimlico, 1999).
——— *A History of Warfare* (London: Pimlico, 1993).
Keir, David, *The House of Collins: The Story of a Scottish Family of Publishers from 1789 to the Present Day* (London: Collins, 1952).
King, Alex, *Memorials of the Great War in Britain: The Symbolism and Politics of Remembrance* (London: Bloomsbury, 2014).
Klein, Holger, ed., *The First World War in Fiction* (London: Macmillan, 1976).
Kramer, Alan, *Dynamic of Destruction: Culture and Mass Killing in the First World War* (Oxford: Oxford University Press, 2007).
Kunitz, Stanley J. and Howard Haycraft, *Twentieth-Century Authors, A Biographical Dictionary of Modern Literature* (New York: H.W. Wilson, 1942).

Lamberti, Elena and Vita Fortunati, eds, *Memories and Representations of War: The Case of World War I and World War II* (New York: Rodolpi, 2009).
Lawrence, A.W., ed., *T.E. Lawrence: By His Friends* (New York: Doubleday, Doran & Company, 1937).
Leed, Eric, *No Man's Land: Combat and Identity in World War* (Cambridge: Cambridge University Press, 1979).
Lengel, Edward, *World War I Memories: An Annotated Bibliography of Personal Accounts Published in English Since 1919* (Oxford: Scarecrow Press, 2001).
MacLeod, Jenny and Pierre Purseigle, eds, *Uncovered Fields: Perspectives in First World War Studies* (Boston: Brill, 2004).
Mayhew, Emily, *Wounded* (Oxford: Oxford University Press, 2014).
McAleer, Joseph, *Popular Reading and Publishing* (Oxford: Clarendon Press, 1992).
McLoughlin, Kate, *Authoring War: The Literary Representation of War from the Iliad to Iraq* (Cambridge: Cambridge University Press, 2011).
——— ed., *The Cambridge Companion to War Writing* (Cambridge: Cambridge University Press, 2009).
Meyer, Jessica, ed., *British Popular Culture and the First World War* (Boston, MA: Brill, 2008).
——— *Men of War: Masculinity and the First World War in Britain* (London: Palgrave Macmillan, 2009).
Moran, C.M., *The Anatomy of Courage* (London: Constable, 1945).
Morgan, Charles, *The House of Macmillan (1843–1943)* (London: Macmillan, 1943).
Mosse, George L., *Fallen Soldiers: Reshaping the Memory of the World Wars* (Oxford: Oxford University Press, 1990).
Moynihan, Michael, *Black Bread and Barbed Wire: Prisoners in the First World War* (London: Leo Cooper, 1978).
Mulligan, William, *The Great War for Peace* (New Haven: Yale University Press, 2014).
Neiberg, Michael, *Fighting the Great War: A Global History* (Cambridge, MA: Harvard University Press, 2005).
Norrie, Ian, *Mumby's Publishing and Bookselling in the Twentieth Century* (London: Bell & Hyman, 1982).
Onions, John, *English Fiction and Drama of the Great War, 1918–1939* (London: Macmillan, 1976).
O'Riordan, Conal, *A Martial Medley, Fact and Fiction* (London: Scholartis Press, 1931).
Overy, Richard, *The Morbid Age: Britain Between the Wars* (London: Allen Lane, 2009).
Parfitt, George, *Fiction of the First World War: A Study* (London: Faber, 1990).
Paris, Michael, *Over the Top: The Great War and Juvenile Literature in Britain* (Westport, CT: Praeger, 2004).
Parker, Peter, *The Old Lie: The Great War and the Public-School Ethos* (London: Hambledon Continuum, 1987).
Philpott, Maryam, *Air and Sea Power in World War I: Combat and Experience in the Royal Flying Corps and the Royal Navy* (London: I.B.Tauris, 2013).
Philpott, William, *War of Attrition: Fighting the First World War* (New York: Overlook, 2014).
Plant, Marjorie, *The English Book Trade: An Economic History of the Making and Sale of Books* (London: Allen & Unwin, 1965).

Potter, Jane, *Boys in Khaki, Girls in Print: Women's Literary Responses to the Great War 1914–1918* (Oxford: Clarendon Press, 2005).
Quinn, Patrick, ed., *Recharting the Thirties* (Cranbury, NJ: Associated University Presses, 1996)
Quinn, Patrick and Steven Trout, eds, *The Literature of the Great War Reconsidered: Beyond Modern Memory* (New York: Palgrave, 2001).
Rachaminov, Alon, *POWs and the Great War: Captivity on the Eastern Front* (Oxford: Berg, 2002).
Raitt, Suzanne and Trudi Tate, eds, *Women's Fiction and the Great War* (Oxford: Oxford University Press, 1997).
Reynolds, David, *The Long Shadow: The Great War and the Twentieth Century* (Simon & Schuster, 2013).
Robb, George, *British Culture and the First World War* (London: Palgrave, 2002).
Roper, Michael, *The Secret Battle* (Manchester: Manchester University Press, 2009).
Roucoux, Michel, ed., *English Literature of the Great War Revisited: Proceedings of the Symposium on the British Literature of the First World War* (Amiens: Presses de l'Universite, Picardie, 1986).
Rubin, Joan Shelly, *The Making of Middlebrow Culture* (Chapel Hill, NC: University of North Carolina Press, 1992).
Rutherford, Andrew, *The Literature of War: Studies in Heroic Virtue* (London: Macmillan, 1978).
Satia, Priya, *Spies in Arabia* (Oxford: Oxford University Press, 2008).
Seymour, Miranda, *Robert Graves: Life on the Edge* (New York: Henry Holt, 1995).
Sheffield, Gary, *Forgotten Victory: The First World War, Myths and Realities* (London: Headline, 2001).
Sheffield, G.D., *Leadership in the Trenches: Officer–Man Relations, Morale and Discipline in the British Army in the Era of the First World War* (New York: Palgrave Macmillan, 2000).
Sheftall, Mark David, *Altered Memories of the Great War: Divergent Narratives of Britain, Australia, New Zealand and Canada* (London: I.B.Tauris, 2009).
Sherry, Vincent, ed., *The Cambridge Companion to the Literature of the First World War* (Cambridge: Cambridge University Press, 2005).
Smith, Angela, *Women's Writing of the First World War: An Anthology* (Manchester: Manchester University Press, 2000).
Stephen, Martin, *The Price of Pity: Poetry, History and Myth in the Great War* (London: Leo Cooper, 1996).
Stevenson, Randall, *Literature and the Great War* (Oxford: Oxford University Press, 2013).
Strachan, Hew, *The First World War: To Arms* (Oxford: Oxford University Press, 2001).
────── *The First World War* (New York: Viking, 2004)
Tal, Kalí, *Worlds of Hurt: Reading the Literatures of Trauma* (Cambridge: Cambridge University Press, 1996).
Terraine, John, *The Smoke and the Fire, Myths and Anti-Myths of War 1861–1945* (London: Sidgwick and Jackson, 1980).
Todman, Dan, *The Great War: Myth and Memory* (London: Hambledon, 2005).
Tombs, Robert and Emile Chabal, *Britain and France in Two World Wars: Truth, Myth and Memory* (London: Bloomsbury, 2013).

Tylee, Claire, *The Great War and Women's Consciousness: Images of Militarism and Womanhood in Women's Writings, 1914–64* (London: Macmillan, 1990).
Unwin, Stanley, *Publishing in Peace and War* (London: Allen & Unwin, 1944).
——— *The Truth About Publishing: An Autobiographical Record* (London: George Allen & Unwin, 1960).
Vance, Jonathan, *Death So Noble: Memory, Meaning and the First World War* (Vancouver: University of British Columbia Press, 1997).
Ward, A.C., *The Nineteen-Twenties: Literature and Ideas in the Post-War Decade* (London: Methuen 1930).
Watson, Alexander, *Enduring the Great War: Combat, Morale, and Collapse in the German and British Armies, 1914–1918* (Cambridge: Cambridge University Press, 2008).
Watson, Janet, *Fighting Different Wars: Experience, Memory, and the First World War in Britain* (Cambridge: Cambridge University Press, 2004).
Waugh, Arthur, *A Hundred Years of Publishing: Being the Story of Chapman & Hall, Ltd.* (London: Chapman & Hall, 1930).
Whitehead, Ian, *Doctors in the Great War* (London: Leo Cooper, 1999).
Wilson, Jean Moorcroft, *Siegfried Sassoon: The Journey from the Trenches, A Biography* (New York: Routledge, 2003).
Wilson, Ross, *Landscapes of the Western Front: Materiality During the Great War* (New York: Routledge, 2011).
Winter, Denis, *Death's Men* (New York: Penguin, 1978).
Winter, Jay, *The Great War and the British People* (New York: Palgrave Macmillan, 2003).
——— *Remembering War* (New Haven: Yale University Press, 2006).
——— *Sites of Memory, Sites of Mourning: The Great War in European Cultural History* (Cambridge: Cambridge University Press, 1995).
Winter, Jay and Antoine Prost, *The Great War in History* (Cambridge: Cambridge University Press, 2005).
Winter, Jay and Emmanuel Sivan, eds, *War and Remembrance in the Twentieth Century* (Cambridge: Cambridge University Press, 1999).
Wohl, Robert, *The Generation of 1914* (Cambridge, MA: Harvard University Press, 1979).

Secondary Sources: Articles

Acton, Carol and Jane Potter, '"These frightful sights would work havoc with one's brain": Subjective Experience, Trauma, and Resilience in First World War Writings by Medical Personnel', *Literature and Medicine* 30:1 (Spring 1012), pp. 61–85.
Adams, Michael C.C., '"Anti-War" isn't Always Anti-War', *The Midwest Quarterly* 31:3 (Spring 1990), pp. 297–313.
Assmann, Jan, 'Collective Memory and Cultural Identity', *New German Critique* 65 (Spring–Summer 1995), pp. 125–33.
Badsey, Stephen, 'The Great War Since the Great War', *Historical Journal of Film, Radio and Television* 22:1 (2002), pp. 37–45.
Ballinger, Pamela, 'The Culture of Survivors: Post-Traumatic Stress Disorder and Traumatic Memory,' *History and Memory* 10:1 (Spring 1998), pp. 99–132.

Booth, Allyson, 'Figuring the Absent Corpse: Strategies of Representation in World War I', *Mosaic* 26:1 (1993), pp. 69–85.

Brown, Matthew, 'Book History, Sexy Knowledge, and the Challenge of the New Boredom', *American Literary History* 16:4 (2004), pp. 688–706.

Brunner, José, 'Psychiatry, Psychoanalysis, and Politics During the First World War', *Journal of the History of the Behavioural Sciences* 17 (October 1991), pp. 352–65.

Campbell, James, 'Combat Gnosticism: The Ideology of First World War Poetry Criticism', *New Literary History* 30:1 (Winter, 1999), pp. 203–15.

Cull, Nicholas, 'Great Escapes: "Englishness" and the Prisoner of War Genre', *Film History* 14 (2002), pp. 282–95.

Cullen, Stephen, '"The Land of my Dreams": The Gendered Utopian Dreams and "Disenchantment" of British Literary Ex-combatants of the Great War', *Cultural and Social History* 8:2 (2011), pp. 195–211.

Darby, Robert, 'Oscillations on the Hotspur–Falstaff Spectrum: Paul Fussell and the Ironies of War', *War in History* 9:307 (2002), pp. 307–31.

Darton, Robert, 'What is the History of Books?', *Daedalus* 111:3 (Summer 1982), pp. 65–83.

Dean, Eric, 'War and Psychiatry: Examining the Diffusion Theory in Light of the Insanity Defence in Post-World War Britain', *History of Psychiatry* 4 (March 1993), pp. 61–82.

Eksteins, Modris, '*All Quiet on the Western Front* and the Fate of a War', *Journal of Contemporary History* 15:2 (1980), pp. 345–66.

——— 'War, Memory, and Politics: The Fate of the Film *All Quiet on the Western Front*', *Central European History* 13:1 (March 1980), pp. 60–82.

Fantauzzo, Justin, '"Buried Alive": Experience, Memory, and the Interwar Publishing of the Egyptian Expeditionary Force in Postwar Britain, 1915–1939', *Journal of the Canadian Historical Association* 23:2 (2012), pp. 212–50.

Ferguson, Niall, 'Prisoner Taking and Prisoner Killing in the Age of Total Warfare: Towards a Political Economy of Military Defeat', *War in History* 11:2 (2004), pp. 148–92.

Fletcher, Anthony, 'Patriotism, Identity and Commemoration: New Light on the Great War from the Papers of Major Reggie Chenevix Trench', *History* 90 (2005), pp. 532–49.

——— 'Patriotism, the Great War and the Decline of Victorian Manliness', *History* 99:334 (2014), pp. 40–72.

Funkenstein, Amos, 'Collective Memory and Historical Consciousness,' *History and Memory* 1:1 (Spring–Summer 1989), pp. 5–26.

Galbraith, John S., 'No Man's Child: The Campaign in Mesopotamia, 1914–1916', *The International History Review* 6:3 (1984), pp. 358–85.

Grayson, Richard, 'Military History from the Street: New Methods for Researching First World War Service in the British Military', *War in History* 21:465 (2014), pp. 465–95.

Grieves, Keith, 'C.E. Montague and the Making of *Disenchantment*, 1914–1921', *War in History* 4:35 (1997), pp. 35–59.

Gullace, Nicoletta F., 'Memory, Memorials, and the Postwar Literary Experience: Traditional Values and the Legacy of World War I', *Twentieth Century British History* 10:2 (1999), pp. 235–43.

Hallett, Christine, 'Portrayals of Suffering: Perceptions of Trauma in the Writings of First World War Nurses and Volunteers,' *CBMH/BCHM* 27:1 (2010), pp. 65–84.
Harari, Yuval Noah, 'Armchairs, Coffee, and Authority: Eye-witnesses and Flesh-witnesses Speak about War, 1100–2000', *The Journal of Military History* 74 (January 2010), pp. 53–78.
——— 'Scholars, Eyewitnesses, and Flesh-witnesses of War: A Tense Relationship', *Partial Answers* 7/2 (2009), pp. 213–28.
——— 'Martial Illusions: War and Disillusionment in Twentieth-Century and Renaissance Memoirs', *The Journal of Military History* 69 (2005), pp. 43–72.
——— 'Military Memoirs: A Historical Overview of the Genre from the Middle Ages to the Late Modern Era', *War in History* 14:3 (2007), pp. 289–309.
Heathorn, Stephen, 'The Mnemonic Turn in the Cultural Historiography of Britain's Great War', *The Historical Journal* 48 (2005), pp. 1103–24.
Howsam, Leslie, 'What is the Historiography of Books? Recent Studies in Authorship, Publishing, and Reading in Modern Britain and North America', *The Historical Journal* 51:4 (2008), pp. 1089–1101.
Isherwood, Ian, "British Publishing and Commercial Memories of the First World War," *War in History* 23:3 (2016), pp. 323–40.
——— '"To fly is more fascinating than to read about flying": British R.F.C. Memoirs of the First World War', in *War, Literature & the Arts* 26 (2014).
——— 'Writing the 'ill-managed nursery': British POW Memoirs of the First World War', *First World War Studies* 5:3 (2014), pp. 267–86.
Jones, Edgar, 'The Psychology of Killing: The Combat Experience of British Soldiers during the First World War', *Journal of Contemporary History* 41:2 (2006), pp. 229–46.
Jones, Heather, 'A Missing Paradigm? Military Captivity and the Prisoner of War, 1914–1918', *Immigrants and Minorities* 25: 1–2 (2008), pp. 19–48.
Kitchen, James, '"Khaki crusaders": Crusading Rhetoric and the British Imperial Soldier during the Egypt and Palestine Campaigns, 1916–18', *First World War Studies* 1:2 (2010), pp. 141–60.
Leed, Eric, 'Class and Disillusionment in World War I', *The Journal of Modern History* 50:4 (1978), pp. 680–99.
——— 'Fateful Memories: Industrialized War and Traumatic Neuroses', *Journal of Contemporary History* 35:1 (2000), pp. 85–100.
Loughran, Tracey, 'A Crisis of Masculinity? Re-writing the History of Shell-shock and Gender in First World War Britain', *History Compass* 11:9 (2013), pp. 727–38.
Lunn, Joe, 'Male Identity and Martial Codes of Honor: A Comparison of the War Memoirs of Robert Graves, Erst Jünger, and Kande Kamara', *The Journal of Military History* 69:3 (2005), pp. 713–35.
MacKenzie, S.P., 'The Ethics of Escape: British Officer POWs in the First World War', *War in History* 15:1 (2008), pp. 1–16.
Madigan, Edward, '"Sticking to a Hateful Task": Resilience, Humour, and British Understandings of Combatant Courage, 1914–1918', *War in History* 20:1 (2013), pp. 76–98.
Marwick, Arthur, 'War and the Arts – Is there a Connection? The Case of the Two Total Wars', *War in History* 2:1 (1995), pp. 65–86.

McCartney, Helen, 'The First World War Soldier and his Contemporary Image in Britain,' *International Affairs* 90:2 (2014), pp. 299–315.

McLoughlin, Kate, 'The Great War and Modern Memory', *Essays in Criticism* 64:4 (2014), pp. 436–58.

Meyer, Jessica, 'Separating the Men from the Boys: Masculinity and Maturity in Understandings of Shell Shock in Britain', *Twentieth Century British History* 20:1 (2009), pp. 1–22.

Petter, Martin, '"Temporary Gentlemen" in the Aftermath of the Great War: Rank, Status and the Ex-Officer Problem', *The Historical Journal* 37:1 (1994), pp. 127–52.

Pilcher, Jane, 'Mannheim's Sociology of Generations: An Undervalued Legacy', *British Journal of Sociology* 45:3 (September 1994), pp. 481–95.

Prior, Robin, 'The Heroic Image of the Warrior in the First World War', *War & Society* 23 (September 2005), pp. 43–51.

Prior, R. and T. Wilson, 'Paul Fussell at War', *War in History* 1:1 (1994), pp. 63–80.

Roper, Michael, 'Nostalgia as an Emotional Experience in the Great War', *The Historical Journal* 54:2 (June 2011), pp. 421–45.

——— 'Re-remembering the Soldier Hero: The Psychic and Social Construction of Memory in Personal Narratives of the Great War', *History Workshop Journal* 50 (Autumn 2000), pp. 181–204.

Rutherford, Andrew, 'Realism and the Heroic: Some Reflections on War Novels', *Yearbook of English Studies* 12 (1984), pp. 194–207.

Showalter, Denis, 'The Great War and its Historiography', *The Historian* 68:4 (2006), pp. 713–21.

Silbey, David, 'The Archaeology of Remembrance: British Memoirs of the Great War, 1918–Present', *Proteus* 20:2 (2003), pp. 81–6.

Smith, Leonard, 'Paul Fussell's *The Great War and Modern Memory*: Twenty-Five Years Later', *History and Theory* 40 (May 2001), pp. 241–60.

——— 'Jean Norton Cru and Combatants' Literature of the First World War', *Modern and Contemporary France* 9:2 (2001), pp. 161–9.

Spitzer, Alan, 'The Historical Problem of Generations', *The American Historical Review* 78:5 (December 1973), pp. 1353–85.

Strachan, Hew, 'John Buchan and the First World War: Fact into Fiction', *War in History* 16:3 (2009), pp. 298–324.

Thomas, T.H., 'Some War Memoirs', *The Journal of Modern History* 2:4 (December 1930), pp. 629–40.

Watson, Alexander, 'Bereaved and Aggrieved: Combat Motivation and the Ideology of Sacrifice in the First World War', *Historical Research* 83:219 (February 2010), pp. 146–64.

——— 'Self-Deception and Survival: Mental Coping Strategies on the Western Front, 1914–18', *Journal of Contemporary History* 41:2 (April 2006), pp. 247–68.

Watson, Alexander and Patrick Porter, 'Bereaved and Aggrieved: Combat Motivation and the Ideology of Sacrifice in the First World War', *Historical Research* 83:219 (February 2010), pp. 146–64.

Wild, Jonathan, '"A Merciful, Heaven-sent Release"? The Clerk and the First World War in British Literary Culture', *Cultural and Social History* 4:1 (2007), pp. 73–94.

Williams, Jeffry, 'The Myth of the Lost Generation: The British War Poets and their Modern Critics', *CLIO* 12:1 (1982), pp. 45–56.

Wilson, Ross, 'Memory and Trauma: Narrating the Western Front 1914–1918', *Rethinking History* 13:2 (June 2009), 251–67.

―――― 'Strange Hells: A New Approach on the Western Front', *Historical Research* 81:211 (February 2008), 150–66.

Winter, Jay, 'Britain's "Lost Generation" of the First World War', *Population Studies* (November 1977), 31:3), 449–66.

―――― 'Shell-shock and the Cultural History of the Great War', *Journal of Contemporary History* 35:1 (2000), pp. 7–11.

INDEX

Adams, Michael, 75
Aldington, Richard, 43, 57, 138
Allenby, Field Marshal Edmund, 29
American Civil War, 69, 148
Armageddon, 14, 112
Armistice, 10, 13, 37, 40, 53, 80, 150
Armistice Day, 11, 113, 143
Arnewood, 102, 104, 107
artillery, 22, 66, 67, 70–2, 102, 128
Asquith, Raymond, 131
Asquith, Violet, 93
attrition, 5, 19, 22, 70–1, 79–80, 89, 122, 152, 155, 157, 162
Audoin-Rouzeau, Stéphane, 7
Australia and New Zealand Army Corps (ANZAC), 92–94

Bairnfather, Bruce, 57
Ball, Albert, 153
Barbusse, Henri, 57
Barczewski, Stephanie, 152,
Baring, Maurice, 55
Bayly, Hugh, 130, 131
Beaman, Ardern, 22
Becker, Annette, 7
Belhaven, The Master of (R.G.A. Hamilton), 59
Bible, 98, 100
bibliography, 56–9

Bishop, Billy, 152
Bishop, H.C.W., 23
Blackwood, George, 40, 52
Blaser, Bernard, 29, 103
Blunden, Edmund, 2, 43, 59–61, 64, 69–72, 74, 76, 84, 103, 116, 119–20
 Undertones of War, 44, 59, 70, 73, 116–17, 129, 163
 War Books, 55–57
Bond, Brian, 9, 114
book dedications, 19–20
Bookseller, The 16–17, 40, 41, 42, 49–51, 53–4
Borden, Mary, 129
Bott, Alan, 40, 52, 104, 150
Bourke, Joanna, 10
Bracco, Rosa Marie, 9, 50
Bray, Norman, 91–2
British Army, units
 1/5 Warwickshire Regiment, 12
 2nd Battalion Leicestershire Regiment, 18, 97
 36th Division, 58
 Black Watch, 22, 79–80, 144
 cavalry, 22, 89
 Guards Division, 31, 131
 Irish Guards, 93
 King's Royal Rifle Corps, 81

Royal Flying Corps, 150–5
Royal Welch Fusiliers, 21–2, 82, 117, 163
Scots Guards, 19, 79–80
Brittain, Vera, 2, 125, 131, 137
Testament of Youth, 28, 48, 51–2, 129–31
Brooke, Rupert, 74
Buchan, John, 17, 50, 93
Buchanan, Angus, 12, 14, 15

Cape, Jonathan, 90–1
Carpenter, Alfred, 42
Carrington, Charles, 12–14, 15, 17–18, 33, 57, 68–9, 115, 119–24, 164
Soldier from the Wars Returning, 161
A Subaltern's War, 17, 31–2, 46, 73, 121

Carstairs, Carrol, 30–1, 46
Cartwright, H.A., 24, 52, 146–7
Cecil, Hugh, 9, 50, 78
Chamberlain, Austen, 92
Chapman, Guy, 25, 74, 119, 120, 161–2, 164
A Passionate Prodigality, 48, 121–4
Vain Glory, 25–26
Chapman and Hall, 40
Churchill, Winston, 42, 54, 57, 140
Coldicott, Rowlands, 26–7, 99
comradeship, 7, 20–2, 33, 67–8, 82, 108, 120, 123–7, 144–5, 156
Conan Doyle, Arthur, 17, 29
Confino, Alon, 59
coping mechanisms, 10
courage, 10, 33, 67, 75–8, 156, 158, 162–3
 of pilots, 152–4
 of prisoners, 145–8
 of soldiers, 139–45
Crozier, Frank, 49, 70
crusade, 87, 97–102, 106–7

Dearden, Harold, 46, 125–6
Dent, J.M., 39
Douie, Charles 4, 13–15, 120, 142–4, 156, 159–61
The Weary Road, 29, 34, 123–5, 158
Dugdale, Geoffrey, 29, 32–3
Durnford, H.G., 25, 32

East Africa, 12
Edmonds, General Sir James, 17
Edward Arnold, Ltd., 50, 88, 92, 93, 94, 96
Edwards, Paul, 34
Eksteins, Modris, 14
emotional resilience, 136, 141
esprit de corps, 7, 19, 22, 82, 130, 162
Evans, A.J., 42, 147
Ewart, Wilfred, 50, 57
Eyre, Giles, 81–2, 84, 144–5

Faber & Faber, 46, 51, 82
Falls, Cyril, 55–6, 160–1
 critic, 83, 94,
 War Books, 57–60
fear, 19–20, 75–7, 115, 121–3, 140–1, 152
Feather, John, 40
Ford, Ford Madox, 42
Frankau, Gilbert, 57
Fraser-Tytler, Neil, 22
Fussell, Paul, 8, 112–14, 117, 119

Gallipoli, 73, 88, 92–4, 133
Gervis, Henry, 125
Gibbons, John, 33
Gibbs, Hamilton, 30
Gibbs, Philip, 30, 142
Gilbert, Vivian, 30, 100–1, 107
Gosse, Edmund, 25, 118
Gosse, Philip, 25, 72
Gough, General Sir Hubert, 28–9
Graham, Stephen, 19, 20, 57, 79–80, 83

Graves, Robert, 2, 43, 73–4, 158, 163
  and Frank Richards 82–3, 84
  Good-bye to All That, 21, 46, 51–5, 73, 117, 119
  reception, 59
  suffering, 116–20
  and T.E. Lawrence 90, 102–3
  truth, 23–4
  unit affiliation, 21–2
Griffith, Llewelyn Wyn, 68, 71–2, 74
  Up to Mametz, 20, 77–8
Grinnell-Milne, Duncan, 147, 152, 154–5, 257

Hallett, Christine, 129
Hamilton, General Sir Ian, 93–4
Hanbury-Sparrow, Arthur, 75–6,
Hardy, J.L., 29–30, 147
Harrison, M.C.C., 24, 52
Hay, Ian, 31–2, 37, 50, 52, 57
Heinemann, 46
Hemingway, Ernest, 43, 57, 138, 156
Herbert, A.P., 57
Herbert, Aubrey, 89, 92–4, 97
Higonnet, Margaret, 129
Hill, C.W., 149
Holy Land, 98, 100, 107
Hope Floyd, Thomas, 27, 32
Hutton, Isabel, 96, 126–7
Hynes, Samuel, 8, 16, 27, 47, 63, 98, 139, 146, 153, 159

Italian front, 13, 73

Jerrold, Douglas, 32, 45–6, 55
Jerusalem, 99, 102
John Murray, Ltd., 12, 88, 91
Johnston, Maurice, 52, 149–50
Jonathan Cape, 46, 90, 164
Jones, E.H., 42, 51, 149
junior officers, 21, 31, 65, 72–8, 96, 100, 115, 124
juvenile books, 39, 150

Kastamuni POW Camp, 134, 147
Keegan, John, 7, 14
Keeling, Edward, 133–5, 149
Kipling, Rudyard, 3–4
  The Irish Guards in the Great War, 3, 42
Kitchen, James, 87
Kut el Amara, 23, 92–3, 102, 105–6, 133–5

Lawrence, T.E., 87, 89–93, 97, 102–3
  Revolt in the Desert, 44, 90
  Seven Pillars of Wisdom, 90
Lawson, John, 95–6
Layton, Lynn, 129
Leed, Eric, 67–8, 139
Lewis, C.S., 1–2
Lewis, Cecil, 48, 151, 154–5, 157, 164
Linton Andrews, William, 22–3, 79–81, 83, 144, 156
literacy, 38, 53
Lucy, John, 48, 82–4, 163

McCudden, James, 153
Macdonnell, A.G., 36–7
Mackenzie, Compton, 94–6, 97
Macmillan, 42, 79
Macmillan, Norman, 152
Madigan, Edward, 10, 141
Manning, Frederic, 43, 50, 59, 74, 79, 81
Mannock, Edward, 153
Marson, Thomas, 46,
masculinity, 10, 34, 67–8, 133
material culture, 28
material shortages, 39
Matthews, E.C., 65–7, 69, 73
mechanised warfare, 10, 75, 140
medical officer, 24, 25, 53, 73, 125–8, 131
Meyer, Jessica, 10, 75, 140, 141
middlebrow, 9, 50, 57, 78, 120
mobilisation, 39
Montague, C.E., 42, 57

INDEX

More, John, 21, 98, 108
Mosse, George, 113
Mottram, R.H., 11, 28, 42–3, 50, 57, 74, 143–4, 156, 164
Mousley, Edward, 134–5,
Murray, John, 39, 41
mythology
  definitions, 63–4, 159
  disillusionment and, 114, 119, 159
  pilots, 150–1, 153
  soldier hero, 75,
  subaltern's war, 75, 78
  war poet, 7, 161

nurses, 41, 53, 88, 124–5, 127–30

Onions, Oliver, 50
Osburn, Arthur, 18–19, 127–8, 131,
other ranks, 65, 79, 84, 135
Overy, Richard, 43, 130
Owen, Wilfred, 2, 103, 111, 116, 138, 159–60

Passchendaele, Battle of, 12, 63, 120–1
Peter Davies, Ltd., 58, 151
Philpott, Maryam, 150
Plowman, Max, 24, 69, 71, 73
Pollard, A.O., 25, 29, 32–3, 74
Potter, Jane, 39, 129
prisoners of war
  escape, 24, 29, 52, 73, 88, 145–50
  suffering, 132–6
  treatment, 134–5
propaganda, 81, 129, 154
Putnam, 45

Raymond, Ernest, 42
Red Cross, 12
Rees, R.T., 21, 31, 71, 72, 76–7, 142, 144
regimental histories, 17, 42, 57,
Remarque, Erich, 43–7, 49, 50, 53, 57, 59, 78, 123, 158
Reynolds, David, 10, 11, 44

Richards, Frank, 46, 48, 82–3
Roper, Michael, 10
Rorie, David, 24, 24, 126
Rutherford, Andrew, 62, 119, 139

Sandes, E.C.W., 133, 134, 135
Sandes, Flora, 96
Sapper (Cyril McNeile), 50
Sassoon, Siegfried, 2, 25, 43–4, 45, 57, 64, 74, 84, 103, 116, 129
  Complete Memoirs of George Sherston, 50–2, 73
  and Robert Graves, 117–18
Satia, Priya, 87, 89, 90
Scott, Robert, 119, 142
Scottish Women's Hospitals, 96, 126
Seely, Major General J.E.B., 29
Shackelton, Ernest, 142
Sheffield, Gary, 7, 114
Sherriff, R.C., 46
Sivan, Emmanuel, 15, 33
Sitwell, Osbert, 30–1
Smith, Richard, 96
Somme, Battle of the, 64, 65, 69, 73, 110, 120, 121, 131, 140, 141, 143–4
Sommers, Cecil, 100, 104
Stein, Gertrude, 2
Still, John, 25, 133, 135
Strachan, Sir Hew, 60, 67
subaltern, 13, 36, 65, 71, 72–8, 84, 101
Swinton, Major General Sir Ernest, 29, 58
Sykes, Mark, 92, 93

Tal, Kali, 27
Tayler, Henrietta, 41
Tennant, John, 105, 106–8
Thompson, E.J., 17–18, 57, 97–8, 101, 108
Thornton Butterworth, 42
Todman, Daniel, 10, 33, 64,
Tomlinson, H.L., 49, 50, 56, 57

Unwin, Stanley, 39

Volunteer Aid Detachment (VAD), 129,
victimization, 139

Wake, Major General Sir Hereward, 81
Walpole, Hugh, 40
war books
　canonization, 55–60
　decline, 41–2
　popularity, 48–53
　revival of, 43–5
　tone, 46
Watson, Alexander, 10
Watson, Janet, 46, 55, 114, 129
Whitehouse, A.G.J., 153

William Blackwood & Sons Ltd., 50, 52, 88, 149, 150
Williamson, Henry, 46, 49, 55, 110–11, 137
Wilson, Charles (Lord Moran), 140–1
Winter, Jay, 8, 15, 20, 33, 118
Wister, Owen, 30
Wohl, Robert, 74–5, 161
World War II, 11, 52, 83, 113, 140, 146, 147, 155, 160, 163–4

Yearsley, Kenneth, 149
Yeats-Brown, Francis, 146, 148–50
Young, Donovan, 96
Young, Hubert, 89, 91–2, 97
Yozgad POW camp, 147, 149
Ypres, 1, 120–2, 131, 141, 143, 158